Essays on Wealth, Generosity, and Legacy

Perspectives from Progressive Christianity

TRAVIS C. MALLETT

VORSTOßEN
ACADEMIC PRESS

VORSTOßEN
ACADEMIC PRESS

First published in 2022 by Vorstoßen Academic Press
www.vorstossen.com

Publisher's Cataloging-in-Publication Data

Names: Mallett, Travis C., author.
Title: Essays on wealth, generosity, and legacy : perspectives from progressive Christianity / Travis C. Mallett.—1st ed.
Description: Includes bibliographical references and index. | Pullman, WA: Vorstoßen Academic Press, 2022.
Identifiers: LCCN: 2021909658 | ISBN: 978-1-953516-06-0 (hardcover) | 978-1-953516-07-7 (pbk.) | 978-1-953516-08-4 (ebook) | 978-1-953516-09-1 (pdf) | 978-1-953516-10-7 (audiobook) | 978-1-953516-11-4 (audiobook)
Subjects: LCSH Wealth—Religious aspects—Christianity. | Finance, Personal—Religious aspects—Christianity. | BISAC RELIGION / Christian Living / General | RELIGION / Biblical Studies / General | BUSINESS & ECONOMICS / Personal Finance / Money Management | BUSINESS & ECONOMICS / Personal Finance / Investing | BUSINESS & ECONOMICS / Personal Finance / Retirement Planning
Classification: LCC BR115.W4 .M35 2022 | DDC 241/.68–dc23

Library of Congress Control Number: 2021909658

Proofreader and copy editor: Kevin O'Malley

Typeset by Travis Mallett in LaTeX using Texmaker 5.1.2 (Copyright © 2003–2021 by Pascal Brachet). Cover design by Travis Mallett with Inkscape 1.1.1 (Copyright © 2021 Inkscape Developers). Cover image credit: iStock.com/naqiewei

FIRST EDITION
D:20220110

Printed in the United States of America
on acid-free paper.

∞

To my parents, Clayton D. & Kristine L. Mallett...
who taught me the ways of financial responsibility,
which I quickly neglected to practice,
but rediscovered later the hard way.

Also to my wife, Andrea R. Mallett...
Thank you for your remarkable patience while I
studied these topics.

"An unexamined faith is not worth having, for it can only be true by accident. A faith worth having is a faith worth discussing and testing."[1] —James Luther Adams

"We hope here not for complete knowledge but for an incomplete ignorance."[2] —Catherine Keller

---

[1] James Luther Adams. *The Essential James Luther Adams: Selected Essays and Addresses.* Ed. by George Kimmich Beach. Boston, MA: Skinner House Books, 1998. ISBN: 978-1558963528, p. 30.

[2] Catherine Keller. *Cloud of the Impossible: Negative Theology and Planetary Entanglement.* New York: Columbia University Press, 2015. ISBN: 978-0-231-17114-4, p. 3.

CONTENTS

INTRODUCTION

As of 2021, it takes about $1 million to be in the wealthiest 1% of the world[1] and $4.4 million to be in the top 1% of wealthiest Americans.[2] Even America's middle class enjoy levels of wealth which far exceed a vast majority of the world's population. However, those who find themselves in the high-net-worth category through either inheritance, fortune, or, for many, discipline over time, there may arise a "problem"[3] of cognitive dissonance. There is a cacophony of voices from culture and religion which preach diverse and contradictory messages about wealth, not all of which promote spiritual wellbeing. Since almost 19 million Americans each have a net worth over $1 million,[4] by far the highest number of millionaires of any other country, many Americans in this category are forced to wrestle with this confusion.

Wealth forces on many individuals a myriad of questions. How should we feel about being wealthy? What is the moral status of wealth? How much should we save, invest, and give away? Do

---

[1] Rachel Cautero. *Are You in the Top 1%?* 2021. URL: www.smartasset. com / financial - advisor / are - you - in - the - top - 1 - percent (visited on 04/19/2021).

[2] Fatma Khaled. *This is How Much You Need to be Worth to be in the Richest 1% in the US—And Other Countries.* 2021. URL: www.businessinsider. com/net-worth-to-be-in-1-percent-top-richest-wealth-2021-2 (visited on 04/19/2021).

[3] Dave Ramsey. *The Legacy Journey: A Radical View of Biblical Wealth and Generosity.* Brentwood, TN: Ramsey Press, 2014. ISBN: 978-1-937-07771-6, pp. 5, 7.

[4] *Global Wealth Databook.* 2019. URL: www . credit - suisse . com/media/ assets/corporate/docs/about-us/research/publications/global-wealth-databook-2019.pdf (visited on 04/20/2021).

we feel ashamed of having wealth? Do we feel "blessed" by it? For those of us who identify with a faith tradition, how does our faith interact with our personal finances? Does it interact at all? How much of our wealth is due to our own hard work and smart decisions, and how much is due to social injustices?

Answers to such questions are not clear. And some of these questions can be uncomfortable, even to entertain. Plenty of tensions arise when the subjects of personal finance, social justice and faith are brought into close proximity with each other. As a result, many people tend to compartmentalize these topics. Faith is relegated to a social activity on Sundays, personal finance is a household chore, and social justice is only a cause to be advocated for with social media posts and voting choices.

This is certainly the *easy* route. With these topics separated, we don't have to feel uncomfortable when our faith challenges the moral status of our wealth. And we can feel proud of the wealth we've worked so hard to earn when we don't realize the privileges which likely played a major role in our success. We can keep the ideas of social justice away from our personal life, and focus on helping "them" at a distance. I suspect that this is not only an unsatisfying way of life, but also that it damages progress towards true human unity.

This book is a collection of essays which explore the interaction between personal finance, social justice, and faith. Each essay brings some combination of these topics into conversation with each other. This is not a book of answers. It is more of an exploration than a declaration. The faith elements in these essays focus primarily on Progressive Christianity, which is deeply concerned with social justice and generally shuns certainty on religious topics. If you are looking for certainty, this is not the book for you. But if you wish to explore with me the questions which wealth imposes on many, then I hope this book will provide some good material to start the conversation.

Chapter Summaries

The chapters are organized following topics presented in Dave Ramsey's course *The Legacy Journey*, which discusses many of these issues from a conservative Evangelical perspective. In this book, I hope to spark the questions in ways that Progressive Christians, in particular, can engage with.

Chapter 1 sets the stage for this grand conversation. Personal finance and social justice seem like unrelated subjects, and yet there is certainly a connection between the two. This essay illustrates that conversations about these topics can be contentious, with strong opinions on both sides of the issues. As a result, it is recommended that conversations on the interactions between these topics start with the heart, that is, *our* hearts. By first focusing on changing *ourselves* and crafting our own identity, we can be better prepared to engage with the tensions rather than evade them.

Chapter 2 explores the moral status of wealth as follows: Is wealth inherently good? Is it inherently evil? Should we be ashamed of having wealth? Proud of it? Indifferent? We bring the sacred texts of Christianity into the conversation and find that it doesn't provide tidy answers to these questions. Instead, the Bible actually adds tension to the discussion. On the one hand, following our faith traditions can produce an increase in wealth. But on the other hand, the same tradition has many harsh words for those who have wealth! We find that the Bible "doesn't do the heavy lifting for us. It alerts us that *we* have to. We cannot escape that sacred responsibility—ever."[5]

Chapter 3 again brings the sacred text into conversation with personal finance. We saw in Chapter 2 that our faith tradition, despite compounding philosophical and moral tensions, can produce positive benefits when allowed to interact with other areas of our life. Here we ask, "What advice does our faith tradition offer that could be useful for investing?" The answer depends on how the Bible is interpreted. Three methods of interpreting the Bible are examined. It is found that our faith traditions advise us to invest with simplicity, diversity, consistency, and with a socially-responsible mindfulness.

Chapter 4 examines the idea of contentment. It is found to

---

[5]Peter Enns. *How the Bible Actually Works: In which I Explain How an Ancient, Ambiguous, and Diverse Book Leads us to Wisdom Rather Than Answers—And Why That's Great News*. New York: HarperOne, 2019. ISBN: 978-0-06-268674-9, p. 34.

be one of the most consistently emphasized virtues throughout recorded history. However, the idea may be in need of a refresh since it is likely to fall on deaf ears in our culture. This essay proposes that the modern secular minimalism movement is well-suited to be the new face of contentment. Practicing minimalism and contentment has profound implications for our personal finances and the way we relate with the world.

Chapter 5 attempts to provide a twist on the dangers of wealth. It is well-known that as wealth increases, so do the associated dangers. Greed has overcome many, nations have fought over wealth, families and marriages are frequently destroyed by it. Yet can the dangers of increased wealth provide the fuel and adrenaline needed to dive deeper into one's faith tradition? Much like the danger of falling causes increased focus in a rock climber, so too can wealth provide a mirror for us to clearly see and improve our spiritual character.

Chapter 6 broadens the focus of the conversation by examining the idea of the afterlife. This essay argues that ideas about the afterlife should not become the focus of our life, following the example of the biblical authors. Instead, we should live in such a way that our life promotes the kingdom of God on earth now, and after we are gone. Keeping faith, personal finance, and social justice compartmentalized serves to keep us blind to this bigger picture.

Finally, **Chapter 7** presents a vision of a unified humanity. The trajectory of our story is one where individual elements come together to produce something new and beautiful. But this vision of unity will be difficult to achieve if we compartmentalize our faith, personal finances, and social justice.

Again, this book is not a collection of answers. Instead, it is an *invitation* to participate in an ancient conversation that has modern implications. I look forward to engaging in this conversation with you, even if we don't arrive at any mutually-agreeable answers to any of the questions raised.

To continue the conversation over your favorite social media platform, visit

www.EssaysOnWealth.com/ContinueTheConversation

Chapter 1

Personal Finance and Social Justice

"The Old Testament is full of invectives against the rich,[1] who with their tricks and demands engender the poor. [...] The opposite of this type of poverty is not wealth. It is justice."[2] —Leonardo Boff, theologian

W EALTH and poverty, justice and injustice, and the symbiotic and parasitic relationships between these issues have been polarizing topics, not only in our day and age, but for thousands of years. On the surface, these topics seem unrelated. Personal finance is about the individual and focuses on their behaviors and situations. Social justice refers to the larger social *systems* in place. The premise of this book is that personal finance, social justice, and religion are topics which many people compartmentalize—for good reason. This chapter illustrates the tension that occurs when these topics are brought into close prox-

---

[1] Isaiah 10:1–2; Amos 2:6–7; Micah 3:1–3; Habakkuk 2:6–8.

[2] Leonardo Boff. *Francis of Assisi: A Model for Human Liberation*. Trans. by John W. Diercksmeier. Maryknoll, NY: Orbis Books, 2006, p. 55; A. Stephen Van Kuiken. *Everyone Does Better When Everyone Does Better*. 3 September 2017, Pullman, WA. Sermon. URL: https://pullmanucc.org/2017/09/06/everyone-does-better-when-everyone-does-better/ (visited on 01/02/2022).

imity with one another. For many, it is easier to keep these topics topics separated and avoid their interaction.

For example, many hardworking Americans have accumulated significant wealth. Without consideration of the systems within which their personal finances are operating, it is reasonable to conclude that they have accumulated wealth *because* they are hardworking, frugal, mindful, and strategic with their finances. And yet, as George Manibot said, "If wealth was the inevitable result of hard work and enterprise, every woman in Africa would be a millionaire."[3] Thus, financial success cannot be divorced from the reality of systemic effects. Some argue that it's a lack of financial literacy which contributes to wealth inequality. If so, the wealthy may feel that they have made superior financial decisions and are thus appropriately being rewarded for their behavior. But others argue that differences in financial literacy may itself be a systemic issue. Again, the results of one's personal finances are inextricably linked to social justice, since social justice is primarily about *systems.* What is the average millionaire supposed to do with that information? Feel shame for having wealth? For working hard? Again, it is often easier to just keep these topics at bay.

Since our personal finances cannot be fully understood apart from the systems within which we operate, it is our responsibility to *not* compartmentalize these two subjects, despite the common tendency to do so. However, this call to avoid compartmentalization comes with a major challenge: both personal finance and social justice are, on their own, high-stakes discussions filled with varying opinions which evoke strong emotions. What of their combination? This chapter suggests that conversations about personal finance and social justice are very often *crucial conversations.* In a discussion where the stakes are high and emotions run strong, the church must be equipped to engage in the conversation with efficacy. The goal is not to suggest where these discussions should end up or even to argue confidently about the relationship between personal finance and social justice—the relationship is complex, and opinions diverge widely. Instead, these topics will be simply allowed to interact while we observe. Since the results of this experiment

---

[3]Frank Lesko. *Bootstraps.* 2017. URL: www.progressivechristianity. org/resources/bootstraps/ (visited on 06/12/2021).

may be diversely interpreted, I argue for a conclusion which transcends the "answers" we may individually come to. Rather than asserting where these conversations should end up (or what conclusions "should" be reached), I suggest where they should *start*: They should start with our hearts.

The Complexity of the Discussion

Western civilization owes its convictions regarding justice to the prophets of the Judeo-Christian tradition, more than to any other.[4] Progressive Christianity connects itself to this tradition by placing a strong emphasis on social justice.[5] Our "sacred responsibility"[6] is to carry on the ancient baton passed down from the prophets, adapt the message to modern times and issues, and preach its truth to culture and society. But the relationship between personal finance and social justice is complex, multifaceted, and provocative, making the execution of this responsibility nontrivial.

For example, some call financial literacy "a great equalizer in the battle against social injustice."[7] They argue that many of the social issues tearing at the fabric of society are "intimately tied"[8] to "disturbingly low"[9] levels of financial literacy, calling this "one of the United States' largest societal problems."[10] According to a

[4]Huston Smith. *The World's Religions*. New York: HarperOne, 2009. ISBN: 978-0-06-166018-4, p. 288.

[5]Matthew S. Hedstrom. *My Brother's Keeper: George McGovern and Progressive Christianity*. Oxford University Press, 2018.

[6]Anna J. Treadway. "The Revolution Begins in the Heart: Exploring the Spiritual Lives of Women Activists for Social Justice." PhD thesis. University of British Columbia, 2005, p. 8.

[7]Carrie Schwab-Pomerantz. *Financial Literacy: A Great Equalizer in the Battle Against Social Injustice*. 2020. URL: www.aboutschwab.com/financial-literacy-a-great-equalizer-in-the-battle-against-social-injustice (visited on 03/28/2021).

[8]Laura Elizabeth Pinto and Hannah Chan. "Social Justice and Financial Literacy." In: *Our Schools, Our Selves* 19.2 (2010).

[9]Theresa F. Henry, Athar Murtuza, Renee E. Weiss, et al. "Accounting as an Instrument of Social Justice." In: *Open Journal of Social Sciences* 3.01 (2015), p. 74.

[10]David R. Poucher. "Teaching Personal Finance as a General Education Course in a Liberal Arts Institution." In: *Christian Business Academy Review* 12 (2017), p. 45.

recent Charles Schwab Financial Literacy Survey, 89% of Americans agree that lack of financial education contributes to some of the biggest social issues our country faces, including poverty (58%), lack of job opportunities (53%), unemployment (53%), and wealth inequality (52%).[11]

However, others vehemently argue the opposite, contending that "harboring this belief may be innocent, but it is not harmless; the pursuit of financial literacy poses costs that almost certainly swamp any benefits."[12] The differences between such opinions are determined by how one answers several questions: how much of a person's finances is predetermined or limited by their environment? What percentage of one's net worth is determined by financial literacy and personal decisions? Answers to such questions seem necessary in order to properly diagnose the problem. But my goal is *not* to answer these questions. Indeed, given the complexity of the topic, answers, if they exist, may be highly individualized. Or, as the name suggests: the relationship between *personal* finance and social justice may in fact be *personal*—tailored to account for the knowledge, background, social position, previous decisions, character and personality of the individual whose situation is in question. Sondra Wheeler says of this issue:

> *"[T]he relation of Christian faith to issues of economic justice and responsibility seems to me one of the areas in which Christians are most confused, divided, and uneasy."*[13]

One of the contributing factors to the complexity of this discussion is that evidence of the problem (or solution) is often given as either anecdotes or as statistics. The problem with anecdotes is that they lack statistical robustness. The problem with statistics is that they lack the personal dimensions evoked by anecdotes. And it seems, based on the competing views mentioned above, that

---

[11] Carrie Schwab-Pomerantz, *Financial Literacy: A Great Equalizer in the Battle Against Social Injustice*, op. cit.

[12] Lauren E. Willis. "Against Financial-literacy Education." In: *Iowa Law Review* 94 (2008), pp. 197–198, 202.

[13] Sondra Ely Wheeler. *Wealth as Peril and Obligation: The New Testament on Possessions*. Grand Rapids, MI: Wm. B. Eerdmans Publishing, 1995, p. xv.

researchers are prone to interpret the same statistical data in different ways, each suggesting the other has the wrong interpretation and diagnosis. To illustrate the complexity of the discussion, we will hear two different true stories of personal finance and see how various views may analyze them. If we dig deep enough, we find it almost impossible to separate our personal finances from the systems within which they operate.

Kate and Tom

In their mid-forties, Kate and Tom appear to be doing well financially.[14] Between their two jobs, they make $160,000, placing them in the top 6% highest-earning households in the U.S..[15] and among the top 0.2% in the world.[16] Living in a high-end neighborhood, they have a large, four-bedroom house with a big yard and a garage. Their three kids attend an expensive private K–12 school.

But behind the facade, their finances are a disaster. Kate and Tom have an insurmountable amount of debt. With 10 or 11 credit cards, eight of them maxed out, and a personal loan, they have close to $80,000 in consumer debt in addition to two mortgages totaling $360,000. The interest payments alone are a major drain on their financial situation, and Kate says, "we're always broke." Yet they spend huge amounts on expensive food—the kids are accustomed to eating sushi. To fund the private education for their kids, Kate and Tom use credit cards. But one of their major concerns is the student loan situation. They aren't even sure what the balance is now. In fact, Tom doesn't even know how to look it up—the only time he ever logs in is to ask the loan provider to push back when they have to start paying it. Last he time he checked, their student loans totaled $90,000. But Kate says that with the interest, their loans have increased to somewhere between $120,000 and $140,000.

---

[14]This story is based on an interview with Kate and Tom (who's real names are not given): A. Goldman. *Debt: A Love Story*. 2018. URL: www . wealthsimple.com/en-us/magazine/couple-debt (visited on 02/27/2021).

[15]According the calculator at *Income Percentile Calculator for the United States in 2020*: https://dqydj.com/income-percentile-calculator/

[16]According to the calculator at *Political Calculations—What is Your World Income Percentile Ranking*: https://politicalcalculations.blogspot.com/2016/10/what-is-your-world-income-percentile.html

Kate and Tom have, in the past, tried to remedy their situation. Once they cashed out their 401(k) to pay off three credit cards and a loan, in addition to funding a "pretty good Christmas that year." But cashing out a 401(k) early comes with taxes and penalties, and when the tax bill of $20,000 arrived, they couldn't pay, and started the cycle all over again by putting it on the credit cards. Another time, Kate's mom gave them $40,000, which helped them pay off a large portion of their consumer debts. But it wasn't long before they had dug themselves right back into a hole, and now they're in exactly the same financial situation again. Kate feels guilty and embarrassed about it because her mom never made more than $30,000 a year during her whole life.

According to Kate, they can't really have fun anymore—there's no real joy, and the stress is taking a toll on their marriage. Tom tries to keep himself distracted to avoid thinking about their situation. He listens to podcasts every night while falling asleep, since otherwise he'd lay awake worrying about the money.[17] Kate and Tom are contemplating filing for bankruptcy, even though that wouldn't get rid of the student loans. Kate imagines that "one of us will die from stress, and the life insurance will pay out."

Ronald Read

Although Kate and Tom's story is tragically all-to-common these days, there are other stories, often with a different outcome. Ronald Read was born in rural Vermont. He was the first person in his family to graduate high school. For 25 years, Ronald worked at a gas station, after which he swept floors at JC Penney for 17 years.[18] He lived a simple and apparently unremarkable life. That is, until he made international headlines after he died in 2014, age 92. To the surprise of his family and friends, Read left in his will $2 million to his caregivers, family, and friends, and more than $6 million to his local hospital and library.[19] Everyone who knew him

---

[17] As the Apocrypha says: "Wakefulness over wealth wastes away one's flesh, and anxiety about it drives away sleep" (Sirach 31:1).

[18] Morgan Housel. *The Psychology of Money: Timeless Lessons on Wealth, Greed, and Happiness.* Hampshire, UK: Harriman House Limited, 2020.

[19] Niall J. Gannon. *Tailored Wealth Management: Exploring the Cause and Effect of Financial Success.* Springer, 2019, p. 11.

was baffled. Had he won the lottery? Gotten a secret inheritance? In fact, Mr. Read had saved what little he could and consistently invested it over the course of his life, waiting for decades on end as his small savings compounded into more than $8 million.

Discussion of the Stories

One of the main points of comparison between personal finance and social justice is that they are both often measured in terms of wealth differences. But that relationship quickly gets complicated when we explore the reasons *why* the differences exist or, from a moral perspective, whether some kinds of inequality *should* exist. When analyzing stories such as those of Kate and Tom or Ronald Read, the common talking points can, in general, be loosely categorized under two main theories regarding the relationship between personal finance and social justice.

Personal Responsibility

The first category emphasizes personal responsibility and focuses primarily on the role individuals play in dictating their results. Responses in this category typically argue against any hint of wealth redistribution, saying that it would only serve as a band-aid that doesn't address the underlying symptoms. To support this stance, these responses may point out that wealth redistribution *did* occur in Kate and Tom's story when Kate's mom gave them $40,000 to pay off their consumer debts. But it wasn't long before they had gotten themselves back into the same financial mess. Why? *Because their behavior didn't change.* Thus, behavior and financial literacy, according to this type of response, are the most important factors to be addressed in order to positively impact wealth inequality.

These responses may also contend that these stories demonstrate how responsible employment of sound financial principles can overcome a great deal of systemic injustice. Even the mere act of planning for the future has been shown in studies to be "a very strong predictor for wealth: those who do not plan get close to retirement with half the amount of wealth of those who have done some planning."[20]

Other responses in this category may suggest that the *real* social injustice was that Ronald Read, who acted responsibly with his money, had a lower salary during his life than Kate and Tom, who are irresponsible. Redistribution of wealth without accounting for individual behavior would be unjust and only continue to promote unhealthy financial behavior.

In summary, since behavior is such a strong predictor of the outcome (e.g., we aren't shocked that Kate and Tom are essentially broke, given their behavior), responses in this category suggest that poor financial literacy and behavioral issues are the primary diseases to be addressed. That is, knowing what to do and actually doing it is where our focus should lie. As Carrie Schwab-Pomerantz said, "At its core, financial literacy is about extending equal opportunities to all, regardless of socioeconomic background. It's about breaking down the barriers between the haves and the have-nots. It's a powerful tool for social justice that can arm people of all economic backgrounds with the knowledge, skill, and training they need to thrive in an increasingly complicated and competitive world."[21] Thus, according to this type of analysis, "issues of equity, and the social problems that reinforce them, are intimately tied to financial literacy."[22]

The Flower's Environment

Another category of responses to these stories focuses not on the behavior of the individuals, but on their environment, and asserts that "a conscientious form of financial literacy [...] acknowledges that one's access to financial resources represents a matter of one's origins."[23] As Alexander Den Heijer put it: "When a flower doesn't

---

[20] Annamaria Lusardi. *Americans' Financial Capability*. Tech. rep. National Bureau of Economic Research, 2011, p. 21.

[21] Carrie Schwab-Pomerantz. *Financial Literacy: A Powerful Tool for Social Justice in 2020 and Beyond*. 2020. URL: www.schwab.com/resource-center/insights/content/financial-literacy-powerful-tool-social-justice-2020-and-beyond (visited on 03/31/2021).

[22] Laura Elizabeth Pinto and Hannah Chan, "Social Justice and Financial Literacy," op. cit.

[23] Thomas A. Lucey. "A Critically Compassionate Approach to Financial Literacy: A Pursuit of Moral Spirit." In: *Education Sciences* 8.4 (2018), pp.

bloom, you fix the environment in which it grows, not the flower."[24]

Responses in this category typically argue that Kate and Tom's financial situation is "not their fault." They may point out that Ronald Read was born in 1921, more than three decades before credit cards were invented in the late 1950s.[25] So while Kate and Tom grew up in an environment where one of the most successfully marketed products of all time is credit card debt,[26] the culture during Ronald Read's formative years didn't even have that terminology. So, Ronald Read had a systemic advantage, because his formative years were not pressured towards financially harmful behavior by the predatory credit systems of our day.

Proponents of this type of response also suggest that focusing on personal responsibility can actually compound the problem of wealth inequality. For example, Dr. Laura E. Pinto of the University of Ontario Institute of Technology says: "It is tempting to think about financial literacy as a neutral construct when, in actuality, it can have the effect of reifying and reproducing inequities in society. Assumptions that all individuals come to financial life on an equal playing field are naïve in that they ignore the very different circumstances which cause individuals and groups to experience personal finance in very different ways."[27] Furthermore, the focus on personal responsibility can muddy the discussion, since "it's easy to reduce the inequities to choice. But [...] decisions are not that simple. [...] This type of choice discourse pathologizes and personalizes inequity, and conceals the systemic barriers [...]."[28] Some take the attack on financial behavior even further, claiming that "harboring this belief [that financial literacy is the

10–11; Annamaria Lusardi, Pierre-Carl Michaud, and Olivia S. Mitchell. "Optimal Financial Knowledge and Wealth Inequality." In: *Journal of Political Economy* 125.2 (2017).

[24]Alexander den Heijer. *Nothing You Don't Already Know: Remarkable Reminders About Meaning, Purpose, and Self-realization.* Scotts Valley, CA: CreateSpace Independent Publishing Platform, 2020.

[25]Dave Ramsey. *Dave Ramsey's Complete Guide to Money.* Brentwood, TN: Ramsey Press, 2011, p. 80.

[26]Ibid., p. 77.

[27]Laura Elizabeth Pinto and Elizabeth Coulson. "Social Justice and the Gender Politics of Financial Literacy Education." In: *Journal of the Canadian Association for Curriculum Studies* 9.2 (2011), pp. 55-56.

[28]Laura Elizabeth Pinto and Hannah Chan, "Social Justice and Financial Literacy," op. cit.

proper diagnosis] may be innocent, but it is not harmless; the pursuit of financial literacy poses costs that almost certainly swamp any benefits. For some consumers, financial education appears to increase confidence without improving ability, leading to worse decisions."[29] Chris Arthur summarizes well the concerns of this type of response:

> "Financial literacy [...] is particularly troubling in a context of massive wealth inequality as it decreases the likelihood that citizens who can provide for their needs through the market (private policing, transportation, healthcare and education) will feel responsible for the conditions faced by those citizens who cannot afford the services or [the] same quality of services that the better off receive. In fact, those who cannot afford to provide for their needs in the market will increasingly appear as irresponsible parasites that are a drain on our collective resources, or objects of pity who can only hope for charity. After all, having been given training on how to spend and save one's money (which is assumed to provide one with the ability to amass wealth and manage economic risk), those who fail to succeed in the market have only themselves to blame."[30]

After explaining the pitfalls of an emphasis on personal responsibility, responses in this category extend their critique to larger systemic issues in macroeconomics. The problem is that focusing on personal finance's relationship to social justice suggests that impoverished people should just "pull themselves up by the bootstraps,"[31] like the rich people supposedly have done. Unfortunately, this diverts attention away from more serious issues of injustice.

---

[29] Lauren E. Willis, "Against Financial-literacy Education," op. cit., pp. 197–198, 202.

[30] Chris Arthur. "Financial Literacy Education for Citizens: What Kind of Responsibility, Equality and Engagement?" In: *Citizenship, Social and Economics Education* 11.3 (2012), p. 168; also quoted in Thomas A. Lucey, "A Critically Compassionate Approach to Financial Literacy: A Pursuit of Moral Spirit," op. cit., p. 7.

[31] Frank Lesko, *Bootstraps*, op. cit.

Instead of being dictated by one's behavior, the wealth of an individual may be dictated primarily by their standing in a sociopolitical economic system, where things like race are the dominant predictors of the outcome.[32] Focusing on the "myth of individualism"[33] actually sustains the class system and the empire. What is needed instead "is to focus on collective transformation— a communal transformation."[34] For example, Walter Bruggeman and Ched Myers, proponents of Sabbath economics, point to the Old Testament practice of the Jubilee Year in Deuteronomy 15 which redistributes wealth through the cancellation of debts and redistribution of the land.[35] The "concern is [for] the oppressed, the broken-hearted, the captives, and the prisoners."[36] But the aim "was not only to protect the poor, but also to prevent the excessive accumulation of wealth in a few hands."[37] However, the idea of wealth redistribution is an emotionally provocative topic for some. Walter Bruggeman relates this personal story:

"A church friend and I never have lunch [during which] he doesn't rail against food stamps. He is so worried that somebody is going to get 'something for nothing.' [. . .] What he misses is that poor people work harder than rich people. That's not known. What interests me, of course, is that he never raises any questions about

[32] Robin DiAngelo. *White Fragility: Why It's So Hard for White People to Talk about Racism*. Boston, MA: Beacon Press, 2018. ISBN: 978-0-8070-4741-5, pp. 30–31.
[33] Walter Brueggemann, Peter Block, and John McKnight. *An Other Kingdom: Departing the Consumer Culture*. Hoboken, NJ: John Wiley & Sons, 2015. ISBN: 978-1-119-19472-9, p. 36.
[34] Ibid., p. 36.
[35] Ched Myers. *The Biblical Vision of Sabbath Economics*. Tell The Word, 2002; Walter Brueggemann, Peter Block, and John McKnight, *An Other Kingdom: Departing the Consumer Culture*, op. cit., pp. 34–35; Walter Brueggemann. *Money and Possessions: Interpretation: Resources for the Use of Scripture in the Church*. Louisville, KY: Westminster John Knox Press, 2016. ISBN: 9780664233648, p. 53; ibid., p. 93; Walter Brueggemann. *Journey to the Common Good*. Louisville, KY: Westminster John Knox Press, 2010. ISBN: 978-0-664-23516, p. 113.
[36] Ibid., p. 113.
[37] Cosimo Perrotta. *Consumption as an Investment: The Fear of Goods from Hesiod to Adam Smith*. Trans. by Joan McMullin. New York: Routledge, 2004. ISBN: 0-415-30619-1, p. 44.

what unearned gifts he might have received. And it only recently occurred to me that he never raises any questions about the huge subsidies to business and industry, which are all 'something for nothing.' But speak of those food stamps or those 'poor people,' and it touches a deep emotional chord."[38]

Indeed, it is extremely difficult to step outside one's privilege[39] and see what benefits we have received that we hypocritically decry for others. In summary, the stories of Kate and Tom and Ronald Read clearly provoke far more complex and emotional issues than just a mere discussion of the relationship between personal finance and social justice in the abstract. The relationship seems to be a complex interaction between at least politics, race, privilege, education, micro- and macro-economics, cultural factors, religion, and psychology.

Risks and Next Steps

As the stories and analysis above demonstrate, the relationship between social justice and personal finance is complex and multi-faceted. Here we find the truth in the ancient Proverb: *"The one who first states a case seems right, until the other comes and cross-examines"* (Proverbs 18:17). Not only do proposed solutions differ, but there is often disagreement over what the problem actually *is*. Some say that some types of wealth inequality *are* just. Others disagree saying no type of wealth inequality is a just outcome. Even a brief survey of the literature on how to reduce inequity shows that it is littered with assertions and "scathing rebuttals."[40]

Engaging in this confusing conversation carries certain risks, both personal and political. And it is tempting to try to avoid these risks. Indeed, some cower in the face of these risks by saying

---

[38]Walter Brueggemann, Peter Block, and John McKnight, *An Other Kingdom: Departing the Consumer Culture*, op. cit., p. 35.

[39]Robin DiAngelo, *White Fragility: Why It's So Hard for White People to Talk about Racism*, op. cit.

[40]Thomas A. Lucey. "The Art of Relating Moral Education to Financial Education: An Equity Imperative." In: *Social Studies Research and Practice* 2.3 (2007), p. 488.

that social justice cannot be defined[41] or even properly tested[42] and therefore "does not belong to the category of error but to that of nonsense."[43] Michael J. Sandel, Harvard University Affiliated Professor of Political Philosophy, argues against this type of philosophical skepticism saying:

> *"In the face of these risks, there is a characteristic evasion. [...] If Aristotle and Lock and Kant and Mill haven't solved these questions after all of these years, who are we to think that we [...] can resolve them? And so maybe it's just a matter of each person having his or her own principles and there's nothing more to be said about it. [...] That's the evasion—the evasion of skepticism. To which I would offer the following reply: It's true—these questions have been debated for a very long time. But the very fact that they have recurred and persisted may suggest that, though they're impossible in one sense, they're unavoidable in another. The reason they're unavoidable, the reason they're inescapable, is that we live some answer to these questions every day. So skepticism, just throwing up your hands and giving up on moral reflection, is no solution. Immanuel Kant described very well the problem with skepticism when he wrote 'Skepticism is a resting place for human reason, where it can reflect upon its dogmatic wanderings, but it is no dwelling place for permanent settlement.'[44] Simply to acquiesce in skepticism, Kant wrote, can never to suffice to overcome the restlessness of reason."[45]*

Reflecting on the complexity of the relationship between personal finance and social justice gives rise to a few observations

---

[41] Michael Novak. "Defining Social Justice." In: *First things* (2000).

[42] Friedrich August Hayek. *Law, Legislation and Liberty: A New Statement of the Liberal Principles of Justice and Political Economy.* Oxfordshire, UK: Routledge, 2012, p. 78.

[43] Ibid., p. 78.

[44] Immanuel Kant. *Critique of Pure Reason.* Trans. by Paul Guyer and Allen W. Wood. 1998, p. 654.

[45] Michael J. Sandel. "Lecture 1: The Moral Side of Murder." In: *Harvard University's Justice [Online Course]* (2005). URL: www.justiceharvard.org/themoralsideofmurder/ (visited on 04/17/2021).

which can guide our first steps into this crucial conversation, while avoiding the pitfalls of arrogance or apathy:

Engage Rather than Evade

We should seek to dialogue with those we disagree with. Otherwise we create our own echo chamber where an *illusion* of conversation is present, but it is only the reaffirmation of our own thoughts, where we succumb to the "social phenomenon of demonizing the Other."[46] Who among the prophets of our tradition spoke only to their own flock and shunned the treacherous waters of truly conversing with others? Without a clear consensus on a diagnosis of the problem that is universally applicable, we should be careful about prescribing universal solutions without first engaging in this difficult conversation with those of a different mindset. After all, "it is not difficult to find adverse consequences resulting from policies that lack meaningful input from all interested parties."[47] Furthermore, if the message and mission of Progressive Christianity has any true value, what good does it do if one "puts it under the bushel basket?"[48]

Consider Delivery as Well as the Message

Engaging with those who disagree with us is difficult. Given sharp disagreements on the relationship between personal finance and social justice, even in academic literature where professionalism is encouraged, it should be no surprise that discussions outside such environments are fraught with even more tension, varying opinions, and strong emotions. In order to be effectual, the church must be equipped to handle the conversation well and promote dialogue, not division. That is, *how* the message of social justice is delivered may have as much of an impact, if not more, than the message itself.

---

[46]A. Stephen Van Kuiken. *Demonizing the Other.* Community Congregational United Church of Christ. 15 July 2018, Pullman, WA. Sermon. URL: www . pullmanucc . org / 2018 / 07 / 18 / demonizing - the - other/ (visited on 05/22/2021).

[47]Thomas A. Lucey, "The Art of Relating Moral Education to Financial Education: An Equity Imperative," op. cit., p. 490.

[48]Matthew 5:15.

Reflect on our own motivations

Finally, in the vast flowing stream of what we call Christianity, we should ask what is our place in this discussion? What are our motivations? Do we dialogue merely to satisfy our intellect? Do we preach the message of social justice simply to feel morally superior? Or, like the prophets, have we had such a radical transformation by God's grace that we long to see the utopia of God's kingdom realized on earth? Our motivations and who our role models are, may affect not only how we think about these topics, but define where we even begin the discussion, and thus dictate the entire trajectory and impact of our part in this grand conversation.

In summary, it is suggested that we commit to engage not evade, promote dialogue which enlightens rather than entrenches,[49] reflect on our opinions, experiences, and motivations rather than blindly point fingers, and critically examine what has been passed down to us through our tradition. As advertised, this chapter does not resolve the topics at hand. To borrow the words of Old Testament scholar and Progressive Christian, Peter Enns, "I do not want to suggest that difficult problems have simple solutions. What I want to offer instead, is a proper starting point for discussing these problems, one that, if allowed to run its course, will reorient us to see the problems in a better light."[50] To increase the probability of a productive outcome when thinking about, discussing, and acting out the mission of social justice in both the personal arena and corporately as part of the church, a healthy starting point for effective communication is proposed next.

A Crucial Conversation

While there are many resources we could consult for navigating difficult conversations, we turn to the business world for inspiration, since it is here that communication has been extensively studied in recent decades. One of the most successful models for com-

---

[49]Peter Enns. *Inspiration and incarnation: Evangelicals and the Problem of the Old Testament*. 2nd ed. Grand Rapids: MI: Baker Academic, 2015. ISBN: 978-0-8010-9748-5, p. 2.

[50]Ibid., p. 5.

munication is the New York Times bestseller and business classic
Crucial Conversations: Tools for Talking When Stakes are High by
Kerry Patterson et al. The authors spent twenty-five years studying
the communication habits of the most effective people in organizations.[51] Patterson et al. argue that "the root cause of many—if not
most—human problems lies in how people behave when others disagree with them about high-stake, emotional issues."[52] Based on
two decades of research involving more than 100,000 people, they
found that "*the* key skill of effective leaders, teammates, parents,
and loved ones is the capacity to skillfully address emotionally- and
politically-risky issues"[53] and "in ways that were far more skilled
than their colleagues."[54]

According to Patterson et al., a *crucial conversation* is a discussion between two or more people which consists of three elements:

1. the stakes are high,

2. opinions vary, and

3. emotions run strong.[55]

Do discussions about the relationship between personal finance
and social justice qualify as a crucial conversation according to
this definition? Yes—these topics often seem to create the perfect
environment for a crucial conversation:

1. Both social justice and personal finance are high-stake topics,
   since they directly affect not only people's quality of life but
   often their ability to survive!

2. Even a brief survey of the topic of social justice shows that
   "versions of justice are as diverse as human culture itself."[56]

---

[51] Kerry Patterson et al. *Crucial Conversations: Tools for Talking When Stakes are High.* McGraw-Hill Education, 2012, p. 21.

[52] Ibid., p. xiii.

[53] Ibid., pp. 9–10.

[54] Ibid., p. 23.

[55] Ibid., p. 3.

[56] Geoff Broughton. "Restorative Justice and Jesus Christ: Why Restorative Justice Requires a Holistic Christology." PhD thesis. Charles Sturt University, 2011, p. 14.

Thus, encountering someone with an opposing opinion is almost unavoidable. It's likely that many people intuitively understand that personal finance is likewise a contentious topic with varying opinions. This can easily be inferred by the fact that "money fights and money problems are the number-one cause of divorce in North America."[57]

3. And finally, it doesn't take much exposure to history or current events to know that opinions about both social justice and money evoke a variety of intense feelings and spark protests, riots, and wars.[58]

Thus, even taken as individual topics, social justice and personal finance are crucial conversations. If there are any additive effects in their combination, this discussion is perilous indeed.

According to Patterson et al., the first step in engaging in a crucial conversation is to "start with the heart."[59]

Start With the Heart

This principle is about as age-old and time-tested as they come. Jesus spoke of it when he asked:

"Why do you see the speck in your neighbor's eye, but do not notice the log in your own eye?" (Matthew 7:3).

The Buddha referred to it when he asserted:

"Easily seen are the faults of others, but one's own are difficult to see. Like chaff, one winnows another's faults but hides one's own, even as a crafty fowler hides behind sham branches."[60]

---

[57]Dave Ramsey, *Dave Ramsey's Complete Guide to Money*, op. cit., p. 27.

[58]David De Cremer and Kees Van den Bos. "Justice and Feelings: Toward A New Era in Justice Research." In: *Social Justice Research* 20.1 (2007); Alan S. Kahan. *Mind vs. Money: The War Between Intellectuals and Capitalism.* New Brunswick, New Jersey: Transaction Publishers, 2010. ISBN: 978-1-4128-1063-0.

[59]Kerry Patterson et al., *Crucial Conversations: Tools for Talking When Stakes are High*, op. cit., pp. 33–50.

[60]Dhammapada 18:252 (Acharya Buddharakkhita. *The Dhammapada—The Buddha's Path of Wisdom.* Trans. by Acharya Buddharakkhita. Kandy, Sri Lanka: Buddhist Publication Society, 2003. ISBN: 978-955-24-0131-2, p. 82).

The famous Rabbi Hillel back in the time of Jesus adds: "Judge not your friend until you have stood in his place."[61]

The Buddha also taught:

> *"One should first establish oneself in what is proper; then only should one instruct others. Thus, the wise man will not be reproached. One should do what one teaches others to do; if one would train others, one should be well controlled oneself. Difficult, indeed, is self-control."*[62]

Likewise, the Chinese Classics agree on the importance of self-reflection as a first step towards supreme wisdom.[63] Thus, many of the greatest teachers of the past tell us that "criticizing others should come only after one's own self-reflection and self-examination."[64] Patterson et al. are well grounded in this

---

[61]Yitzhak Buxbaum. *The Life and Teachings of Hillel.* Plymouth, UK: Rowman & Littlefield Publishers, 2004, p. 108.

[62]Dhammapada 12:158–159.

[63] "If you know the enemy and know yourself, you need not fear the result of a hundred battles. If you know yourself but not the enemy, for every victory gained you will also suffer a defeat. If you know neither the enemy nor yourself, you will succumb in every battle" (The Art of War 3:18; Sūnzǐ. *Sun Tzu's The Art of War: Bilingual Edition Complete Chinese and English Text.* Ed. by John Minford. Trans. by Lionel Giles. 1st ed. Tokyo: Tuttle Publishing, 2012. ISBN: 978-0-8048-3944-0, p. 13). | "Someone who knows men has only knowledge, but to know yourself is perception" (Tao Te Ching 33; Lǎozǐ and James Trapp. *Tao Te Ching.* Ed. by Sarah Uttridge. Trans. by James Trapp. New York: Chartwell Books, 2015. ISBN: 978-0-7858-3319-2, p. 41). | "Whenever one acts to no avail, one should turn within and examine oneself. When one has made one's own person correct, the rest of the world will follow" (Mencius 4A4; Mèngzǐ. *Mencius.* Ed. by Philip J. Ivanhoe. Trans. by Irene Bloom. Translations from the Asian Classics. New York: Columbia University Press, 2009. ISBN: 978-0-231-12204-7, p. 76). | "The ancients who wished to illustrate illustrious virtue throughout the kingdom, first ordered well their states. Wishing to order well their states, they first regulated their families. Wishing to regulate their families, they first cultivated their persons. Wishing to cultivate their persons, they first rectified their hearts" (The Great Learning 1:2; Kǒng Fūzǐ. *The Sacred Books of China: The Texts of Confucianism.* Ed. by Friedrich Max Müller. Trans. by James Legge. Vol. 28. The Sacred Books of the East. Oxford: Clarendon Press, 1885, p. 411–412).

[64]John D. Mayer. *Why Confucius Had No Time to Judge.* 2009. URL: www.psychologytoday.com/us/blog/the-personality-analyst/200903/why-confucius-had-no-time-judge (visited on 04/18/2021).

wisdom when they teach their first principle for successful crucial conversations:

> *"This is the first principle of dialogue—Start with Heart. That is, your own heart. If you can't get yourself right, you'll have a hard time getting dialogue right. [...] Although it's true that there are times when we are merely bystanders in life's never-ending stream of head-on collisions, rarely are we completely innocent. More often than not, we do something to contribute to the problems we're experiencing. People who are best at dialogue understand this simple fact and turn it into the principle 'Work on me first, us second.' They realize not only that they are likely to benefit by improving their own approach, but also that they're the only person they can work on anyway.[65] As much as others may need to change, or we may want them to change, the only person we can continually inspire, prod, and shape—with any degree of success—is the person in the mirror."[66]*

So where should the discussion of personal finance and social justice begin? According to Patterson et al., it is best to start by reflecting on *our* personal finances and *our* work in the field of social justice. For example, before criticizing Kate and Tom for their out-of-control consumer spending habits and debt, I should reflect on my own habits. Even if my own habits aren't as extreme as Kate and Tom's, what are the opportunities for improvement in my own life? Before criticizing corporate greed, I should diligently squash any semblance of greed in my own life and thoughts. And before asserting ideas about justice on others, I should ask myself hard questions such as: "In a pluralistic world full of varying conceptions of justice, what place does *my* Christian conception of

---

[65] As René Descartes said, "there is nothing that is completely within our power except our thoughts" (René Descartes. *Discourse on Method and Meditations on First Philosophy.* Trans. by Donald A. Cress. 4th ed. Indianapolis, IN: Hackett Publishing, 1998, p. 15).

[66] Kerry Patterson et al., *Crucial Conversations: Tools for Talking When Stakes are High*, op. cit., pp. 33–35.

justice occupy? Is it just another rival version of justice?"[67] What do I *really* want as an outcome for myself, my community, and ultimately the world?

A possible objection is to ask what difference does it make, in the grand scheme of things, if I "work on *me* first, us second?"[68] Even if I were completely irresponsible with my finances or engaged in a few activities which promote social injustice, these are only a tiny fraction of the world's problems; wouldn't my time be better spent focusing on the "outward journey" and work to cause changes in the world which are larger than the impact of my insignificant personal life? Not so, according to decades of research on effective communication: Focusing first on our inward journey makes *all* the difference. Not because changes to my small sphere of influence are really that important but because starting with *my* heart and mastering *my* stories defines and flavors the entire trajectory and impact of the greater conversation. If our starting point is really a major predictor of our effectiveness in this conversation, then ignoring this call to self-reflection before outward discussion may greatly reduce the effectiveness of, if not bring to futility, our attempts to spread the message and enact the mission of social justice.

Summary

The analysis of Kate and Tom and Ronald Read illustrates how difficult it is to discuss our personal finance in any depth without considering the social structures within which they operate. That is, our personal finances can never be divorced from the larger systems. Major questions of interest include: How much of an individual's wealth is a result of the system? How much can be attributed to behavior? We find conclusive answers to these questions elusive. As Walter Brueggemann points out, even casual conversations with friends and family can erupt into emotionally-charged arguments. Even academic literature on the subject exhibits a thinly-veiled

---

[67] Geoff Broughton, "Restorative Justice and Jesus Christ: Why Restorative Justice Requires a Holistic Christology," op. cit., p. 14.

[68] Kerry Patterson et al., *Crucial Conversations: Tools for Talking When Stakes are High*, op. cit., p. 34.

vehemence towards opposing perspectives.

The easy way out is to compartmentalize these topics, as many people do. But I contend that we may miss the humility and grace that comes when studying the relationship between personal finance and social justice. For example, it can be easy to feel proud of building some wealth and criticize the poor for not doing the same, if inequities in the system are not taken into account. Likewise, we can feel disdain for those who receive more benefit from the economic systems than we do—believing that it's their fault. In many cases, it is not that the rich are immoral people. As Reinhold Niebuhr explains in his famous book *Moral Man and Immoral Society*, a society could consist of perfectly moral people individually, but they can still be participating in a societal sin by nature of the system they participate in.[69] Recognizing this allows us to turn our criticism towards unjust systems and show grace to the individual.

Great care must be taken by the modern Christian in navigating this high-stake discussion with a plethora of opinions and strong emotions. I argue, based on decades of research on effective communication which is in-line with ancient wisdom, that the best place to begin this discussion is with ourselves—focusing first on *our* inward journey before engaging with the outward journey, or telling others what *their* inward journey should look like. As Mahatma Gandhi said,

> *"If we could change ourselves, the tendencies in the world would also change. As a man changes his own nature, so does the attitude of the world change towards him. This is the divine mystery supreme. A wonderful thing it is and the source of our happiness. We need not wait to see what others do."*[70]

As Richard Rohr said, "None of us can dialogue with others

---

[69]Reinhold Niebuhr. *Moral Man and Immoral Society: A Study in Ethics and Politics*. New York: Continuum, 2005. ISBN: 0-8264-7714-3.

[70]Margaret W. Fisher. "The Collected Works of Mahatma Gandhi, Volumes I–XII (1884–1914)." In: *American Political Science Review* 60.1 (1966), p. 158.

until we can calmly and confidently hold our own identity."[71] So, let's start by changing *ourselves* and crafting our own identity. To this end, the following chapters continue to explore the interaction between faith, personal finance, and social justice while challenging us to live in the tension they create and integrate them in our own lives before preaching a message of their unification for others.

---

[71] Richard Rohr. *Falling Upward: A Spirituality for the Two Halves of Life.* San Francisco, CA: John Wiley & Sons, 2011. ISBN: 978-0-470-90775-7, p. 42.

Chapter 2

The Moral Status of Wealth

"As soon as we become aware of money, we develop beliefs about it—beliefs we cling to, sometimes for the rest of our lives, often at the cost of our souls."[1] — George Kinder, Spiritual Teacher and Life Planner

EVEN though I advocate for the unification of personal finance, faith, and social justice, this vision poses a perpetual challenge: tensions arise which have no tidy solution for relief, and it is our responsibility to lean into the tension rather than avoid it. For example, mindfulness is an important part of many faith traditions. When applied to personal finance, profound benefits can be realized. In my experience, wealth can increase exponentially when one is mindful of the flow of money in one's life. Thus, spirituality can have a profoundly positive influence on finances. However—and this is where the problem lies—many of our ancient texts criticize those who have obtained some measure of wealth. Some texts paint such a disparaging image of wealth that they can hardly be read without cultivating suspicion that merely possessing some wealth is a participation in evil. Furthermore, the ancient

---

[1] George Kinder. *The Seven Stages of Money Maturity: Understanding the Spirit and Value of Money in Your Life.* New York: Dell Publishing, 2012, p. 33.

texts provide a diverse array of opinions regarding the moral status
of wealth. Some cite it as a blessing from God and others suggest
that wealth and material possessions should be dispensed with entirely in favor of spiritual treasures. The tension is this: the Bible
may give us a proverb which, if followed, increases our wealth. But
then the very same Bible appears to simultaneously criticize those
who have some wealth!

As a result, some people "get confused about things when they
finally have a little money."[2] The culture of shame in Evangelicalism which Progressive Christians so often condemn[3] can quietly
work its way into our lives regarding wealth.[4] Should those of us
who find our net worth exceeds others in our global society feel
shame about that position? Is wealth inherently immoral? Is it
inherently a blessing? Or is it amoral, having no moral qualities in
itself until it is used to perform a moral or immoral action? Does
the moral status of wealth just depend on our attitude? As Shakespeare famously said: *"There is nothing either good or bad, but
thinking makes it so."*[5] Should we shun wealth and follow Jesus'
command to the Rich Ruler to *"go, sell your possessions, and give
the money to the poor, and you will have treasure in heaven; then
come, follow me"*?[6] These questions all relate on some level to the
moral status of wealth, which is one of the most confused areas in

---

[2]Dave Ramsey, *The Legacy Journey: A Radical View of Biblical Wealth
and Generosity*, op. cit., p. 37.

[3]Polk Culpepper. *Churches Teaching the Doctrine of Shame*. 2015. URL:
www.progressivechristianity.org/resources/churches-teaching-the-
doctrine-of-shame/ (visited on 02/13/2021); Frank Lesko. *How Toxic Shame
Turns Evangelization Into Abuse*. 2015. URL: www.progressivechristianity.
org/resources/how-toxic-shame-turns-evangelization-into-abuse/
(visited on 02/13/2021); Polk Culpepper. *Shame Based Prayers: 'You May
Be a Child of God, But You Are Still an Unworthy Human Being'*. 2015.
URL: https://www.progressivechristianity.org/resources/shamed-based-
prayers-you-may-be-a-child-of-god-but-you-are-still-an-unworthy-
human-being/ (visited on 02/13/2021); Linda Kay Klein. *Pure: Inside the
Evangelical Movement that Shamed a Generation of Young Women and How
I Broke Free*. Simon and Schuster, 2018.

[4]J. W. Bennison. *The Affliction of Affluence: Reconciling Gratitude, Generosity and Greed*. 2012. URL: www.wordsnways.com/the-affliction-
of-affluence-reconciling-gratitude-greed-generosity (visited on
02/13/2021).

[5]*Hamlet* 2.2.244–245.

[6]Matthew 19:21.

Christian theology and one that causes much division.[7]

This essay first motivates the issue by examining the results of mindfulness in finance. Application of spiritual principles to personal finance can raise questions of the moral status of wealth. We then explore what the Bible says on the topic and shed some light on the roles of the Old and New Testaments. Finally, the essay argues that the Bible, as Peter Enns says, "doesn't do the heavy lifting for us. It alerts us that *we* have to. We cannot escape that sacred responsibility—ever."[8] Following the precedent set in the previous essay, we here undertake not to answer once and for all these perennial questions. Instead, by shedding light on the motivations driving some to these questions and by critically examining how the Bible behaves, we can hope to open the door for further exploration as we seek to build our own "theology" of personal finance and wealth.

FIRE and Mindfulness

Mindfulness can improve a variety of aspects of life, including personal finance.[9] Although current research on the relationship between mindfulness and personal awareness is sparse, it is known that cultivating mindfulness strengthens the reflexive and reflective systems of the mind, thus impacting behavior and decisions relating to personal finance.[10] Evidence of the power of mindfulness applied to finance can be found in a recent lifestyle movement called FIRE (Financial Independence, Retire Early), which has attracted a wide following, especially among millennials.[11] It seeks

---

[7]Sondra Ely Wheeler, *Wealth as Peril and Obligation: The New Testament on Possessions*, op. cit., p. xv.

[8]Peter Enns, *How the Bible Actually Works: In which I Explain How an Ancient, Ambiguous, and Diverse Book Leads us to Wisdom Rather Than Answers—And Why That's Great News*, op. cit., p. 34.

[9]Wray Herbert. "Mindfulness and Heuristics." In: *The Wiley Blackwell Handbook of Mindfulness* (2014).

[10]Dan Stone. "Cultivating Financial Mindfulness: A Dual-process Theory." In: *Consumer Knowledge and Financial Decisions*. Springer, 2011.

[11]Ann Brenoff. *7 Things You Can Learn From The 'FIRE' Early Retirement Movement*. 2018. URL: https://bit.ly/3ncRv4I (visited on 04/21/2021); Kristin Wong. *The Basics of FIRE (Financial Independence and Early Retirement)*. 2019. URL: www.twocents.lifehacker.com/the-basics-of-fire-

freedom, not only from "the labor market, but also from materialism, consumerism, and consumer debt."[12] Those seeking to attain FIRE intentionally maximize their savings rate by finding ways to increase income and/or decrease expenses in order to accumulate assets until the resulting passive income provides enough money for living expenses throughout one's retirement years.[13] The movement began in 1992 with the bestselling book, *Your Money or Your Life,* by Vicki Robin.[14]

Robin argues that money is one's life energy: "Money is something you trade your life energy for. You sell your time for money."[15] Based on this premise, Robin teaches a mindfulness-based "spiritual practice for living in a very material world."[16]

financial-independence-and-early-re-1820129768 (visited on 04/21/2021); S. Wills. *Meet the Young People Who Are Retiring in Their 30s.* 2018. URL: www.vice.com/en/article/qvnwvq/financial-independence-retire-early (visited on 04/21/2021); Greg Daugherty. *What 30-Year-Old Retirees Can Teach The Rest Of Us.* 2014. URL: www.forbes.com/sites/nextavenue/2014/03/21/what-30-year-old-retirees-can-teach-the-rest-of-us/?sh=12ac29e437b0 (visited on 04/21/2021); Money. *A Growing Cult of Millennials Is Obsessed With Early Retirement. This 72-Year-Old Is Their Unlikely Inspiration.* 2018. URL: www.money.com/vicki-robin-financial-independence-retire-early/ (visited on 04/21/2021).

[12]Nick Taylor and William Davies. "The Financialization of Anti-capitalism? The Case of the 'Financial Independence Retire Early' Community." In: *Journal of Cultural Economy* (2021).

[13]J. L. Collins and Peter (Mr. Money Mustache) Adeney. *The Simple Path to Wealth: Your Road Map to Financial Independence and a Rich, Free Life.* Scotts Valley, CA: CreateSpace Independent Publishing Platform, 2016. ISBN: 9781533667922; J. L. Fisker. *Early Retirement Extreme: A Philosophical and Practical Guide to Financial Independence.* Scotts Valley, CA: CreateSpace Independent Publishing Platform, 2010; Vicki Robin, Joe Dominguez, and Monique Tilford. *Your Money or Your Life: 9 Steps to Transforming Your Relationship With Money and Achieving Financial Independence.* New York: Penguin, 2008; Scott Rieckens and Peter Adeney. *Playing with FIRE (Financial Independence Retire Early).* Novato, CA: New World Library, 2019.

[14]Vicki Robin, Joe Dominguez, and Monique Tilford, *Your Money or Your Life: 9 Steps to Transforming Your Relationship With Money and Achieving Financial Independence*, op. cit.

[15]Ibid., p. 48.

[16]Vicki Robin. *Your Money or Your Life: An Interview with Author Vicki Robin [Podcast].* 2017. URL: www.madfientist.com/vicki-robin-interview/ (visited on 04/20/2021); Vicki Robin, Joe Dominguez, and Monique Tilford, *Your Money or Your Life: 9 Steps to Transforming Your Relationship With Money and Achieving Financial Independence*, op. cit., pp. 70–71.

The goal is to "train the mind to be here now, 'in the moment'"[17] by tracking one's life energy.[18] Robin teaches a 9-step program to incorporate mindfulness in personal finance:[19]

Step 1: Making Peace with the Past Find out your total lifetime earnings—the sum total of your gross income. What have you to show for it? Do this without judgment, just take note of it.

Step 2: Being in the Present—Tracking Your Life Energy How much are you trading your life energy for? Establish the actual costs in time and money required to maintain your job and compute your *real* hourly wage. Factor in commuting, clothing, meals, time and money spent on daily decompression, time and money spent on "escape entertainment," vacations, job-related illnesses, and other job-related expenses.

Step 3: Where Is It All Going? (The Monthly Tabulation) Every month, total all your expenses within categories generated by your own unique spending pattern. Convert dollars spent in each category to "hours of life energy," using your real hourly wage from Step 2.

Step 4: Three Questions That Will Transform Your Life On your Monthly Tabulation, ask these three questions of each category, total expressed as hours of life energy, and record your responses:

1. Did I receive fulfillment, satisfaction, and value in proportion to life energy spent?

2. Is this expenditure of life energy in alignment with my values and life purpose?

3. How might this expenditure change if I didn't have to work for money?

---

[17]Ibid., p. 70.
[18]Ibid., p. 57.
[19]Ibid., p. 307–309.

For each question in each category, evaluate whether the expense should increase, decrease, or stay the same for your optimal fulfillment. The remaining steps deal with making life energy visible through a large wall chart, valuing your life energy by minimizing spending, valuing your life energy by maximizing income, tracking progress towards financial independence, and investing.

The heart of the program is contained in Steps 2–4. Step 2 often reveals that one's real hourly wage is often far lower than we may realize. For example, Lisa, who makes \$25/hr may find that, after taxes and all her job-related expenses, her real hourly wage is \$14/hr. Once this is realized, the goal is to ask whether the things we spend money on are *actually* providing enough value in return for our life energy. Lisa may be considering purchasing a new car for \$20,000, which translates into over 1,400+ hours of her life energy. The question is: "Will the new car bring enough satisfaction and fulfillment to overcome the additional 35 weeks of full-time labor?" If so, then this transaction will produce a net positive in happiness. If not, then purchasing the car actually results in an overall decrease in happiness. Similarly, a \$12 margarita would cost Lisa 51 mins of labor. Is the happiness derived from the drink worth this extra hour of labor? Maybe, maybe not. That's for Lisa to decide. As the prophet Isaiah said,

> *"Why do you spend your money for that which is not bread, and your labor for that which does not satisfy? Listen carefully to me, and eat what is good, and delight yourselves in rich food"* (Isaiah 55:2).

Vicki Robin's program charges us to track every cent that comes into or out of our lives, convert to life energy, and create a list of all our transactions. Then, without judgment, mark next to each transaction whether it produced a net positive, neutral, or negative effect in our life.

After several months of performing this exercise, the mind becomes trained to see the flow of life energy and starts to naturally redirect it towards things that maximize happiness. Many people find that the majority of things they spend their money on actually decrease happiness rather than increase it and that they don't do enough of the things which genuinely are worth it to them. Increased spending in those areas has a net increase in happiness and satisfaction.

What is the consequence of applying mindfulness to finance? Does it only slightly decrease one's spending overall and give a little extra money for saving? In fact, Robin's book is full of stories from people whose lives have been completely transformed by employing mindfulness in their finances. As one who has followed this program, my story can illustrate the potential for impact.

After graduating college, getting married, and entering the workforce, my wife and I weren't very good at managing money. Correction: *I* wasn't very good at managing money. Every paycheck that came in went out quickly without much, if any, being retained. To be sure, our net worth did increase during the first few years, but progress was hampered by increasing levels of debt. As the debt increased, so did the stress levels. After a few years, desperate to reduce the financial stress, and having read the formative writings of the FIRE movement, I finally decided to employ them. As shown in Fig. 2.1, the results of applying mindfulness to finance are unmistakable; the yearly rate of increase in wealth nearly tripled. If sustained and compounded with a 10% rate of return[20] over a working lifetime of 30 years, the trajectory of the mindfulness path in Fig. 2.1 results in several million dollars *more* than the non-mindfulness path at retirement age. But the benefits of this path extend far beyond the finances. By spending less on things that produce a net negative impact on life and increasing spending on things that are actually meaningful, such as giving, the quality of one's life is improved. The consequences of mindfulness in finance are clearly far-reaching and potentially massive.

Although application of mindfulness to finances may not immediately place one in the "wealthy" category, even a change of trajectory raises new questions. What should we *do* with our money? How should we feel about being on this trajectory, potentially leading towards being considered wealthy? Popular options include feelings of shame or pride, neither of which are spiritually healthy perspectives. Should we try to avoid this trajectory by giving away any excess beyond our minimum necessary expenses? If so, what

---

[20]See Appendix A "Stock Market Growth Calculations" on page 147 for an explanation of long-term stock market returns.

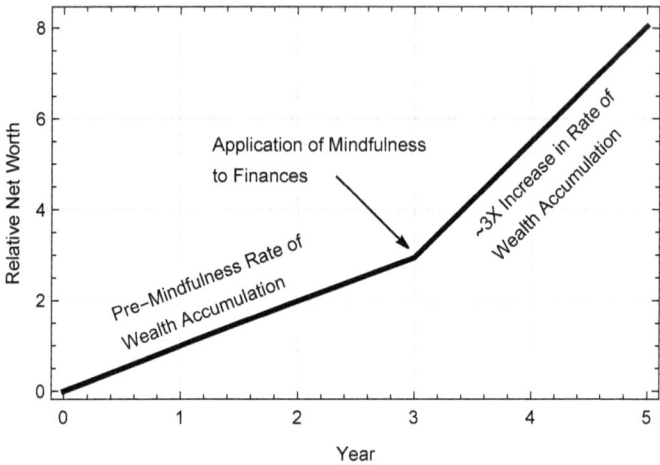

Figure 2.1: Effect of Mindfulness in Finances

is considered a "necessary" expense? How much should we be saving for retirement? In the wake of pervasive global poverty, is it morally acceptable to enjoy wealth? How much is morally acceptable to enjoy? These are all questions which may be sparked, even if unintentionally, by simply following the spiritual practice of mindfulness.

To explore these questions, we now turn to the Bible. Given its importance, not only in the formation of the Christian tradition, but in Western society, its influence and voice are palpable. Its set of diverse opinions on this topic must either be dealt with, at a minimum, or better, be allowed to be part of the conversation.

The Moral Status of Wealth in the Bible

The Bible has much to say which relates to the moral status of wealth. However, its presentation is by no means systematic— "messy"[21] is a better descriptor. Hermeneutical problems abound

---

[21]Peter Enns, *How the Bible Actually Works: In which I Explain How an Ancient, Ambiguous, and Diverse Book Leads us to Wisdom Rather Than*

as questions arise regarding whether certain texts are prescriptive or descriptive. Far from being "univocal,"[22] the Bible presents a plethora of divergent opinions. Wealth is treated as both a blessing to be enjoyed and a spiritual distraction to be shunned. It is considered both a mark of God's favor on the righteous and as a symptom of economic injustice and oppression. Wealth is described as being a systematic result of diligent labor and a result of seemingly random distribution from God.[23] As Bart Ehrman says, even within the New Testament, views are divergent:

> *"Historians who have carefully examined the New Testament have found that its authors do, in fact, embody remarkably diverse points of view. These scholars have concluded that the most fruitful way to interpret the New Testament authors is to read them individually rather than collectively."*[24]

Christian Smith thus argues:

> *"Where scripture is sometimes internally at odds with itself, even apparently self-contradictory, we would do better to let stand the tensions and inconsistencies than*

Answers—And Why That's Great News, op. cit., p. 81.

[22] Sondra Ely Wheeler, *Wealth as Peril and Obligation: The New Testament on Possessions*, op. cit., p. 125.

[23] For example, in the Deuteronomic view of the world, God's relationship with humans is described in very transactional terms. Do good and God will bless you with abundance, do evil and God will curse you with its removal (Deuteronomy 28). Other biblical authors point out that this is not, in fact, how the world actually appears to work. As the author of Ecclesiastes says, "there is a vanity that takes place on earth, that there are righteous people who are treated according to the conduct of the wicked, and there are wicked people who are treated according to the conduct of the righteous. I said that this also is vanity" (Ecclesiastes 8:14). Thom Stark. *The Human Faces of God: What Scripture Reveals When it Gets God Wrong (and Why Inerrancy Tries to Hide It)*. Eugene, OR: Wipf and Stock Publishers, 2011. ISBN: 978-1-60899-323-9, pp. 6–12.

[24] Bart D. Ehrman. *The New Testament: A Historical Introduction to the Early Christian Writings*. 2nd ed. Oxford: Oxford University Press, 2000, p. 13; Bart D. Ehrman. *Jesus, Interrupted: Revealing the Hidden Contradictions in the Bible (And Why We Don't Know About Them)*. New York: HarperOne, 2009, p. 99.

to force them into an artificial harmony. "[25]

Accordingly, this biblical survey, at the risk of oversimplification, organizes the biblical authors' views into two broad categories, positive and negative judgments about the moral status of wealth. Some observations about the differences between the Old and New Testaments are discussed, and the reader is encouraged to develop for themselves, their own "theology" of wealth and finance.

Wealth as Blessing and Reward

In many passages, wealth is treated in a positive light, either as inherently good or as evidence of diligence and wisdom and as a reward from God for living a moral and faithful life. Wealth is described as the blessing on the faithful[26] as well as the reward of diligence, labor, and "worldly prudence."[27]

Wealth—A Blessing from God to be Enjoyed

Throughout the Hebrew scriptures, the reward of faithfulness is abundance and prosperity. Wealth, in this view, is a "mark of God's favor and its withdrawal a sign of his judgment."[28] As Sondra Wheeler puts it:

> *"The same Deuteronomic and prophetic traditions which excoriate the apostasy, oppression, and heartlessness of the rich, promise all manner of abundance as the consequence of fidelity to God and God's covenant. There is no trace of irony as both the law and the prophets depict the overflowing of grain and wine and oil, the proliferation of flocks and herds, and even the*

---

[25] Christian Smith. *The Bible Made Impossible: Why Biblicism Is Not a Truly Evangelical Reading of Scripture.* Grand Rapids, MI: Brazos Press, 2012, p. 133.

[26] Sondra Ely Wheeler, *Wealth as Peril and Obligation: The New Testament on Possessions,* op. cit., p. 125.

[27] Ibid., p. 126.

[28] Ibid., p. 125.

flow of golden tribute from vassal states that will be the result of faithfulness."[29]

Although wealth brings many benefits, it is meaningless if not enjoyed. Qohelet says,

> *"There is an evil that I have seen under the sun, and it lies heavy upon humankind: those to whom God gives wealth, possessions, and honor, so that they lack nothing of all that they desire, yet God does not enable them to enjoy these things, but a stranger enjoys them. This is vanity; it is a grievous ill"* (Ecclesiastes 6:1–2).

We find a similar mentality throughout the Hebrew scriptures—one that views wealth and income as a positive blessing from God and encourages us to enjoy it and share it with others. For example, in a passage on regulations concerning tithes in Deuteronomy 14, the ancient Israelites were told to gather their yearly tithes and consume them in a great feast.

> *"Set apart a tithe of all the yield of your seed that is brought in yearly from the field. In the presence of the Lord your God, in the place that he will choose as a dwelling for his name, you shall eat the tithe of your grain, your wine, and your oil, as well as the firstlings of your herd and flock, so that you may learn to fear the Lord your God always. But if, when the Lord your God has blessed you, the distance is so great that you are unable to transport it, because the place where the Lord your God will choose to set his name is too far away from you, then you may turn it into money. With the money secure in hand, go to the place that the Lord your God will choose; spend the money for whatever you wish—oxen, sheep, wine, strong drink, or whatever you desire. And you shall eat there in the presence of the Lord your God, you and your household rejoicing together. As for the Levites resident in your towns, do*

---

[29]Leviticus 26:3–5; Leviticus 26:9–10; Deuteronomy 11:13–15; Isaiah 54:11–12; Isaiah 60:9–16; Jeremiah 33:6–9; ibid., p. 125.

> *not neglect them, because they have no allotment or in-*
> *heritance with you. Every third year you shall bring*
> *out the full tithe of your produce for that year, and*
> *store it within your towns; the Levites, because they*
> *have no allotment or inheritance with you, as well as*
> *the resident aliens, the orphans, and the widows in your*
> *towns, may come and eat their fill so that the Lord your*
> *God may bless you in all the work that you undertake"*
> (Deuteronomy 14:22–29).

As Qohelet said: "Feasts are made for laughter; wine gladdens life, and money meets every need,"[30] and the Apocrypha adds: "Wealth and wages make life sweet."[31] But the benefits of wealth extend beyond the direct enjoyment of them. According to several passages, wealth also brings friends,[32] honor,[33] glory,[34] security,[35] and an occasion to rejoice.[36]

It is important to note that this positive view of wealth is coupled with the refrain throughout the Hebrew scriptures that wealth (and the enjoyment of it) is a gift from God—a fact we will do well to remember:[37] "All to whom God gives wealth and possessions and whom he enables to enjoy them, and to accept their lot and find enjoyment in their toil—this is the gift of God" (Ecclesiastes 5:19). "But remember the Lord your God, for it is he who gives you power to get wealth" (Deuteronomy 8:18). These positive emotions evoked by this view are captured well by the psalmist's exclamation: "Happy are those who fear the Lord! [...] Wealth and riches are in their houses, and their righteousness endures forever" (Psalm 112:3).

---

[30] Ecclesiastes 10:19.
[31] Sirach 40:18.
[32] Proverbs 19:4.
[33] Sirach 10:30–31.
[34] Isaiah 61:6; Greek Esther 10:2.
[35] Proverbs 18:11; Proverbs 10:15; Ecclesiastes 7:12.
[36] Isaiah 6:10.
[37] Psalm 105:44; Sirach 11:14.

Wealth as a Reward for Labor, Diligence, and Wisdom

Although wealth is overwhelmingly described as being a gift from God, the element of human responsibility is not neglected. Wealth is also described as a result of "hard work, thrift, and discipline"[38] but "laziness, waste, and self-indulgence are responsible for poverty and want."[39] We are told that "the lazy do not roast their game, but the diligent obtain precious wealth (Proverbs 12:27); "wealth hastily gotten will dwindle, but those who gather little by little will increase it" (Proverbs 13:11); "By your great wisdom in trade you have increased your wealth" (Ezekiel 28:5); and "the good leave an inheritance to their children's children, but the sinner's wealth is laid up for the righteous" (Proverbs 13:22).

This dependence on human responsibility is also implied by curses found in various passages. A common theme among God's curses towards the unfaithful is the removal of their wealth.[40] Wealth must therefore have some positive status since otherwise its removal wouldn't make for much of a punishment. Thus, it is also intimately connected with wisdom, faithfulness, and upright moral character and obedience to God. On this basis, many individuals in the Bible are described as wealthy, where the term has positive and praiseworthy connotations.[41] In fact, in the Apocrypha, a lengthy hymn is devoted to the famous men of old, many of whom were wealthy:

> *"Let us now sing the praises of famous men [such as Enoch, Noah, Abraham, Moses, Aaron, Phinehas, etc.], our ancestors in their generations. [...] their wealth will remain with their descendants, and their inheritance with their children's children"* (Sirach 44:1–11).

In summary, wealth, according to these texts, is something to be desired. It is a mark of God's favor—a motivator for faithfulness

---

[38] Proverbs 10:4; Proverbs 12:11; Proverbs 12:24; Proverbs 13:4; Proverbs 14:23; Proverbs 21:5; Sondra Ely Wheeler, *Wealth as Peril and Obligation: The New Testament on Possessions*, op. cit., p. 126.

[39] Proverbs 20:4; Proverbs 20:13; Proverbs 21:17; Proverbs 21:20; Proverbs 23:5; Proverbs 23:21; ibid., p. 126.

[40] Jeremiah 15:13; Jeremiah 17:3; Jeremiah 20:5; Ezekiel 27:12; Ezekiel 29:19; Ezekiel 30:4; Zephaniah 1:13; Zechariah 9:4; Sirach 40:13; 2 Esdras 15:63.

[41] 1 Samuel 9:1; 2 Samuel 19:32; 2 Kings 4:8; Genesis 26:13.

and hard work. Wealth is described as a reward for faithfulness, righteousness, hard work, and worldly prudence. Those who are wealthy are accordingly worthy of admiration and praise. Despite these elements of human responsibility, wealth is still ultimately a gift from God, a fact that we are warned not to forget. But it is a gift which is intended to be enjoyed and shared. God apparently smiles on his children when they rejoice and feast in their abundance with an attitude of gratefulness.

Wealth as Peril and a Symptom of Injustice

While the strand of tradition which supports a positive and celebratory view of wealth is vibrant, even more abundant and forceful are the warnings about the dangers of wealth and commands regarding our obligations concerning it. It is described as an occasion for idolatry,[42] a competing object of devotion,[43] and a stumbling block or practical hindrance to those who would follow Jesus.[44]

Wealth as a Spiritual Impediment

In the Old Testament, material wealth "is repeatedly associated with apostasy, as the comforts of prosperity lead the people to rely on their wealth, or, more commonly, on the adopted gods of their pagan neighbors as the source of their safety and their well-being."[45] In the New Testament, wealth and prosperity are practically antithetical to communion with God. Wealth is a spiritual impediment, as evidenced most clearly in Jesus' teaching that "No one can serve two masters; for a slave will either hate the one and love the other, or be devoted to the one and despise the other. You cannot serve God and wealth."[46] With vivid imagery, Jesus describes the lures of wealth as choking the Divine word, causing it to

---

[42]Sondra Ely Wheeler, *Wealth as Peril and Obligation: The New Testament on Possessions*, op. cit., p. 123.

[43]Ibid., p. 129.

[44]Ibid., p. 127.

[45]Ibid., p. 123.

[46]Matthew 6:24; Luke 16:13; A. Stephen Van Kuiken. *Whom do you serve?* Community Congregational United Church of Christ. 9 Aug. 2020, Pullman, WA. Sermon. URL: www.pullmanucc.org/2020/08/10/whom-do-you-serve/ (visited on 02/13/2021).

yield nothing.[47] The Wisdom of Sirach adds agreement: "One who loves gold will not be justified; one who pursues money will be led astray by it."[48] Wealth in this view seems to have no moral properties which can propel us towards communion with God. Rather, its magnetic pull drags us outside the kingdom of God. As Jesus said to his disciples, "How hard it will be for those who have wealth to enter the kingdom of God!"[49] Even following all God's commandments and living a moral and upright life is apparently not enough to overcome the allurement of wealth's spiritual barricade. Jesus' command to the Rich Ruler was: "If you wish to be perfect, go, sell your possessions, and give the money to the poor, and you will have treasure in heaven; then come, follow me."[50] The question of whether Jesus was simply teasing out a moral shortcoming in the life of that specific individual or whether he was making a claim about the fundamental moral status of wealth has been debated for 2,000 years. But it would be hard to sustain an interpretation of Jesus' teachings that shows he was promoting a *positive* view of wealth's moral status. At best, wealth is either morally neutral or, at worst, practically demonic.

The bulk of the teachings which cast wealth as a spiritual impediment center around one's attitude towards money. Pride,[51] arrogance,[52] and the love of money[53] are consistently condemned. Wealth is said to be a particularly dangerous catalyst for these attitudes. Do not say to yourself, "My power and the might of my own hand have gotten me this wealth,"[54] as did Ephraim.[55] As Habakkuk said: "Wealth is treacherous; the arrogant do not endure. They open their throats wide as Sheol; like Death they never have enough."[56] Jeremiah adds: "Thus says the Lord: Do not let the wise boast in their wisdom, do not let the mighty boast in their

---

[47] Matthew 13:22; Mark 4:19.
[48] Sirach 31:5.
[49] Mark 10:23; Luke 18:24.
[50] Matthew 19:21; Mark 10:21; Luke 18:22.
[51] Ezekiel 28:5.
[52] Wisdom 5:8.
[53] Ecclesiastes 5:10.
[54] Deuteronomy 8:17.
[55] Hosea 12:8.
[56] Habakkuk 2:5.

might, do not let the wealthy boast in their wealth."[57] Job even denied rejoicing in his wealth because that "would be an iniquity to be punished by the judges."[58] Furthermore, "The love of money is a root of all kinds of evil, and in their eagerness to be rich some have wandered away from the faith and pierced themselves with many pains."[59] In the pastoral epistles, the love of money is listed alongside drunkenness, violence and arrogance, and disqualifies one for church leadership.[60]

In addition to being considered a direct spiritual impediment, pursuit of wealth is also discouraged since it is simply not as worthy of our attention when compared to more spiritual options. Pursuit of wealth is not satisfying,[61] not as good as generosity,[62] inferior to wisdom and knowledge,[63] and transitory and unreliable.[64] Even suffering for the Christ is considered to be better than the treasures of Egypt.[65] Jesus thus commands: "Sell your possessions, and give alms. Make purses for yourselves that do not wear out, an unfailing treasure in heaven, where no thief comes near and no moth destroys. For where your treasure is, there your heart will be also."[66]

Wealth as the Fruit of Injustice

While most scholars agree that Israel received its concern for social justice from the Near Eastern cultures surrounding it,[67] "Israel knew well what social justice was because it had been born in that condition. Israel came into being in a situation of op-

---

[57] Jeremiah 9:23.

[58] Job 31:24–28.

[59] 1 Timothy 6:10.

[60] 1 Timothy 3:2–4; 1 Timothy 3:8; 2 Timothy 3:2.

[61] Ecclesiastes 5:10.

[62] Tobit 12:8.

[63] 2 Chronicles 1:11; Sirach 51:25; Wisdom 7:8.

[64] Psalm 49:16; Psalm 52:7; Sirach 5:1; Sirach 5:8; Luke 16:9.

[65] Hebrews 11:26.

[66] Luke 12:33–34.

[67] Bruce V. Malchow. *Social Justice in the Hebrew Bible: What is New and What is Old.* Collegeville, MN: Liturgical Press, 1996, p. 1; F. Charles Fensham. "Widow, Orphan, and the Poor in Ancient Near Eastern Legal and Wisdom Literature." In: *Journal of Near Eastern Studies* 21.2 (1962).

pression in Egypt."[68] Thus, suspicion of wealth and concern for justice are major themes throughout the prophets, from Isaiah to Malachi. They make the accusation that "the rich have become so by using false dealing and dishonest weights and measures (e.g., Micah 6:10–12) and by taking advantage of the poor, especially widows and orphans who are without any protection (e.g., Isaiah 10:1–3)."[69] Theologian José Miranda says: "The fact that differentiating wealth is unacquirable without violence and spoliation is presupposed by the Bible in its pointed anathemas against the rich; therefore almsgiving is nothing more than restitution of what has been stolen, and thus the Bible calls it justice."[70] The indictments against the wealthy are "fierce and colorful."[71] As Jeremiah said: "Like the partridge hatching what it did not lay, so are all who amass wealth unjustly; in mid-life it will leave them, and at their end they will prove to be fools."[72]

The association of wealth with evil and oppression continues into the New Testament. The "announcement of the gospel is portrayed as bringing blessing to the poor and woe to the rich."[73] As Jesus turns upside down the commonsense notions of the day regarding who belongs in the kingdom of God, the rich are constantly pitted against the poor where, in this redemptive eschatology, the poor and oppressed are favored in the end.[74] As Jesus said: "Woe to you who are rich, for you have received your consolation."[75] But the New Testament takes things even further since judgment is "not reserved solely for those who actively rob and exploit the poor or use their wealth for corruption. Unjust distribution is condemned

---

[68]Bruce V. Malchow, *Social Justice in the Hebrew Bible: What is New and What is Old*, op. cit., p. 5.

[69]Sondra Ely Wheeler, *Wealth as Peril and Obligation: The New Testament on Possessions*, op. cit., p. 124.

[70]José Porfirio Miranda. *Marx and the Bible: A Critique of the Philosophy of Oppression*. Eugene, OR: Wipf and Stock Publishers, 2004, p. 19.

[71]Sondra Ely Wheeler, *Wealth as Peril and Obligation: The New Testament on Possessions*, op. cit., p. 124.

[72]Jeremiah 17:11.

[73]Luke 1:51–53; Luke 4:18–19; Luke 6:21; Luke 16:19–26; Sondra Ely Wheeler, *Wealth as Peril and Obligation: The New Testament on Possessions*, op. cit., p. 131.

[74]Luke 16:19–26; Matthew 25:31–46; James 5:2–3.

[75]Luke 6:24.

along with unjust accrual and unjust use."[76]

A Case for the Old Testament

In line with the plurality of viewpoints offered by the Christian tradition, financial guru and conservative Christian Dave Ramsey teaches a two-sided message: "Wealth is powerful, and, therefore dangerous,"[77] *but* "it's okay to enjoy wealth"[78] and you should "build wealth so you can change not only your family tree but also your whole community."[79] To support the warnings about wealth, Ramsey quotes passages from both the Old and New Testaments. But to support the idea that "a person's quest for profit and wealth [is] inherently moral,"[80] a phrase he borrows from Jewish Rabbi Lapin,[81] Ramsey's citations consist of only Old Testament passages. He cites New Testament passages only to disarm[82] texts which he describes as "the most-often-misinterpreted passages in the whole Bible."[83] These include stories such as The Rich Ruler (Luke 18:22–27), Jesus and Zaccheus (Luke 19:1–10), and Jesus Denounces the Scribes and The Widow's Offering (Luke 20:45–21:4). For each passage, Ramsey has to explain why the text is *not* speaking negatively about wealth itself. Once these New Testament passages are disarmed, the ancient wisdom of the Old Testament can shine through. That is, Ramsey uses only the Old Testament to *support* positive views about building and managing wealth while the New Testament seems to present a contradictory position that needs to be explained away.

---

[76] Sondra Ely Wheeler, *Wealth as Peril and Obligation: The New Testament on Possessions*, op. cit., p. 132.

[77] Dave Ramsey, *The Legacy Journey: A Radical View of Biblical Wealth and Generosity*, op. cit., p. 36.

[78] Ibid., p. 53.

[79] Ibid., p. 56.

[80] Ibid., p. 20.

[81] Rabbi Daniel Lapin. *Thou Shall Prosper: Ten Commandments for Making Money.* Hoboken, NJ: John Wiley & Sons, 2002.

[82] Ramsey's treatment of the New Testament passages is similar to John Shelby Spong's method of disarming misused passages in John Shelby Spong. *The Sins of Scripture: Exposing the Bible's Texts of Hate to Reveal the God of Love.* New York: HarperOne, 2005. ISBN: 978-0-06-077840-8.

[83] Dave Ramsey, *The Legacy Journey: A Radical View of Biblical Wealth and Generosity*, op. cit., pp. 44–52.

Why does Ramsey treat the Old and New Testaments so differently? The answer is found in the contents and overall thrust of the two Testaments. What is striking in the previous analysis is that the strands of tradition in the Old Testament which treat wealth and prosperity as signs of God's favor toward the righteous or as the fruit of wisdom and diligence are notably *missing* in the New Testament.[84] The interested reader can even refer back to the previous biblical survey and see that the sections promoting positive views of wealth cite no passages from the New Testament. Even more shocking is that the wisdom tradition of the Old Testament is completely turned upside down in the New Testament: righteousness is *not* expected to bring riches. In fact, there is an expectation that the earthly reward of faithfulness is suffering and persecution.[85] Conservative preacher Randy Alcorn describes this difference between the Old and the New Testaments, and suggests an explanation:

> *"In the Old Testament, material blessing was given for obedience,*[86] *yet in the New Testament, many of the saints were poor.*[87] *Enjoying worldly wealth is emphasized in the Old Testament,*[88] *yet the New Testament talks of giving away possessions.*[89] *By their obedience, the Israelites avoided persecution,*[90] *but by their obedience Christians incur persecution.*[91] *Why this disparity? Because God was determined that the New Testament saints would understand that their home is in another world."*[92]

The reason for this great omission may be even deeper than

---

[84]Sondra Ely Wheeler, *Wealth as Peril and Obligation: The New Testament on Possessions*, op. cit., p. 133.

[85]ibid., p. 133; Randy Alcorn. *Money, Possessions, and Eternity.* Carol Stream, IL: Tyndale House Publishers, Inc., 2011. ISBN: 978-0-8423-5360-1, p. 77; 2 Timothy 3:12; 1 Peter 5:9.

[86]Deuteronomy 28:2.

[87]Matthew 9:20; 2 Corinthians 11:27; James 2:5.

[88]Deuteronomy 28:11; Joshua 1:15; Proverbs 15:6.

[89]Mark 10:17–21; 1 Timothy 6:17–18.

[90]Deuteronomy 28:7.

[91]Matthew 5:11–12; 2 Timothy 3:12; 1 Peter 1:6.

[92]Randy Alcorn, *Money, Possessions, and Eternity*, op. cit., p. 162.

this. The New Testament is infused with an expectation of Jesus' imminent return which undergirds and flavors its teachings. The author of the Letter to the Hebrews writes: "For yet in a very little while, the one who is coming will come and will not delay" (Hebrews 10:37). And it is this expectation that drives many of the commands in the New Testament. Paul even tells people it is better not to marry because "the appointed time has grown short."[93] For the same reason, he says to "let those who buy [do so] as though they had no possessions."[94] That is, if you engage in any "dealings of the world,"[95] that's fine—just act as if it's a meaningless activity because " the present form of this world is passing away."[96]

The problem for modern Christians is that these moral assertions are based on an expectation that the end of the world is imminent—an assertion which has remained unfulfilled for 2,000 years. It seems more relevant for us to ask not "how should we live knowing that Jesus is coming tomorrow?"—on which the New Testament seems to offer much advice—but "how should we live, knowing that Jesus has not returned and, dare we say, may never return in a literal, bodily form?"—a question the New Testament is not exactly designed to answer with clarity. Some, coming to this apparent impasse, "may not even wish to be seriously challenged or instructed by [the moral rules in the New Testament]."[97] As Sondra Wheeler puts it, "the expectation [. . .] of Christ's imminent return has often been treated as a 'condition contrary to fact' that limits the relevance and vitiates the force of biblical norms."[98] That is, Jesus' failure to fulfill the expectation of imminent return causes us to ask whether we should take seriously some teachings which seem wholly dependent on this "flawed eschatology".[99]

While much ink has already been spilled in attempts to answer such questions in a plurality of ways, a simple observation can give

---

[93] 1 Corinthians 7:29.

[94] 1 Corinthians 7:29–30.

[95] 1 Corinthians 7:31.

[96] 1 Corinthians 7:31.

[97] Sondra Ely Wheeler, *Wealth as Peril and Obligation: The New Testament on Possessions*, op. cit., p. 11.

[98] Ibid., p. 17.

[99] Richard J. Callahan. "R3AL HOPE: Living with the End in Mind." PhD thesis. George Fox University, 2013, p. vi.

us some hope for a path forward. One of the beautiful things about the Bible and Christianity is that diverse points of view are not eliminated or harmonized in the Scriptures; they are *canonized*! The Bible does not speak with a single sustainable voice on our most important questions. Although shunned in modern circles for its primitive warrior-God theology and seemingly barbaric cultural practices, the Old Testament speaks of those who, like us, struggle with God's apparent abandonment. While the New Testament was written over a very small period of time, the Old Testament was written over a vast time scale—plenty of time to have a faith crisis and struggle with questions that only occur over the generations. It is in the Old Testament that we find the psalmist asking: "Why, O Lord, do you stand far off? Why do you hide yourself in times of trouble?" (Psalm 10:1; Psalm 89:46) It is here we find the Books of Psalms, Proverbs, Ecclesiastes, and Job questioning the transactional model of ethics and causality we find in Deuteronomy. And it is here that we witness people who seem to "trust God enough to get in his face and call him a liar."[100] Peter Enns uses this observation as his "advertisement" for the value of the Old Testament:

> *"Amid persecutions and other struggles that Christians endured, the tone of the New Testament writers was* urgency *to keep the faith because ultimate* triumph *is near at hand: "Hold on. It won't be long. Soon Jesus will return, and God will set all things in order and your present sufferings will be over and justice will be served."*[101]
>
> *The problem we face today, of course, is that after 2,000 years, the "end" hasn't come yet. And frankly, I don't know of many Christians who are gearing up for it. Most of us go about our lives without ever seriously thinking of Stage Two. I suppose we could go on living "as if" it were imminent, but it's hard shutting out the rest of life waiting by the door with your bags packed.*

---

[100] Psalm 89; Peter Enns. *The Sin of Certainty: Why God Desires Our Trust More Than Our 'Correct' Beliefs.* New York: HarperOne, 2016. ISBN: 978-0-06-227208-9, p. 65.

[101] Hebrews 10:37; Revelation 22:12; 1 Peter 5:10.

> *So here is my point: when it comes to living day in and day out in a messy world where things keep drudging on as they have been since forever and will continue on for the foreseeable future, the New Testament sense of urgency is hard to connect with.*
>
> *In that respect, Christians today have more in common with the Israelites wandering through a lonely and threatening desert or exiled to a hostile land than with Paul and most other New Testament writers. The Old Testament doesn't speak in the booming voice of imminent triumph. It speaks of generation after generation of the faithful and not so faithful, of successes and failures, of God's presence and God's absence."[102]*

Thus, some propose that "Jesus' demands were so radical because he believed the kingdom, understood as a divinely-wrought utopia, to be so close. His injunctions were issued in the conviction that normal, ordinary, day-to-day existence was soon to be a thing of the past. Why not be rid of wealth, if shortly it will have no value?"[103]   Although somewhat counter-intuitive, this argument suggests that returning to the Old Testament for inspiration on this topic actually becomes *more* progressive as expectation of the imminent *parousia* continues to fade into the past.

How, Then, Should We Handle the New Testament?

Does this mean that we should abandon the radical teachings of the New Testament? I would like to suggest not, for at least two reasons:

---

[102] Peter Enns, *The Sin of Certainty: Why God Desires Our Trust More Than Our 'Correct' Beliefs*, op. cit., p. 197.

[103] Dale C. Allison. *The Sermon on the Mount: Inspiring the Moral Imagination.* New York: Crossroad Publishing Company, 1999, p. 12; Bart D. Ehrman. *Jesus: Apocalyptic Prophet of the New Millennium.* New York: Oxford University Press, 1999, pp. 167–170.

The Kingdom of God

While certainly a major factor, the entire New Testament does not always "clearly ground its imperatives in near eschatological expectation."[104] Many of Jesus' teachings are better understood as being centered on the idea of the kingdom of God. In the judgment of virtually all scholars, the kingdom of God was a central part of Jesus' teachings.[105] Despite its centrality, a century of scholarly research has failed to reach a consensus on its meaning.[106] However, there are some broad themes for this important *symbol* in the teachings of Jesus. Marcus Borg explains that,

> *"His use of the phrase "kingdom of God" subverted and negated the kingdoms of his day by affirming a different king and kingdom—what life would be like on earth if God were Lord and the lords of this earth were not. Most simply, his use of the word "kingdom" challenged the kingdoms of this world. Third, the kingdom of God was not only for the earth, but involved a transformed world. It is a blessed state of affairs, a utopia brought about by God, God's dream for the earth."*[107]

John Dominic Crossan gives a similar interpretation:

> *"The kingdom of God" was a standard expression for what I have been calling the Great Divine Cleanup of this world. It was what this world would look like if and when God sat on Caesar's throne."*[108]

And Dale C. Allison says the following about one of the most famous passages about the kingdom of God, the Sermon on the Mount:

---

[104]Dale C. Allison, *The Sermon on the Mount: Inspiring the Moral Imagination*, op. cit., p. 12.

[105]Marcus J. Borg. *Conflict, Holiness, and Politics in the Teachings of Jesus.* London: Continuum International Publishing Group, 1998, p. 256.

[106]Ibid., p. 256.

[107]Marcus J. Borg. *Jesus: Uncovering the Life, Teachings, and Relevance of a Religious Revolutionary.* New York: HarperCollins e-books, 2006, p. 187.

[108]John Dominic Crossan. *God and Empire: Jesus Against Rome, Then and Now.* New York: HarperCollins e-books, 2007, p. 116.

"The Beatitudes promise that the kingdom of God will bring eschatological comfort, a permanent inheritance, true satisfaction, the vision of God, and unprecedented intimacy with God."[109]

Whatever this "kingdom of God" is, it must be good. Progressive Christians feel the call to continue imagining what it means to bring God's kingdom to earth, and wrestling with questions of the moral status of wealth in this context is inevitable, and thus, the voice of the New Testament on this topic should be taken seriously.

Eschatology and Death

Even though much of the energy of the New Testament comes from the expectation that Christ will return soon, it has continued to inspire generations of people for two thousand years. Taken as a metaphor for death, the expectation of imminent return can continue to inspire us today. As the author of James puts it,

"Come now, you who say, 'Today or tomorrow we will go to such-and-such a town and spend a year there, doing business and making money.' Yet you do not even know what tomorrow will bring. What is your life? For you are a mist that appears for a little while and then vanishes" (James 4:12–14).

Knowing that life is fleeting, and that our time on earth is short, the voice of the New Testament can still speak into our lives. Given our imminent and inevitable demise, we should endeavor to do something meaningful with our lives. Knowing that "sometimes one who has toiled with wisdom and knowledge and skill must leave all to be enjoyed by another who did not toil for it,"[110] what value is the pursuit of wealth? How can we make the most impact for the kingdom of God in our short lives knowing that we cannot take any possessions with us at death? The New Testament speaks directly to this question and suggests a model for how to live when the imminence of this expectation crystallizes in our minds.

---

[109] Dale C. Allison, *The Sermon on the Mount: Inspiring the Moral Imagination*, op. cit., p. 57.
[110] Ecclesiastes 2:21.

Summary—Building Your Own Theology of Wealth

In an increasingly global society, differences in wealth become evermore apparent. Even the middle class in America are wealthy compared to many parts of the world. For some unsuspecting individuals, questions about the moral status of wealth are thrust upon them from seemingly unlikely sources. Even the application of spiritual principles applied to personal finance, such as mindfulness, can force one to deal with major questions about the moral status of wealth. Our faith tradition, when allowed to interact with our personal finances can both cause an increase in wealth *and* criticize us for having wealth!

When we turn to the Bible, we don't find clear, unambiguous answers to these questions. Instead, we find ourselves listening in on an ancient conversation about the moral status of wealth, an invitation to participate in this conversation, and a call to develop for ourselves a "theology of wealth." Richard Rohr likens the Christian faith to a tricycle consisting of three wheels: Experience, Scripture, and Tradition.[111] In this essay, we discussed the wheel of scripture and found it to consist of a multiplicity of views regarding the moral status of wealth. Flowing from these scriptures is a broad river of tradition carrying a plethora of views and practices relating to wealth and finances. Based on the teachings of Jesus, Catholicism recognizes voluntary poverty and asceticism as one of the *evangelical counsels*, or *counsels of perfection*.[112] Calvinist and Puritan theologies on the other hand view the pursuit of wealth as not only acceptable but as a religious calling or duty, and emphasize hard work and frugal lifestyles as spiritual acts in themselves. John Wesley and his Methodists said: "Gain all you can, save all you can and give all you can,"[113] and were famous for their consistently large contributions to charity.

---

[111]Richard Rohr. *Universal Christ: How a Forgotten Reality Can Change Everything We See, Hope For, and Believe.* New York: Convergent Books, 2019, p. 213.

[112]John P. Beal, James A. Coriden, and Thomas Joseph Green. *New Commentary on the Code of Canon Law.* Paulist Press, 2000, can. 600.

[113]John S. Knox. *John Wesley's 52 Standard Sermons: An Annotated Summary.* Eugene, OR: Wipf and Stock Publishers, 2017, Sermon 50.

Finally, our experiences often play a more important role in a formation of our beliefs about wealth than our sacred scriptures. In Richard Rohr's model of faith, the wheel of experience is at the forefront, often steering our faith in ways that overpower scripture and tradition. As Æsop said, "What we know from experience we know well."[114] In wrestling with these questions we can find in scripture and tradition views which resonate with our experience as well as challenge it.

Given the tensions that erupt when our personal finances interact with our faith traditions, many naturally choose to keep these topics compartmentalized. Although this essay offers no definitive answers to these important questions, we cannot escape the responsibility for bringing their inevitable interaction into focus. After all, "we live some answer to these questions every day."[115]

---

[114] Æsop, Fables 83. The Shepherd Turned Merchant (Æsop and Munro Leaf. *Æsop's Fables—A New Version.* Trans. by John Warrington. Norwalk, CT: Easton Press, 1979, pp. 111-112).

[115] Michael J. Sandel, "Lecture 1: The Moral Side of Murder," op. cit.

Chapter 3

Biblicism, Evolutionary Wisdom, and Investing

"Many Christians have been taught that the Bible is Truth downloaded from heaven, God's rulebook, a heavenly instructional manual—follow the directions and out pops a true believer; deviate from the script and God will come crashing down on you with full force. If anyone challenges this view, the faithful are taught to 'defend the Bible' against these anti-God attacks. Problem solved. That is, until you actually read the Bible." [1] —Peter Enns, Old Testament Scholar

As the last two chapters illustrated, allowing faith, personal finance, and social justice to interact with each other poses some formidable challenges and tensions. But I contend that it is our responsibility to engage with the tension rather than evade it. In this chapter, I will show a positive, albeit somewhat obscure, synergy between our faith traditions and personal finance.

One of the primary ways most people build wealth is through investing. What does our tradition have to offer this important part of our financial journey? I argue that the answer to that question depends on *how* the ancient scriptures are interpreted.

---

[1] Peter Enns. *The Bible Tells Me So: Why Defending Scripture Has Made Us Unable to Read It.* New York: HarperOne, 2014, pp. 3–4.

A dominant form of Christianity today contends that the Bible contains objective "truth that transcends time and space and therefore inform[s] our decisions today."[2] If that is true, then we should be able to find objective truth to inform our investing decisions. However, this way of looking at the Bible suffers from the problem of *pervasive interpretive pluralism* which makes this way of reading the Bible irrelevant—perhaps even fundamentally wrong. The problem is that, even if the Bible contains objective truth as advertised, it doesn't operate that way *in practice*. In fact, a multitude of diverse interpretations are reached regarding *every* passage of scripture. Hence, this method of reading the Bible fails to deliver on its promises.

Since biblicism fails to give us answers regarding investing, we next examine an older tradition that *embraces* the fact that the scripture seems capable of being interpreted in very creative ways. Although this tradition of *creative interpretations* offers a valuable invitation to join an ancient conversation, it still doesn't provide definitive answers regarding investing.

To solve these problems, I develop a way of looking at the ancient text called the *interfaith hermeneutic of evolutionary wisdom*. This method examines the ancient sources and attempts to identify pearls of wisdom which have endured over time. These elements of wisdom are the result of a long process of trial and error, an evolutionary process, if you will. They are found across multiple faith traditions and have stood the test of time. Once the interfaith hermeneutic of evolutionary wisdom is explained, I apply it to the topic of investing to better understand if there are any "objectively true guidelines" that improve the probability of financial success. It is found that simplicity, diversity, consistency, and social responsibility are key to promoting financial success in an ethically responsible and satisfying manner.

There are a lot of details to cover to support the conclusion, so pack a lunch! This journey is a bit long and complex.

---

[2]Walter C. Kaiser et al. *Four Views on Moving Beyond the Bible to Theology.* Ed. by Stanley N. Gundry and Gary T. Meadors. Counterpoints. Grand Rapids, MI: Zondervan Academic, 2009. ISBN: 978-0-310-27655-5, p. 7.

Biblicism—The Failed Hypothesis

As science continues to plumb the depths of creation as never before, revealing the "mighty process, which manifests itself in the indefinitely small and in the indefinitely great—in the infinitesimal life which is revealed through the microscope and in the vast movements of the heavenly spheres,"[3] we find that the ancients likely knew not how deep the truth in their words would ring: "The heavens declare the glory of God" (Psalm 19:1), and God's "eternal power and divine nature have been clearly perceived, ever since the creation of the world, in the things that have been made" (Romans 1:20). As the poet said, "The world is charged with the grandeur of God."[4] Yet despite its breathtaking majesty, the scope of creation is not the most sublime feature of creation according to Genesis. It was humanity—the "very good" of all that was made,[5] the "crowning jewel of His creation,"[6] and the very image of the divine[7]—that was placed in the "blissful seat"[8] of lordship over creation.[9]

The Forbidden Question

Despite these glorious beginnings, mankind was quickly evulsed from Paradise and cursed with a life of fruitless toil and pain.[10] What initiated this grotesque plunge? What could lead to such a fantastic demise and cause the entirety of creation to groan with the pains of childbirth?[11] Surely it required an unrelenting force bent on tearing down God's handiwork! But alas, it was only a question

---

[3]J. Gresham Machen. *Christianity and Liberalism.* J. J. Little & Ives Company, 1923, p. 63.

[4]G. M. Hopkins. *"God's Grandeur" and Other Poems.* Dover Publications, 1995, p. 15.

[5]Genesis 1:31.

[6]Eugene H. Merrill, Mark F. Rooker, and Michael A. Grisanti. *The World and the Word: An Introduction to the Old Testament.* B&H Publishing Group, 2011, p. 185.

[7]Genesis 1:27.

[8]John Milton, E. Fenton, and S. Johnson. *Paradise Lost.* John Bumpus, 1821, p. 3.

[9]Genesis 1:26.

[10]Genesis 3.

[11]Romans 8:22.

that toppled the created order. This infamous inquiry poked a tiny hole in the taut fabric of creation, a hole that soon ripped into an insurmountable chasm between creation and creator. The serpent opened his dialog with the crafty question, *the forbidden question*:

"Did God really say [. . .]?" (Genesis 3:1)

Was that all it took to cause a rebellion[12] with near-infinite consequences? The whole of creation in all its majesty and infinitude was undermined by the insignificant suggestion of a serpent. *"Did God really say [. . .]?"* was not a direct accusation at first.[13] It was not a carefully-constructed syllogism of "abstract [and] intellectual"[14] knowledge, nor a powerful personal experience that caused humanity to succumb to temptation and cause the universe to crumble. Perhaps creation was poorly constructed—fragile and designed with no margin to survive even the slightest whiff of doubt. Surely not! For God Himself saw that everything was "very good."[15] It's nigh inconceivable that the divine design should be upset by the slightest examination. This must be "the most dangerous question of them all!"[16] What power courses through its veins? It seems that *"Did God really say [. . .]?"* is a "life-and-death question"[17] which unlocks the door to Hell itself through the asking alone. Consider all the pain and suffering of this world—all the suffering that has ever occurred, is currently taking place, and is yet to be experienced by every man, woman, child, and beast on this earth—and now realize it all began with "a tiny seed of

---

[12]Marjorie Suchocki. *The Fall to Violence: Original Sin in Relational Theology.* A&C Black, 1994, p. 17.

[13]Ken Ham and Britt Beemer. *Already Gone: Why Your Kids Will Quit Church and What You Can Do To Stop It.* New Leaf Publishing Group, 2009, p. 99.

[14]Abraham Kuyper. *The Work of the Holy Spirit.* Cosimo, Inc., 2007, p. 61.

[15]John M. Frame. *The Doctrine of the Word of God.* P&R Publishing, 2010, p. 5.

[16]D. Earley. *The 21 Most Dangerous Questions of the Bible.* Barbour Publishing, Incorporated, 2013, p. 10.

[17]Peter Enns et al. *Five Views on Biblical Inerrancy.* Ed. by James R. A. Merrick, Stephen M. Garrett, and Stanley N. Gundry. Grand Rapids, MI: Zondervan Academic, 2013, p. 31.

doubt."[18] This, then, is the story of *the forbidden question*: The Word of God, handed to us in a book, opens with a "stern warning"[19] in its first pages not to doubt any of its contents lest we invite the curse of God upon us—or so we are told by evangelicals and fundamentalists.

Their narrative continues: If this is an example "written down as a warning to us,"[20] dare we flirt with this devious question? Some treat it like Voldemort in the Harry Potter series: "the one who must not be named."[21] Doubting or questioning is tantamount to sin.[22] "Don't doubt, just believe,"[23] they preach. Others see any suggestion that could cast the slightest shadow on the truthfulness of God's word as a vicious attack on Christianity and the human soul.[24] The battle cries to "defend the faith!"[25] and "sound the alarm"[26] reverberate across evangelicalism. These may be reasonable reactions considering the infinite damage reportedly caused by this "first attack,"[27] which resulted in many being "plunged into

[18]Charles Van Divier Darnell. *Who Art Thou, Lord?—The Good News Jesus Preached*. Xlibris, 2013, p. 13.

[19]David Limbaugh. *Finding Jesus in the Old Testament*. Simon and Schuster, 2015, Ch. 9.

[20]1 Corinthians 10:11.

[21]Robert T. Henderson. *The Church and the Relentless Darkness*. Wipf and Stock Publishers, 2013, p. 99; Dominic Done. *When Faith Fails: Finding God in the Shadow of Doubt*. Thomas Nelson, 2019, p. 12.

[22]Romans 14:23; Theodore Parker. "The Transient and Permanent in Christianity." In: *Electronic Texts in American Studies* (1908). Ed. by George Willis Cookie, p. 146; Dominic Done, *When Faith Fails: Finding God in the Shadow of Doubt*, op. cit., p. 12; Steven B. Cowan, Stanley N. Gundry, and William Lane Craig. *Five Views on Apologetics*. Grand Rapids, MI: Zondervan, 2000, p. 65.

[23]James 1:6; John 20:27; Bobby Conway. *Doubting Toward Faith: The Journey to Confident Christianity*. Harvest House Publishers, 2015, p. 52; Gordon Kainer. *God's Solution to the Doubting Dilemma*. Lulu, 2016, p. 49; J. G. Morrow. *The Listening Heart: Hearing God in Prayer*. Baker Publishing Group, 2013, November 16; C. Cloninger. *More E-Mail from God for Teens*. David C. Cook Publishing Company, 2003, p. 59.

[24]Ken Ham and Britt Beemer, *Already Gone: Why Your Kids Will Quit Church and What You Can Do To Stop It*, op. cit., pp. 99–105.

[25]Henry Morris. *Defending the Faith: Upholding Biblical Christianity and the Genesis Record*. New Leaf Publishing Group, 1999, p. 12.

[26]F. David Farnell et al. *Vital Issues in the Inerrancy Debate*. Wipf & Stock Publishers, 2016, p. xvi.

[27]Arthur W. Pink. *The Divine Inspiration of the Bible*. Swengel, PA: Bible

a sea of doubt."[28] It seems better not to ask questions, especially not the forbidden ones. But if entertained, it is imperative that the proper conclusions be reached since the stakes are so high. As one fundamentalist said,

> "Make sure [your kids] grasp the doctrine of the Trinity. Make sure they possess correct Christology and soteriology. Make sure they understand the Bible is the inspired, infallible, inerrant, sufficient Word of God. After all, their souls depend upon it."[29]

It is not uncommon to look upon "those who doubt [as] clearly participating in evil."[30] When confronted with the forbidden question, Christians are told to "question the questioner"[31] rather than take the question seriously. Those who do wrestle with doubt are subject to "thinly-veiled questioning" of their salvation.[32] Others warn of becoming casualties for asking questions about scripture— the moral: don't risk being "publicly shamed"[33] and shunned for your faithlessness.[34] Others are stunned, tears welling up in their eyes when someone crosses the line and dares to ask too much.[35] And if you "keep asking questions,"[36] you eventually become an outsider to those who take seriously these words of scripture:[37]

Truth Depot, 1917, p. 7.

[28] Ibid., p. 8.

[29] Todd Friel. *Reset for Parents: How to Keep Your Kids from Backsliding.* New Leaf Publishing Group, 2017, p. 135.

[30] E. Roberts and J. Eyl. *Christian Tourist Attractions, Mythmaking, and Identity Formation.* Bloomsbury Publishing, 2018, p. 71.

[31] Douglas J. Rumford. *Questions God Asks, Questions Satan Asks.* Wheaton, Ill. : Tyndale House, 1998, p. 14.

[32] Denis O. Lamoureux et al. *Four Views on the Historical Adam.* Grand Rapids, MI: Zondervan Academic, 2013, p. 88.

[33] Rachel Held Evans. *Searching for Sunday: Loving, Leaving, and Finding the Church.* Nashville, TN: Thomas Nelson, 2015. ISBN: 978-0-7180-2212-9, p. 64.

[34] Peter Enns, *The Bible Tells Me So: Why Defending Scripture Has Made Us Unable to Read It*, op. cit., p. 8.

[35] Bart D. Ehrman. *How Jesus Became God: The Exaltation of a Jewish Preacher from Galilee.* 2014, p. 87.

[36] Justin Lewis-Anthony. *You Are the Messiah and I Should Know: Why Leadership is a Myth (and Probably a Heresy).* London: Bloomsbury Publishing, 2013, p. 270.

[37] Gregory A. Boyd. *Benefit of the Doubt: Breaking the Idol of Certainty.*

"Take care, brothers, lest there be in any of you an evil, unbelieving heart, leading you to fall away from the living God" (Hebrews 3:12).

Biblicism

This carefully crafted and staunchly defended way of reading the Bible is based on a group of ideas and assumptions about the sacred text which, taken together, are called *biblicism,* or as some say, *bibliolatry.*[38] Christian Smith defines biblicism as a "constellation [of] ten assumptions or beliefs:"[39]

1. Divine Writing: The Bible, down to the details of its words, consists of and is identical with God's very own words, written inerrantly in human language.

2. Total Representation: The Bible represents the totality of God's communication to and will for humanity, both in containing all that God has to say to humans and in being the exclusive mode of God's true communication.

3. Complete Coverage: The divine will about all of the issues relevant to Christian belief and life are contained in the Bible.

4. Democratic Perspicuity: Any reasonably intelligent person can read the Bible in his or her own language and correctly understand the plain meaning of the text.

5. Commonsense Hermeneutics: The best way to understand biblical texts is by reading them in their explicit, plain, most obvious, literal sense, as the author intended them at face value, which may or may not involve taking into account their literary, cultural, and historical contexts.

Grand Rapids, MI: Baker Books, 2013, p. 41.

[38] A. Stephen Van Kuiken. *Bibliolatry.* Community Congregational United Church of Christ. 22 Jan. 2017, Pullman, WA. Sermon. URL: `www.pullmanucc.org/2017/01/26/bibliolatry/` (visited on 05/01/2021).

[39] Christian Smith, *The Bible Made Impossible: Why Biblicism Is Not a Truly Evangelical Reading of Scripture*, op. cit., pp. 4–5.

6. Solo Scriptura: The significance of any given biblical text can be understood without reliance on creeds, confessions, historical church traditions, or other forms of larger theological hermeneutical frameworks, such that the theological formulations can be built up directly out of the Bible from scratch.

7. Internal Harmony: All related passages of the Bible on any given subject fit together almost like puzzle pieces into single, unified, internally-consistent bodies of instruction about right and wrong beliefs and behaviors.

8. Universal Applicability: What the biblical authors taught God's people at any point in history remains universally valid for all Christians at every other time, unless explicitly revoked by subsequent scriptural teaching.

9. Inductive Method: All matters of Christian belief and practice can be learned by sitting down with the Bible and piecing together through careful study the clear "biblical" truths that it teaches.

The prior nine assumptions and beliefs generate a tenth viewpoint that—although often not stated in explications of biblicist principles and beliefs by its advocates—also commonly characterizes the general biblicist outlook, particularly as it is received and practiced in popular circles:

10. Handbook Model: The Bible teaches doctrine and morals with every affirmation that it makes, so that together these affirmations comprise something like a handbook or textbook for Christian belief and living, a compendium of divine and therefore inerrant teachings on a full array of subjects—including science, economics, health, politics, and romance.

Based on these presuppositions, many biblicists advertise, and reasonably so if these points are correct, that their worldview offers access to "objective" truth, as recorded in the Bible.[40]

---

[40]William J. Martin. "Special Revelation as Objective." In: *Revelation*

Pervasive Interpretive Pluralism

The goal of this essay is not to argue that the assumptions of biblicism are wrong *per se*, though each point may be subject to severe criticism. Instead, it is argued that *even if* the assumptions are true, the claim to objectivity is demonstrably irrelevant in the wake of the "vast variety of interpretive differences that biblicists themselves reach when they actually read and interpret the Bible."[41] The fifth century Gallic monk, Vincent of Lérins, observed that "all do not accept it in one and the same sense, but one understands its words in one way, another in another, so that it seems capable of as many interpretations as there are interpreters."[42] D. A. Carson notes that "it is very distressing to contemplate how many differences there are among us as to what Scripture actually says. [...] The fact remains among those who believe the canonical 66 books are nothing less than the Word of God, there is a disturbing array of mutually-incompatible theological opinions."[43] Topics of such

---

and the Bible: Contemporary Evangelical Thought. Edited by Carl F. H. Henry (1958); Carl F. H. Henry. "The Priority of divine revelation: a review article." In: *Journal of the Evangelical Theological Society* 27.1 (1984), p. 78; James Bannerman. *Inspiration: The Infallible Truth and Divine Authority of the Holy Scriptures.* Edinburgh: T. and T. Clark, 1865, p. 163; Edward D. Andrews et al. *Biblical Criticism: Beyond the Basics.* Cambridge, Ohio: Christian Publishing House, 2017. ISBN: 978-1-945757-71-6, p. 201.

[41] Christian Smith, *The Bible Made Impossible: Why Biblicism Is Not a Truly Evangelical Reading of Scripture*, op. cit., Goodreads product description: www.goodreads.com/book/show/11342171-the-bible-made-impossible.

[42] Vincent of Lérins. "A Commonitory." In: *Nicene and post-Nicene fathers—Second Series.* Ed. by Philip Schaff and Henry Wallace. Vol. 11. (originally published circa 434). New York: Cosmo Classics, 2007, Commonitory 2.5, p. 132; cited in Christian Smith, *The Bible Made Impossible: Why Biblicism Is Not a Truly Evangelical Reading of Scripture*, op. cit., p. 21.

[43] Donald A. Carson. *Exegetical Fallacies.* Grand Rapids, MI: Baker Books, 1996, p. 18; cited in Christian Smith, *The Bible Made Impossible: Why Biblicism Is Not a Truly Evangelical Reading of Scripture*, op. cit., pp. 18–19.

importance as Hell,[44] salvation,[45] eternal security,[46] the Trinity,[47] Canaanite genocide,[48] and sanctification[49] are all disputed on the basis of biblical interpretation.

This is not just the case between individuals from opposite sides of the Christian spectrum, such as liberal and conservative. Even theologians who all "unequivocally affirm the divine inspiration and authority of the Bible"[50] cannot agree on how to interpret it and use *the same exegetical tools* to "reach diametrically-opposed conclusions" regarding interpretation of the same passage of Scripture.[51] As John Hick so eloquently put it, "here we are on the edge of the 'bottomless pit' of biblical interpretation, for virtually nothing that any scholar has said in this field has remained uncontradicted by some other scholar."[52]

Given the supposed importance of evangelizing to "save souls," one would think the Bible would provide a clear approach for evangelicals. But even here there are major disputes about what is the best or proper way to spread the gospel, proponents of each apologetic method confidently stating that the Bible best supports *their* position. Conservative theologian John Frame says:

---

[44] Denny Burk et al. *Four Views on Hell.* Ed. by Preston Sprinkle and Stanley N. Gundry. 2nd ed. Grand Rapids, MI: Zondervan Academic, 2016.

[45] John Hick, Clark H. Pinnock, and Alister E. McGrath. *Four Views on Salvation in a Pluralistic World.* Ed. by Stanley N. Gundry, Dennis L. Okholm, and Timothy R. Phillips. Counterpoints. Grand Rapids, MI: Zondervan, 1996.

[46] Michael Horton et al. *Four Views on Eternal Security.* Ed. by J. Matthew Pinson and Stanley N. Gundry. Grand Rapids, MI: Zondervan Academic, 2011.

[47] Stephen R. Holmes et al. *Two Views on the Doctrine of the Trinity.* Ed. by Jason S. Sexton and Stanley N. Gundry. Grand Rapids, MI: Zondervan Academic, 2014.

[48] Daniel L. Gard et al. *Show Them No Mercy: 4 Views on God and Canaanite Genocide.* Ed. by Stanley N. Gundry. Grand Rapids, MI: Zondervan Academic, 2003.

[49] Melvin E. Dieter et al. *Five Views on Sanctification.* Ed. by Stanley N. Gundry. Grand Rapids, MI: Zondervan Academic, 1996.

[50] Walter C. Kaiser et al., *Four Views on Moving Beyond the Bible to Theology,* op. cit., p. 280.

[51] ibid., p. 280; P. Andrew Sandlin. "Two Paradigms for Adherents of Sola Scriptura." In: *Reformation & Revival* 9.4 (2000), p. 40; Christian Smith, *The Bible Made Impossible: Why Biblicism Is Not a Truly Evangelical Reading of Scripture,* op. cit., pp. x–xi; ibid., p. 17.

[52] John Hick, Clark H. Pinnock, and Alister E. McGrath, *Four Views on Salvation in a Pluralistic World,* op. cit., pp. 52–53.

"Through much of the twentieth century, American evangelical apologists have been battling one another vigorously over apologetic method."[53] Dr. Mark L. Ward Jr. in his review of the book *Five Views on Apologetics* gives a poignant anecdote from his own personal life:

> *"Once upon a time, a fellow Christian young man, age 20 or so, like me, invited me to go witnessing in the downtown area where I live. We ran into a young lady [...], but as I began to speak, my partner began to feel uncomfortable with my approach. Deeper than that, he disagreed with the doctrine behind it. And he felt the necessity to say so—in front of the girl we were witnessing to. I remember the incredulity on her face: 'You guys don't even agree on this?' It's a little disconcerting to see how apparently equally-committed and intelligent Christians tear apart each other's justifications of the Christian faith. [...] If even Christian apologists can't agree on the best strategy for defending and promoting Christian truth, then something deeper must be going on than what the eyes can see. All of these Christians have access to the same divine words and the same divine world. What causes them to come to different conclusions about how to persuade non-Christians to repent and believe the gospel? Presuppositions, I'd think."[54]*

Voltaire (1694–1778), the French Enlightenment writer, noticed the variety of beliefs in Christianity when he said:

> *"Have not things the most venerable, the most sacred, the most divine, been obscured by the ambiguities of language? Ask two Christians of what religion they are. Each will answer, I am a Catholic. You think they are both of the same communion; yet one is of the Greek,*

---

[53]Steven B. Cowan, Stanley N. Gundry, and William Lane Craig, *Five Views on Apologetics*, op. cit., p. 358.

[54]Mark L. Ward. *Goodreads Review of Five Views on Apologetics*. 2013. URL: `www.goodreads.com/review/show/639892599?book_show_action=true&from_review_page=1` (visited on 05/01/2021).

the other of the Latin church; and they are irreconcil-
able. If you seek to be further informed, you will find
that by the word Catholic each of them understands uni-
versal, in which case universal signifies a part."[55]

Even if one dogmatically asserts the idea of democratic perspicuity (the belief that any reasonably intelligent person can read
the Bible and understand the plain meaning of the text), it doesn't
change the fact that, as Galileo Galilei put it, "[the Bible] is often
very abstruse, and may say things which are quite different from
what its bare words signify."[56] Of course, Jesus, like a good rabbi
of the time,[57] did not exactly avoid ambiguity: In the canonical
gospels, "Jesus is asked 183 questions and only directly answers
three."[58] Teaching dogma to the contrary does not change the fact
that some passages are so complex that "different interpreters, even
learned ones, will sometimes diverge widely in their understanding
of the details—and of the whole."[59] The fundamental assumptions
of biblicism are called into question since "if scripture were trans-
parent and unambiguous, then there would be no need for biblical
exegesis. If God were self-evidently just and good, then there would
be no need for theodicy."[60] As Peter Enns says:

"If God is behind the Bible, why doesn't he just get to it
in a five-point summary, or perhaps a white paper with
clear answers to everything we need to know so we're
not left scratching our heads, and so theologians don't

[55]Voltaire. *The Works of Voltaire: A Contemporary Version.* Vol. 18. St. Hubert Guild, 1901, p. 142.

[56]Galileo Galilei. "Letter to the Grand Duchess Christina of Tuscany." In: *Published online at Modern History Sourcebook* (1999), p. 3.

[57]A. Stephen Van Kuiken. *Disagreeing with Jesus.* Community Congrega- tional United Church of Christ. 22 Mar. 2021, Pullman, WA. Sermon. URL: www.pullmanucc.org/2021/03/22/disagreeing-with-jesus/ (visited on 05/06/2021).

[58]Jared Byas. *Love Matters More: How Fighting to Be Right Keeps Us from Loving Like Jesus.* Grand Rapids, MI: Zondervan, 2020, p. 115.

[59]Adele Berlin, Marc Zvi Brettler, et al. *The Jewish Study Bible: Jewish Publication Society Tanakh Translation.* 2nd ed. Oxford University Press, USA, 2014, p. 1489.

[60]Stuart Ingrouille. *Unbelievable: Christianity as a House of Cards.* Lulu.com, 2013, pp. 198–199.

have to debate for centuries and write fifteen-hundred-page books on 'the nature of God'?"[61]

Although biblicists may *claim* to be starting from a position of objective truth, at best, they are championing *their interpretation* of that truth. In order to make their point, they actually need *their interpretation* of scripture to be divinely inspired, inerrant, and objectively true, not the scripture itself.[62]

Consequences of Biblicism

The problem with biblicism is not that pervasive interpretive pluralism is inherently undesirable or that it can lead to questioning the divine authorship of the Bible. Perhaps diversity of human thought on religious matters was God's intention—part of the Divine plan; if so, the success on that front is remarkable. Brian D. McLaren asks:

> *"What if the Christian faith is supposed to exist in a variety of forms rather than just one imperial one? What if it is both more stable and more agile—more responsive to the Holy Spirit—when it exists in these many forms? And what if, instead of arguing about which form is correct and legitimate, we were to honor, appreciate, and validate one another and see ourselves as servants of one grander mission, apostles of one greater message, seekers on one ultimate quest?"*[63]

No. The issue, in my opinion, is that biblicists often cultivate a sense of pride and arrogance because apparently *they* have a monopoly on truth. Some project those attitudes towards those who offer alternative viewpoints, not realizing that interpretive

---

[61]Peter Enns, *The Bible Tells Me So: Why Defending Scripture Has Made Us Unable to Read It*, op. cit., p. 135.

[62]Rachel Held Evans. *Evolving in Monkey Town: How a Girl Who Knew All the Answers Learned to Ask the Questions.* Grand Rapids, MI: Zondervan, 2010. ISBN: 978-0-310-29399-6, p. 188.

[63]Brian D. McLaren. *A New Kind of Christianity: Ten Questions That are Transforming the Faith.* New York: HarperOne, 2010. ISBN: 978-0-06-185398-2, p. 164.

pluralism is pervasive even among their own ranks, thus causing division among biblicists themselves. Topics of arguably lesser importance such as whether Adam was a literal person,[64] remarriage after divorce,[65] baptism,[66] inerrancy,[67] and church government,[68] regularly cause denominational in-fighting and church splits.[69] N. T. Wright observes: "It seems to be the case that the more you insist that you are based on the Bible, the more fissiparous you become; the church splits up into more and more little groups, each thinking that they have got biblical truth right."[70] The saying,

---

[64]Denis O. Lamoureux et al., *Four Views on the Historical Adam*, op. cit.

[65]Gordon John Wenham, William A. Heth, and Craig S. Keener. *Remarriage after Divorce in Today's Church*. Ed. by Mark L. Strauss. Grand Rapids, MI: Zondervan Academic, 2009.

[66]John Castelein et al. *Understanding Four Views on Baptism*. Ed. by John H. Armstrong and Paul E. Engle. Grand Rapids, MI: Zondervan Academic, 2009.

[67]Peter Enns et al., *Five Views on Biblical Inerrancy*, op. cit.

[68]Peter Toon et al. *Who Runs the Church?: 4 Views on Church Government*. Ed. by Steven B. Cowan and Stanley N. Gundry. Grand Rapids, MI: Zondervan Academic, 2009.

[69]Christian Smith writes, "Ask a biblicist about the matter and a common response is, 'Well, yeah, but most of those disagreements are about minor issues. On important matters most of us pretty much read the Bible as teaching similar things.' Such a response is natural for American evangelicals, who comprise a transdenominational religious movement that has sought to transcend its differences in order to work together toward certain common activities and goals, particularly evangelism, world missions, and 'ministries of mercy.' It is also a highly useful response for protecting biblicism from the problems of interpretive pluralism. But this response is in the end a form of denial. It is simply not true. It is like a member of a dysfunctional, conflict-ridden family telling her friends that, 'Yeah, we all get along pretty well in our family.' Disagreements among biblicists (and other Bible-referring Christians) about what the Bible teaches on most issues, both essentials and secondary matters, are many and profound. If biblicists hope to maintain intellectual honesty and internal consistency they must acknowledge them and explain them" (Christian Smith, *The Bible Made Impossible: Why Biblicism Is Not a Truly Evangelical Reading of Scripture*, op. cit., pp. 61–62). As Rachel Held Evans says, "Those who decry the evils of selective literalism tend to be rather clumsy at spotting it in themselves" (Rachel Held Evans. *A Year of Biblical Womanhood: How a Liberated Woman Found Herself Sitting on Her Roof, Covering Her Head, and Calling Her Husband 'Master'*. Nashville, TN: Thomas Nelson, 2012. ISBN: 978-1-59555-367-6, p. 52).

[70]Nicholas Thomas Wright. "How Can the Bible be Authoritative?" In: *Vox Evangelica* 21.1991 (1991); cited in Christian Smith, *The Bible Made Impossible: Why Biblicism Is Not a Truly Evangelical Reading of Scripture*,

"let's make like a Baptist church and split,"[71] is unfortunately no joke. As people divide over various matters, "biblicists (and most other Christians) who interpret the Bible in the same way have a very strong tendency to cluster together into homogeneous social networks of similarly believing people,"[72] creating loud echo chambers which only serve to entrench and keep true dialogue at bay.

Another problem with this method of handling the Bible is that any worldview based on the foundation of biblicism is very fragile: "all it takes is one minuscule disagreement with the Bible for the whole house of cards to come tumbling down."[73] Christian Smith warns that,

> "Biblicism also has the pastorally problematic tendency to set up some young, committed believers for unnecessary crises of personal faith, when some of them come to realize (rightly, yet without warning) that biblicism is untenable. Having been taught as youth to stake their faith fully on one (faulty) theory of the Bible, their faith can later founder and sometimes collapse when antagonistic nonbiblicists point out and press home real problems with biblicist theory. [...] When some of those youth give up on biblicism and simply walk away across the wet paint, it is flawed biblicism that is partly responsible for those losses of faith."[74]

John Shelby Spong suggests that biblicism is a "Gentile heresy,"[75] which needs to be addressed in the church for it to

---

op. cit., p. 18.

[71] Dale B. Martin. *New Testament History and Literature*. New Haven: Yale University Press, 2012; Dale B. Martin. *Introduction to the New Testament History and Literature*. 2009. URL: https://oyc.yale.edu/religious-studies/rlst-152/lecture-12 (visited on 05/01/2021).

[72] Christian Smith, *The Bible Made Impossible: Why Biblicism Is Not a Truly Evangelical Reading of Scripture*, op. cit., p. 60.

[73] Thom Stark, *The Human Faces of God: What Scripture Reveals When it Gets God Wrong (and Why Inerrancy Tries to Hide It)*, op. cit., p. 17.

[74] Christian Smith, *The Bible Made Impossible: Why Biblicism Is Not a Truly Evangelical Reading of Scripture*, op. cit., pp. 88–89.

[75] John Shelby Spong. *Biblical Literalism: A gentile Heresy: A Journey Into a New Christianity Through the Doorway of Matthew's Gospel*. New York: HarperCollins, 2016.

survive:

> *"Unless biblical literalism is challenged overtly in the
> Christian church itself, it will, in my opinion, kill the
> Christian faith. It is not just a benign nuisance that
> afflicts Christianity at its edges; it is a mentality that
> renders the Christian faith unbelievable to an increasing
> number of the citizens of our world."*[76]

In summary, biblicism touts objectivity, but this claim turns
out to be only an illusive vapor disconnected from the reality of
pervasive interpretive pluralism. It comforts many with a "false
sense of certainty [and] provides people [with] the illusion that they
have some semblance of control over their lives."[77] To be clear, I am
not saying that all the underlying assumptions of biblicism, such
as the doctrine of divine inspiration, are false—especially since the
claims are often carefully worded with legal precision so as to make
them impossible to refute... or verify. I am only arguing that *even
if* all the words in the Bible are divinely inspired, even if they hold
objective truth, and even if the sacred text is inerrant in precisely
the way evangelicals and fundamentalists assert, it *still*, as Rob
Bell says, "has to be interpreted. And if it isn't interpreted, then
it can't be put into action. [...] It is not possible to simply do what
the Bible says. We must first make decisions about what it means
at this time, in this place, for these people."[78] In practice, the act
of interpretation births a multitude of diverse meanings,[79] a result
which is irreconcilable with the illusory advertisement of biblicism.
This disconnect, coupled with worship of the "idol of certainty,"[80]

---

[76]Ibid., p. 4.

[77]Thom Stark, *The Human Faces of God: What Scripture Reveals When it
Gets God Wrong (and Why Inerrancy Tries to Hide It)*, op. cit., p. 241.

[78]Rob Bell. *Velvet Elvis: Repainting the Christian Faith*. Grand Rapids,
MI: Zondervan, 2006, p. 46.

[79]"There is no such thing as a text that is not interpreted, and disagreements emerge over what seems the most obvious meaning of a text. Every
reader brings cultural, social, and personal perspectives to a text, which always
influences interpretation" (John R. Donahue. "Guidelines for Reading and Interpretation." In: *The New Interpreter's Study Bible: New Revised Standard
Version with the Apocrypha*. Ed. by Walter J. Harrelson et al. Nashville, TN:
Abingdon Press, 2003. ISBN: 978-0-687-27832-9, p. 2261).

[80]Gregory A. Boyd, *Benefit of the Doubt: Breaking the Idol of Certainty*,
op. cit., pp. 54–72.

often causes division in the church and results in losses of faith.

If "an objective interpretation of Scripture [cannot] be achieved, and as such, [is] not a particularly valuable endeavor to pursue,"[81] as the Jewish scholar Abraham Geiger (1810-1874) insisted, is there a better way to engage the sacred text? Is our quest for investing advice from the sacred text utterly futile?

Multiple Creative Interpretations

In contrast to the biblicist approach, there is another strand of tradition, stronger and more ancient, which *embraces* the phenomenon of pervasive interpretive pluralism rather than denies it. It is well known that the Jewish rabbinic traditions reveled in creative interpretation of their scriptures. They even had a phrase for this— "the seventy faces of the Torah,"[82] their euphemism for an "inexhaustible fount of meaningfulness."[83] "Turn it around and around, for everything is in it,"[84] they said. An old saying captures this perfectly: "When two rabbis argue, there will be three opinions."[85] This way of handling the sacred text is not just an incidental characteristic of Jewish interpretation; it is perhaps the fundamental *essence* of the Jewish religion. As the *Jewish Study Bible* notes,

> *"The tradition of biblical interpretation has been a constant conversation, at times an argument, among its*

---

[81] Adele Berlin, Marc Zvi Brettler, et al., *The Jewish Study Bible: Jewish Publication Society Tanakh Translation*, op. cit., p. 1968.

[82] Stephen M. Wylen. *The Seventy Faces of Torah: The Jewish Way of Reading the Sacred Scriptures*. New York: Paulist Press, 2005, p. 63; Adele Berlin and Marc Zvi Brettler. "Introduction: What is The Jewish Study Bible?" In: *The Jewish Study Bible: Jewish Publication Society Tanakh Translation*. Ed. by Adele Berlin, Marc Zvi Brettler, et al. 2nd ed. Oxford University Press, USA, 2014, p. ix.

[83] David Stern. "Midrash and Jewish Exegesis." In: *The Jewish Study Bible: Jewish Publication Society Tanakh Translation*. Ed. by Adele Berlin, Marc Zvi Brettler, et al. 2nd ed. Oxford University Press, USA, 2014, p. 1889.

[84] Bamidbar Rabbah 13:15.

[85] William E. Phipps. *The Wisdom & Wit of Rabbi Jesus*. Louisville, KY: Westminster John Knox Press, 1993, p. 64; A. Stephen Van Kuiken. *Disagreeing with Jesus*. Community Congregational United Church of Christ. 22 Mar. 2021, Pullman, WA. Sermon. URL: `www.pullmanucc.org/2021/03/22/disagreeing-with-jesus/` (visited on 05/06/2021).

participants; at no period has the text been interpreted in a monolithic fashion. If anything marks Jewish biblical interpretation, it is the diversity of approaches employed and the multiplicity of meanings produced.[86] *[...] It is often remarked that what is Jewish about the Bible is not the Bible itself, not even the Hebrew text of the Bible, but the Jewish* interpretation *of the Bible."*[87]

The Jewish interpreters "clearly believed that sacred texts contain timeless wisdom; but when preserved in writing, this timeless wisdom becomes in time obscure or difficult to understand, and must therefore be explained."[88] To them, "each letter [of the sacred text] and the spaces between the letters are available for interpretive work."[89]

Studying the Bible "was an *ad hoc* activity directed essentially to an audience hungry for a response to its immediate needs and to the desire to have Scripture speak in the present moment."[90] It was vital that the Scriptures be rendered "relevant to the communities they addressed."[91] The act and process of interpretation was so important that early nonrabbinic sources often claimed the

---

[86] Adele Berlin and Marc Zvi Brettler, "Introduction: What is The Jewish Study Bible?" Op. cit., p. ix.

[87] David Stern, "Midrash and Jewish Exegesis," op. cit., p. 1879.

[88] Yaakov Elman. "Classical Rabbinic Interpretation." In: *The Jewish Study Bible: Jewish Publication Society Tanakh Translation.* Ed. by Adele Berlin, Marc Zvi Brettler, et al. 2nd ed. Oxford University Press, USA, 2014, p. 1859; Of course conservative scholars disagree: John Frame says, "Others have said that although God's personal words may have occurred in the past, they are no longer available to us as personal words because of the problems of hermeneutics and canon. If those theologies are true, all is lost" (John M. Frame, *The Doctrine of the Word of God,* op. cit., p. 6).

[89] Wilda C. Gafney. *Womanist Midrash: A Reintroduction to the Women of the Torah and the Throne.* Louisville, KY: Westminster John Knox Press, 2017, p. 5; cited in Rachel Held Evans. *Inspired: Slaying Giants, Walking on Water, and Loving the Bible Again.* Nashville, TN: Thomas Nelson, 2018. ISBN: 978-0-7180-2231-0, p. 23.

[90] David Stern, "Midrash and Jewish Exegesis," op. cit., pp. 1889–1890.

[91] Hindy Najman. "Early Nonrabbinic Interpretation." In: *The Jewish Study Bible: Jewish Publication Society Tanakh Translation.* Ed. by Adele Berlin, Marc Zvi Brettler, et al. 2nd ed. Oxford University Press, USA, 2014, p. 1850.

authority of divine revelation "not only for the prophetic text, but also for its interpretation."[92]

The most well-known interpretive method of the Jewish tradition is called *midrash*, which is a "cross between biblical commentary and fan fiction,"[93] but which introduces the reader to "a sort of delighted reverence for the text unencumbered by the expectation that it must behave itself to be true."[94] "Unlike their postmodern descendants, in which [ambiguity] signifies an indeterminacy that reflects the fundamental instability of meaning, multiple interpretation as found in midrash is actually a sign of its stability, the guarantee of a belief in Scripture as an inexhaustible fount of meaningfulness."[95]

The tradition of multiple creative interpretations continued into the Christian tradition as the New Testament authors and early church "pored over their sacred texts of the past to discover new meanings by which they might understand and interpret experiences that were occurring in their present."[96] However, this tradition eroded over time as more gentile interpreters, who did not have access to the Jewish ways of thinking, engaged the text.[97] But the tradition is not relegated only to Jewish rabbinic interpreters; "a constant reworking of biblical material is a hallmark of Jewish literature, a hallmark that is already prominent in the Bible itself."[98]

---

[92] Ibid., p. 1846, 1850.

[93] Rachel Held Evans, *Inspired: Slaying Giants, Walking on Water, and Loving the Bible Again*, op. cit., p. 23.

[94] Ibid., p. 23.

[95] David Stern, "Midrash and Jewish Exegesis," op. cit., p. 1889.

[96] John Shelby Spong. *Liberating the Gospels: Reading the Bible with Jewish Eyes*. HarperSanFrancisco, 1996, p. 52.

[97] Ibid., p. 35.

[98] Benjamin D. Sommer. "Inner-biblical Interpretation." In: *The Jewish Study Bible: Jewish Publication Society Tanakh Translation*. Ed. by Adele Berlin, Marc Zvi Brettler, et al. 2nd ed. Oxford University Press, USA, 2014, p. 1841.

Inner-biblical Interpretation

The act of creative interpretation "is as old as the Bible itself."[99] Even "before the biblical canon had been completed, readers and authors were already interacting with the texts they possessed in creative ways."[100] The "biblical authors frequently commented on other biblical texts; they revised them, they argued with them, and they alluded to them,"[101] typically not merely quoting the earlier works, but interpreting them.[102] In many instances of inner-biblical interpretation, "the new text presents an innovative variation of the older text's ideas or even argues against it. Instead of saying, 'Here is how you ought to understand the older text,' the new composition tells the reader, 'There are some ideas in the older text that need to be revised or extended or discarded. Here's my proposal for a replacement.'"[103]

For example, the author of Daniel appropriated Jeremiah's "seventy years" prophecy that had already been fulfilled in the sixth century, and "retooled it"[104] to make it relevant to the concerns of his audience in the second century BCE.[105] The stories of liberation from Egypt and the wilderness wanderings are retold in Psalm 78 and Psalm 105, while Psalm 104 is a retelling of the creation narrative of Genesis 1.[106] They even rewrote the history of

---

[99] John R. Donahue, "Guidelines for Reading and Interpretation," op. cit., p. 2261.

[100] Howard Jacobson. "Biblical Interpretation in Pseudo-Philo's *Liber Antiquitatum Biblicarum*." In: *A Companion to Biblical Interpretation in Early Judaism*. Ed. by Matthias Henze. Grand Rapids, MI: Wm. B. Eerdmans Publishing, 2012, p. 180.

[101] Benjamin D. Sommer, "Inner-biblical Interpretation," op. cit., p. 1835.

[102] Marc Zvi Brettler. "The Hebrew Bible's Interpretation of Itself." In: *The New Oxford Annotated Bible with Apocrypha: New Revised Standard Version*. Ed. by Michael D. Coogan et al. 5th ed. New York: Oxford University Press, 2010, p. 2254.

[103] Benjamin D. Sommer, "Inner-biblical Interpretation," op. cit., p. 1839.

[104] Thom Stark, *The Human Faces of God: What Scripture Reveals When it Gets God Wrong (and Why Inerrancy Tries to Hide It)*, op. cit., p. 20.

[105] Benjamin D. Sommer, "Inner-biblical Interpretation," op. cit., pp. 1837–1838; Peter Enns, *Inspiration and incarnation: Evangelicals and the Problem of the Old Testament*, op. cit., p. 108; Marc Zvi Brettler, "The Hebrew Bible's Interpretation of Itself," op. cit., p. 2256.

[106] John R. Donahue, "Guidelines for Reading and Interpretation," op. cit., p. 2261.

Israel in the Book of Chronicles.[107] The books of 1 Samuel through
2 Kings tell the five-hundred year story of Israel's monarchy. In
the modern canon, the books of 1 Chronicles and 2 Chronicles
are located directly after the books of Samuel and Kings. But in
the Jewish Bible, they were located at the *end*, because they are a
"retelling of those books from a much later point in Jewish history.
In fact, it is nothing less than an act of reimagining God."[108]

Probably most striking is how the New Testament uses the Old
Testament. For example, Jesus quotes the phrase "the God of
Abraham, and the God of Isaac, and the God of Jacob," from
Exodus 3:6 to make a theological point about the resurrection.[109]
To a modern reader who was taught that the "proper" way to
interpret scripture is with the historical-grammatical method, Jesus' interpretation is very strange. The original passage in Exodus
says nothing about resurrection. But this creative reworking of
the text was praised by some of the teachers of the law who "re-
sponded, 'Well said, teacher!' And no one dared to ask him any
more questions."[110] That is, in Jesus' day, creative interpretations
were *celebrated* rather than condemned.

The New Testament, especially the Gospels of Matthew and
John (usually considered the "most Jewish" of the Gospels),[111] and
"rabbinic midrash both contain a form of interpretation called 'fulfillment narrative.'"[112] To give one example, Matthew cites Hosea
1:11, "out of Egypt I have called my son" as a messianic prophecy

---

[107]Marc Zvi Brettler. "Jewish Interpretation in the Premodern Era." In: *The
New Oxford Annotated Bible with Apocrypha: New Revised Standard Version.*
Ed. by Michael D. Coogan et al. 5th ed. New York: Oxford University Press,
2010, p. 2261.

[108]Peter Enns, *How the Bible Actually Works: In which I Explain How an
Ancient, Ambiguous, and Diverse Book Leads us to Wisdom Rather Than
Answers—And Why That's Great News*, op. cit., p. 108; John R. Donahue,
"Guidelines for Reading and Interpretation," op. cit., p. 2261.

[109]Luke 20:34–38; Peter Enns, *Inspiration and incarnation: Evangelicals and
the Problem of the Old Testament*, op. cit., p. 104.

[110]Luke 20:39–40; ibid., pp. 104–105.

[111]Ruth Sheridan. "Scripture Fulfillment." In: *The Jewish Annotated New
Testament.* Ed. by Amy-Jill Levine and Marc Zvi Brettler. 2nd ed. New York:
Oxford University Press, 2011. ISBN: 978-0-19-046185-0, p. 727.

[112]David Stern. "Midrash and Parables." In: *The Jewish Annotated New
Testament.* Ed. by Amy-Jill Levine and Marc Zvi Brettler. 2nd ed. New York:
Oxford University Press, 2011. ISBN: 978-0-19-046185-0, p. 707.

concerning Jesus. The problem is that "it would take a tremendous amount of mental energy to argue that Matthew is respecting the historical context of Hosea's words, that is, that there is actually something predictive in Hosea 1:11."[113] These "interpretive methods used, especially by Matthew and Paul, have much in common with those used by other Jews in the same period."[114]

While a full treatment of this subject is outside the scope of this essay (after all, 1,200-page books have been written on the topic!),[115] it is clear that creative engagement of the ancient text is not only relegated to the Jewish tradition, it is *inscripturated* in the Bible itself. Since both the tradition and the scriptures themselves are grounded in this method of creative engagement with ancient texts, which method of interpretation takes the text and tradition more seriously, as a model for us today?

Adapting to Survive—A Model for Christians Today

Engaging with the text creatively and adapting it for our modern issues and questions is our "sacred responsibility."[116] A consequence of engaging with our faith tradition in this way is that it "must be progressive. Theology must be the ever-reformed and reforming renewal and reconsideration of the belief mosaic of Christianity in light of its primary sources and norms."[117] Thus "theology is progressive in that it is an ongoing discipline that repeatedly gives rise

---

[113]Peter Enns, *Inspiration and incarnation: Evangelicals and the Problem of the Old Testament*, op. cit., p. 123.

[114]Pheme Perkins. "The New Testament Interprets the Jewish Scriptures." In: *The New Oxford Annotated Bible with Apocrypha: New Revised Standard Version*. Ed. by Michael D. Coogan et al. 5th ed. New York: Oxford University Press, 2010, p. 2258.

[115]Gregory K. Beale and Donald A. Carson. *Commentary on the New Testament Use of the Old Testament*. Grand Rapids, MI: Baker Books, 2007. ISBN: 978-0-8010-2693-5.

[116]Peter Enns, *How the Bible Actually Works: In which I Explain How an Ancient, Ambiguous, and Diverse Book Leads us to Wisdom Rather Than Answers—And Why That's Great News*, op. cit., p. 34; ibid., p. 271.

[117]Roger E. Olson. *Reformed and Always Reforming (Acadia Studies in Bible and Theology): The Postconservative Approach to Evangelical Theology*. Grand Rapids, MI: Baker Academic, 2007. ISBN: 978-0-8010-3169-4, p. 148.

to new ways of looking at old questions, brings into views previously undervalued aspects of the Christian belief-mosaic, and occasionally even advances the church's knowledge of theological truth."[118] In fact, the progressive nature of our faith is nothing less than the story of Christianity itself. Theodore Parker (1810–1860), the American transcendentalist and Unitarian minister, said:

> *"Anyone who traces the history of what is called Christianity, will see that nothing changes more from age to age than the doctrines taught as Christian, and insisted on as essential to Christianity and personal salvation. What is falsehood in one province passes for truth in another. The heresy of one age is the orthodox belief and 'only infallible rule' of the next."*[119]

While it may be tempting to interpret this history of theological development as proof that objective doctrines were not "once for all entrusted to the saints" as Jude 1:3 claims, this misses the importance of a progressive faith—development is *necessary* for the relevance, utility, and survival of the faith. While John Shelby Spong says bluntly that "Christianity must change or die,"[120] Peter Enns provides a more subtle summary of the Progressive approach to faith:

> *"For the ancient tradition to survive, it had to transform [and] adapt to changing circumstances. To seek to remain as it always was would simply ensure its isolation, if not its death. The* act *of transformation is, therefore, a sacred responsibility on the part of people of faith in order to maintain their faith. [...] When*

---

[118]Stanley J. Grenz. *Renewing the Center: Evangelical Theology in a Post-theological Era.* Grand Rapids, MI: Baker Academic, 2006. ISBN: 0-8010-2239-8, p. 343; cited in Roger E. Olson, *Reformed and Always Reforming (Acadia Studies in Bible and Theology): The Postconservative Approach to Evangelical Theology*, op. cit., p. 148.

[119]Theodore Parker, "The Transient and Permanent in Christianity," op. cit., p. 10.

[120]John Shelby Spong. *Why Christianity Must Change or Die: A Bishop Speaks to Believers in Exile.* HarperSanFrancisco, 1998. ISBN: 0-06-067536-5; John Shelby Spong, *The Sins of Scripture: Exposing the Bible's Texts of Hate to Reveal the God of Love*, op. cit., p. 178.

we engage that process today, we are simply doing what the Bible itself, as well as Jews in the centuries before the time of Jesus, had already modeled. Our experiences, what life throws at us, drive us to think about what God is like here and now, and consequently what it means to believe in this God. And without making these wise adaptations, however diverse and even conflicting they might have been, and regardless of whether some lasted and others didn't, Judaism would not have survived. And neither would Christianity. In fact, it never would have gotten off the ground.[121] *[...] Christians, just like their Jewish ancestors, have always been re-imagining God, adapting the sacred past to discern God's presence here and now. And we can never simply appeal to the Bible as an unchanging standard, for the Bible itself—Old and New Testaments alike—never sits still. Its authors have already accepted their sacred responsibility to employ wisdom. As should we—always respectful of the past, but never assuming that we are meant to recreate it and live in it; always tied to this ancient tradition, but without expecting it to do the heavy lifting for us. The life of faith has always been about respecting this tension and living by wisdom.*"[122]

Although the tradition of creative interpretation leads us to thoughtfully consider how the ancient texts may apply to our present situations, presents a call for progressive adaptation, and invites us to participate in an ancient conversation, it still makes no promises to objective truths similar to those we find in science and mathematics. Thus, this way of reading the Bible, while it provides more hope for seeking wisdom regarding investing, it makes no promises regarding "answers" to our questions.

---

[121]Peter Enns, *How the Bible Actually Works: In which I Explain How an Ancient, Ambiguous, and Diverse Book Leads us to Wisdom Rather Than Answers—And Why That's Great News*, op. cit., p. 189.
[122]Ibid., p. 271.

An Interfaith Hermeneutic of Evolutionary Wisdom

While biblicism advertises objective truth, that promise is, in practice, utterly irrelevant, due to pervasive interpretive pluralism. The progressive approach, on the other hand, invites us to participate in an ancient conversation. In this tradition, the Bible is seen as "an honest conversation between humanity and God. And when we see it this way, it invites us into a conversation with God within our own soul. It invites us into the struggle."[123] Rachel Held Evans writes that "the tensions and questions produced by Scripture aren't obstacles to be avoided, but rather opportunities for engagement, invitations to join in the Great Conversation between God and God's people that has been going on for centuries and to which everyone is invited."[124] When posed with a theological, moral, or practical question, the biblicist might respond with the quip, "the Bible, in such and such a proof text, clearly answers that question. If you don't immediately accept *my* interpretation, then you are really questioning God. Go read the book of Job and see how God responds to those who question him." But when posed with the same question, the progressive response is more invitational: "that's a great question—one that people have been wrestling with for thousands of years!"[125] This is where biblicism fails: it neither explains why pervasive interpretive pluralism exists nor engages with it in a healthy manner. The approach of Progressive Christianity, on the other hand, both explains and engages the phenomenon in a way that is arguably more orthodox than sects which claim that descriptor.[126] In fact, Brian D. McLaren calls

---

[123]A. Stephen Van Kuiken. *Bibliolatry*. Community Congregational United Church of Christ. 22 Jan. 2017, Pullman, WA. Sermon. URL: www.pullmanucc. org/2017/01/26/bibliolatry/ (visited on 05/01/2021).

[124]Rachel Held Evans, *Inspired: Slaying Giants, Walking on Water, and Loving the Bible Again*, op. cit., p. 23.

[125]Peter Enns. "Episode 54: Ask Pete—Answering Questions from The Bible For Normal People Community." In: *The Bible for Normal People [Podcast]*. 2019. URL: www.peteenns.com/ask-pete-episode-55/ (visited on 05/02/2021).

[126]The tradition of creative interpretation, however, requires a note of caution. Since our presuppositions and prejudices greatly influence our interpretation of a text, simply acknowledging them is not enough to avoid dangerous

this a "generous orthodoxy":

> *"We must never underestimate our power to be wrong*
> *when talking about God, when thinking about God, when*
> *imagining God, whether in prose or in poetry. [...] A*
> *generous orthodoxy, in contrast to the tense, narrow, or*
> *controlling orthodoxies of so much of Christian history,*
> *doesn't take itself too seriously. It is humble. It doesn't*
> *claim too much. It admits it walks with a limp."*[127]

Unfortunately for many individuals, the modernist mindset, deeply influenced by the Scientific Revolution and Enlightenment, may be too overpowering to allow a meaningful foothold in the apparent subjectivity of these religious traditions which seem to lack real and objective answers. This is likely why biblicism is so appealing to some: it *claims* that "theology [...] is also a science, differing from the natural and social sciences only with respect to the data it seeks to explain."[128] However, we do not find in the sciences the same level of pervasive interpretive pluralism as biblical studies. For example, one would be hard-pressed to find multiple "interpretations" of Ohm's Law, even though science continues to progress, showing that Ohm's Law is but a simplification of Maxwell's Equations, which are simplifications of quantum electrodynamics.

---

interpretations. As Rachel Held Evans said, "For those who count the Bible as sacred, interpretation is not a matter of *whether* to pick and choose, but *how* to pick and choose. We are all selective. We all wrestle with how to interpret and apply the Bible to our lives. We all go to the text looking for something, and we all have a tendency to find it. So the question we have to ask ourselves is this: are we reading with the prejudice of love, or are we reading with the prejudices of judgment and power, self-interest and greed?" (Rachel Held Evans, *A Year of Biblical Womanhood: How a Liberated Woman Found Herself Sitting on Her Roof, Covering Her Head, and Calling Her Husband 'Master'*, op. cit., p. 296).

[127]Brian D. McLaren. *A Generous Orthodoxy: Why I am a Missional, Evangelical, Post/Protestant, Liberal/Conservative, Mystical/Poetic, Biblical, Charismatic/Contemplative, Fundamentalist/Calvinist, Anabaptist/Anglican, Methodist, Catholic, Green, Incarnational, Depressed-yet-hopeful, Emergent, Unfinished Christian.* Grand Rapids, MI: Zondervan, 2004. ISBN: 978-0-310-25803-2, pp. 170–171.

[128]David W. Diehl. "Evangelicalism and General Revelation: An Unfinished Agenda." In: *Journal of the Evangelical Theological Society* 30.2 (1987), p. 452.

While this may be a somewhat misguided quest, can our ancient faith be further updated to appeal to those of us influenced by modernity without falling into the pit of biblicism? As Galileo said, "I do not feel obliged to believe that the same God who has endowed us with senses, reason and intellect has intended us to forego their use and by some other means to give us knowledge which we can attain by them."[129] "Indeed, who wants the human mind put to death?"[130] For those of us who ask if there is nothing in religion of which it can be said, "this is objectively true," I offer, for lack of a better name, *an interfaith hermeneutic of evolutionary wisdom.*

Food Rules

To develop this method, we will draw an analogy to nutrition and diets. One would think that, if God designed this world specifically for human life and activity, that there'd be some instructions provided for some of the most basic and essential activities for life, such as what to eat. Instead, we find a veritable minefield in nature. About 90% of white or yellow berries are poisonous, and nearly 50% of reddish-colored berries are poisonous as well. Several dozen species of mushrooms are fatal if ingested. And some fruits such as the fruit of the strychnine plant, contain a poison so toxic that even a small amount can be fatal.[131] For many living in first-world societies, our primary food sources come from grocery stores, which fare no better. They are often packed with highly-processed foods and meats with lots of added fat, sugar and refined grains—the staples of the industrialized Western diet.[132] It is well-established that "virtually all of the obesity, type 2 diabetes, 80% of cardiovascular disease, and more than a third of all cancers can be linked to this diet. Four of the top ten killers in America are

---

[129]Galileo Galilei, "Letter to the Grand Duchess Christina of Tuscany," op. cit., p. 5.

[130]Galileo Galilei. *The Galileo Affair: A Documentary History.* Vol. 1. Univ of California Press, 1989, p. 96.

[131]Walter H. Lewis and Memory P. F. Elvin-Lewis. *Medical Botany: Plants Affecting Human Health.* John Wiley & Sons, 2003, p. 77.

[132]Michael Pollan. *Food Rules: An Eater's Manual.* New York: Penguin Group USA, 2009. ISBN: 978-0-14-311638-7, p. xii.

chronic diseases linked to this diet." [133]

As a result, there is also a non-stop, confusing array of ever-changing advice from nutrition science. Food products capitalize on this, advertising *"no cholesterol!"* one year, *"no trans fats!"* the next, depending on the prevailing winds of dietary opinion. [134] During the past several decades, reduction in fat intake has been the main focus of national dietary recommendations, [135] only to later have been found to be based on little scientific evidence. [136]

The journalist Michael Pollan, in his book *In Defense of Food: An Eater's Manifesto*, [137] endeavored to sort through the noise of nutritionalism and determine what is truly good for us to eat. Pollan noticed that through the barrage of contradicting opinions on the subject, "two facts are not in dispute. All the contending parties in the nutrition wars agree on them:" [138]

1. The Western industrialized diet, for whatever reason, causes a myriad of health problems, [139] and when people get off this diet, they see dramatic improvements in their health. [140]

2. Populations eating a remarkably wide range of traditional diets generally don't suffer from these chronic diseases. [141] This seems to be the case even when the nutritional content differs largely from the usual mixed traditional diets. Pollan cites a couple of extreme examples which range "from ones in very high fat (the Inuit in Greenland subsist largely on seal blubber), to ones high in carbohydrates (Central American Indians subsist largely on maize and beans), to ones very high in protein (Masai tribesmen in Africa subsist chiefly on cattle blood, meat, and milk)." [142]

---

[133] Ibid., p. xii.
[134] Michael Pollan. *In Defense of Food: An Eater's Manifesto*. New York: Penguin Group USA, 2008. ISBN: 978-1-59420-145-5, p. 27.
[135] Ibid., p. 42.
[136] Ibid., p. 43.
[137] Ibid.
[138] Idem, *Food Rules: An Eater's Manual*, op. cit., p. xi.
[139] Ibid., p. xii.
[140] Ibid., p. xiii.
[141] Ibid., p. xii–xiii.
[142] Ibid., pp. xii–xiii.

Based on these observations, Pollan asks,

> "*So whom did we rely on before the scientists (and, in turn, governments, public health organizations, and food marketers) began telling us how to eat? We relied of course on our mothers and grandmothers and more distant ancestors, which is another way of saying, on tradition and culture. We know there is a deep reservoir of food wisdom out there, or else humans would not have survived and prospered to the extent we have. This dietary wisdom is the distillation of an evolutionary process involving many people in many places figuring out what keeps people healthy (and what doesn't), and passing that knowledge down in the form of food habits and combinations, manners and rules and taboos, and everyday and seasonal practices, as well as memorable sayings and adages. Are these traditions infallible? No. [...] But much of this food wisdom is worth preserving and reviving and heeding.*"[143]

Objectivity and Certainty in Science and Mathematics

Before proposing the interfaith hermeneutic of evolutionary wisdom, a little clarification is in order regarding "objectivity" in science. One might think that the "laws of nature," carry with them a perfect epistemological certainty, but in fact, they are only empirically verified and limited by test methodologies. When a hypothesis or theory is proposed, it is confirmed or refuted with repeated measurements and tests. After this theory continues to be proved consistent and true, it becomes a so-called "law," but it is still limited by the methods of confirmation. That is why Ohm's Law, which was developed from repeated tests to discover the relationship between voltage, current, and resistance, first formulated by George Ohm in the early 1800s, was later supplanted by Maxwell's Equations, and more recently by quantum electrodynamics. The field effects, and certainly quantum effects, were not

---

[143]Ibid., pp. xvi–xvii.

really measurable in Ohm's work. A far as we can tell, all such laws of nature are only *approximations*, albeit very good ones.

Like Pollan's "food rules," science can also be said to undergo an evolutionary process. Many theories have been proposed over time, some of them good and valid, others not so much. As they are tested, confirmed, and refuted, we see an evolutionary curation through survival of the fittest: the weaker theories become discarded over time while the stronger theories stand the test of time, continuing to evolve and become more refined. Despite this empirical messiness, it seems there is *something* underneath it all which is objective and certain.

Galileo thought, and I would agree, that this underlying objectivity is related to or identical with mathematics, and that God has written the book of nature in the language of mathematics.[144] Dr. Morris Kline (1908–1992) explains that "mathematics is immanent in nature; it is the truth about its structure, or, as Plato would have it, the reality of the physical world. Moreover, human reason could penetrate the divine plan and reveal the mathematical structure of nature."[145] For Galileo, "the certainty of mathematics was [...] a way to God. The certainty of mathematics [...] was the only way to epistemological perfection."[146] Galileo claimed that mathematics "allow[s] the utmost epistemological certainty that [can] possibly be attained."[147] Unlike the empirical sciences, mathematics can be said to have an unparalleled objectivity and certainty. The idea that $2 + 2 = 4$, while it can be examined in a myriad of ways (for example in abstract algebra and group theory), is never qualified with a measure of uncertainty.

Does science contain objective truth? If by 'objective' we mean that it can be independently verified by many different individuals, then yes, science is objective. If by 'truth' we mean the kind of "epistemological perfection" we find in mathematics, then no— science does not have that kind of certainty.

---

[144]Teun Koetsier and Luc Bergmans. *Mathematics and the Divine: A Historical Study.* Elsevier, 2004, p. 355.

[145]Morris Kline. *Mathematics for the Nonmathematician.* Courier Corporation, 1967, p. 194.

[146]Teun Koetsier and Luc Bergmans, *Mathematics and the Divine: A Historical Study*, op. cit., p. 354.

[147]Ibid., p. 353.

An Interfaith Hermeneutic of Evolutionary Wisdom

We are now ready to propose the interfaith hermeneutic of evolutionary wisdom. This way of reading the Bible and other ancient texts is predicated on the assumption that God is *not* their author, at least in the way biblicists describe. What if God has *not* "spoken to us personally,"[148] with "clarity and fullness,"[149] through a special revelation which is authoritative,[150] inerrant,[151] and objective?[152] What if the Bible is *not* "a corpus of divinely guaranteed truths"[153] which "very far excel all other writings"[154] and are "the only reliable source for the continuing disclosure and delivery of God's mercy to human creatures?"[155] What if we do not have God's "recorded utterances"[156] and "true knowledge concerning Himself,"[157] a question which apparently risks "grave peril

---

[148] John M. Frame, *The Doctrine of the Word of God*, op. cit., p. 6.

[149] Bruce Milne. *Know the Truth: A Handbook of Christian Belief.* InterVarsity Press, 2009, p. 31.

[150] John Piper. *How Are General and Special Revelation Different?* 2009. URL: www.desiringgod.org/interviews/how-are-general-and-special-revelation-different (visited on 04/17/2020); David Basinger. "Biblical Paradox: Does Revelation Challenge Logic?" In: *Journal of the Evangelical Theological Society* 30.2 (1987), p. 207; Carl F. H. Henry, "The Priority of divine revelation: a review article.," op. cit., p. 77.

[151] John Piper, *How Are General and Special Revelation Different?* Op. cit.; Eugene H. Merrill, Mark F. Rooker, and Michael A. Grisanti, *The World and the Word: An Introduction to the Old Testament*, op. cit., p. 91; Gordon R. Lewis. "Is Propositional Revelation Essential to Evangelical Spiritual Formation?" In: *Journal of the Evangelical Theological Society* 46.2 (2003), p. 271.

[152] William J. Martin, "Special Revelation as Objective," op. cit.; Carl F. H. Henry, "The Priority of divine revelation: a review article.," op. cit., p. 78.

[153] John Kelman Sutherland Reid. *The Authority of Scripture: A Study of the Reformation and Post-Reformation Understanding of the Bible.* Methuen, 1962, p. 162 cited in James I. Packer. "Contemporary Views of Revelation." In: *Revelation and the Bible: Contemporary Evangelical Thought. Edited by Carl F. H. Henry* (1959), p. 95.

[154] John Calvin. *Institutes of the Christian Religion.* Trans. by John Allen. Vol. 1. 1816, Ch. VII.4 (p. 84).

[155] Robert Kolb. "Reality Rests on the Word of the Lord: Martin Luther's Understanding of God's Word." In: *Reformation & Revival* 9.4 (2000), p. 50.

[156] James I. Packer, "Contemporary Views of Revelation," op. cit., p. 90.

[157] Leonard de Moor. "The Idea of Revelation in the Early Church." In: *The Evangelical Quarterly* 50.3 (1978), p. 170.

to the soul"[158] to ask?

It is clear that God did not provide an instruction manual for what is safe and not safe to eat in nature,[159] and it has always been up to *us* to figure out. Presumably the first person to eat the "death cap" mushroom served as an "empirical test" that refuted the theory, if you will, that it was safe for consumption. This empirically-tested truth was passed down from generation to generation as the first people told the story of that individual's demise, later generations forgetting the details but remembering the lesson.

Instead of an instruction manual written on stone tablets and handed to Moses on Mount Sinai, perhaps people have been asking questions about theology, ethics and morality, and how to live life, proposing theories, and testing them all along. As ideas become tested, the weaker, less useful, morally and spiritually harmful are discarded. This is what the hermeneutic of evolutionary wisdom is all about. We find in the Bible ideas which have been curated, tested over time, and found to be spiritually healthy—ideas which become wisdom. We also find recorded in scripture many ideas which have *not* withstood the test of time or proved spiritually healthy. The goal of this hermeneutic is to find those things in the ancient text and tradition which seem to have been proved true time-and-time again.

While the Christian tradition has had a remarkable effect on the world and remains the largest religion today, it is still a minority compared to the combination of all other religions. It is only in modern times that the Bible has been unshackled from the hands of the priests and given to lay people to read, interpret, and test its ideas for themselves, and few people throughout history were raised in a thoroughly Christian culture. To increase the objectivity of this hermeneutic and decrease uncertainty in its empirically-tested results, I propose that an interfaith approach be employed. We in fact, already used this method in the section "Start With the Heart" in Chapter 1 where we found that self-reflection before

---

[158] Arthur W. Pink, *The Divine Inspiration of the Bible*, op. cit., p. 9.

[159] Although the Bible does contain a great deal of dietary restrictions, many of these seem quite arbitrary and unrelated to health. Even if one were to follow the Jewish dietary restrictions exactly, it still wouldn't preclude someone from eating a poisonous plant.

entering a crucial conversation is encouraged in Christianity,[160] Judaism,[161] Buddhism,[162] Hinduism,[163] and the Chinese Classics.[164]

Likewise, nearly all religions teach some sort of prayer or meditation—perhaps because people have discovered it causes profound and positive changes in our brains, as we now know from the new field of neurotheology.[165] Furthermore, the "three jewels of Taoism," compassion, frugality, and humility, are clearly confirmed in other religions as superior spiritual virtues. As another example, it is well-known that the "golden rule" is independently confirmed as a superior rule for life in a variety of religious traditions: Christianity,[166] Buddhism,[167] Judaism,[168] Confucianism,[169] Taoism,[170] and many other religions all contain a version of the golden rule

---

[160]Matthew 7:3.

[161]Yitzhak Buxbaum, *The Life and Teachings of Hillel*, op. cit., p. 108.

[162]Dhammapada 18:252; Dhammapada 12:158–159.

[163]Margaret W. Fisher, "The Collected Works of Mahatma Gandhi, Volumes I–XII (1884–1914)," op. cit., p. 158.

[164]The Art of War 3:18; Sūnzǐ, *Sun Tzu's The Art of War: Bilingual Edition Complete Chinese and English Text*, op. cit., p. 13 | Tao Te Ching 33; Lǎozǐ and James Trapp, *Tao Te Ching*, op. cit., p. 41 | Mencius 4A4; Mèngzǐ, *Mencius*, op. cit., p. 76 | The Great Learning 1:2; Kǒng Fūzǐ, *The Sacred Books of China: The Texts of Confucianism*, op. cit., p. 411–412.

[165]Mike McHargue. *Finding God in the Waves: How I Lost My Faith and Found It Again Through Science*. New York: Convergent Books, 2016. ISBN: 978-1-101-90605-7, pp. 177–178.

[166]Matthew 7:12: "In everything do to others as you would have them do to you; for this is the law and the prophets."

[167]Dhammapada 10:131: "One who, while himself seeking happiness, oppresses with violence other beings who also desire happiness, will not attain happiness hereafter" (Acharya Buddharakkhita, *The Dhammapada—The Buddha's Path of Wisdom*, op. cit., p. 43).

[168]Tractate Shabbath 31a: "What is hateful to you, do not do to your fellow: this is the whole Torah; the rest is the explanation; go and learn."

[169]Analects of Confucius 5:12: "What I do not want others to do to me, I also do not want to do to others" (Kǒng Fūzǐ. *The Analects of Confucius: Chinese-English Bilingual Edition*. Trans. by Pan Fuen et al. 1st ed. Jinan, China: Qi Lu Press, 1993. ISBN: 7-5333-0283-4, p. 45).

[170]Tao Te Ching 49: "The enlightened man has no will of his own. He follows the will of the people. I am kind to those who are kind themselves. I am also kind to the unkind. The virtue of kindness" (Lǎozǐ and James Trapp, *Tao Te Ching*, op. cit., p. 59).

in their sacred texts. Even Æsop[171] and the ancient Egyptians[172] arrived at the same principle, worded in nearly the same way. This teaching has persisted even through modern philosophy: Immanuel Kant proposed his "categorical imperative,"[173] which is nothing more than a generalization of the golden rule.[174]

Thus, we can engage our tradition and sacred text by looking for those principles which have been tested, confirmed and developed by a variety of people and cultures. In this way, we can approach the objectivity and certainty advertised by biblicists without neglecting *our* responsibility in the matter[175] and the role humans have played in this evolutionary process of developing wisdom.

Does this method produce objective truth? I suggest that yes, it does, since this hermeneutic purposely sorts through the subjectivity in religion to find principles which have been independently verified elsewhere. Can we be certain about its results? Again, I propose yes, but not with the kind of epistemological certainty we find in mathematics. This hermeneutic results in a kind of certainty more akin to that found in the natural sciences—its certainty depends on how long the principle has been tried and found true and how many people and cultures have independently come to the same conclusions. If we are looking for something to anchor our need for certainty and objectivity, to satisfy the cravings of our postmodern mindsets, I suggest that this is a good foundation. But it is only that—a starting place, a foothold for the individual still under the spell of modernity allowing them to dig deeper into their tradition.

---

[171] Æsop, Fables 81. The Eagle & the Fox (Æsop and Munro Leaf, *Æsop's Fables—A New Version*, op. cit., pp. 108–109).

[172] P.Brooklyn 47.218.135 7:7–8: "That which you hate to be done to you, do not do it to another" (Richard L. Jasnow. *A Late Period Hieratic Wisdom Text (P. Brooklyn 47.218.135)*. Ed. by Thomas A. Holland and Thomas G. Urban. Vol. 52. Studies in Ancient Oriental Civilization. Oriental Institution of the University of Chicago, 1992. ISBN: 0-918986-85-0, p. 95.

[173] "I ought never to act except in such a way that I can also will that my maxim should become a universal law" (Immanuel Kant and H. J. Paton. *The Moral Law—Kant's Groundwork of the Metaphysic of Morals*. Trans. by H. J. Paton. 3rd ed. London: Hutchinson & Co., 1964 [1797], p. 70).

[174] Robert Charles Sproul. *The Consequences of Ideas*. Wheaton, IL: Crossway Books, 2000. ISBN: 978-1-4335-0314-6, p. 130.

[175] I.e., while avoiding the idea that the Bible is an instruction manual which suggests we don't need to work things out on our own.

An important caveat is that this method, if left unfettered, may tend to reduce all the religions to their lowest common (and probably least interesting) denominator. As John Shelby Spong says:

> *"Does the interfaith future mean that all the religious traditions of the world must seek to come together in an attempt to find our lowest common denominator? I do not think so. That would only reduce each tradition to something bare and bleak. It would be nothing more than a manifestation of our least divisive and therefore least characteristic affirmations. No richness, no uniqueness would be found there. Is our only alternative then to seek to honor positive traditions in all religious systems, creating in the process a pantheon large enough to hold us all together, a religion of consensus where the edges are blurred and the divisions are papered over? Some traditions, like Bahá'í, seek to do that, and they do it with great integrity, but that pathway, while positive for many, does not seem to me to offer the best hope for either religious toleration or a religious future."*[176]

Spong makes an insightful argument that we should consider carefully. He essentially argues that the "religion of consensus" is devoid of richness and uniqueness, which is certainly true. The common ground across the faiths is likely uncomplicated, perhaps not even that insightful. However, there is one aspect of this result which I believe should enter the discussion: the relationship between simplicity and truth. Many great minds have claimed that truth is simple. George S. Clason said: "Deride not what I say because of its simplicity. Truth is always simple."[177] Tolstoy is famous for saying: "There is no greatness where there is not simplicity, goodness, and truth."[178] Isaac Newton also said: "Truth is

---

[176] John Shelby Spong, *The Sins of Scripture: Exposing the Bible's Texts of Hate to Reveal the God of Love*, op. cit., p. 243.
[177] George S. Clason. *The Richest Man in Babylon*. New American Library, 1988, p. 27.
[178] Leo Tolstoy. *War and Peace*. Trans. by Ann Dunnigan. New York:

ever to be found in the simplicity, and not in the multiplicity and confusion of things."[179]   And Albert Einstein said: "I am not a genius, I am just curious. I ask many questions. And when the answer is simple, then God is answering."[180] Thus, the simplicity of the "blurred edges" Spong speaks of may actually be an indicator of their truthfulness. That is, to borrow Spong's imagery, perhaps flowing underneath all the religions is the seemingly illusive river of objective truth—and maybe this truth is somehow simple.

But more to Spong's point, I should make it clear that I am *not* proposing that the interfaith hermeneutic of evolutionary wisdom supplant the rich traditions of multiple creative interpretation found in Judaism and carried forward throughout Christianity and more recently championed by the Progressive Christian movement. This is simply *another* way of looking at the sacred text, another refraction of the light off its multifaceted surface. My hope is simply that this can provide a solid foothold for some as well as help guide the phenomenon of pervasive interpretive pluralism towards meanings which are in-line with the time tested, "objective" and "certain" truths, as "proven" by empirical verification across multiple cultures.

"Objectively True" Guidelines for Investing

All of the previous material serves as an elaborate (and admittedly overly-dramatic) prolegomenon for our topic at hand: investing— the *what* and *how* of investing. There is a *lot* of noise in the culture and media today regarding investing. Daily headlines offer a dizzying array of advice such as:

"7 Reasons to Ditch Dogecoin and Buy These Stocks Now"

Penguin Group (USA), 1968 [1869], p. 1279; cited in John C. Bogle. *John Bogle on Investing: The First 50 Years*. Hoboken, NJ: John Wiley & Sons, 2015. ISBN: 978-1-119-08836-3, p. 308.

[179]Cited in Corey Powell. *God in the Equation: How Einstein Transformed Religion*. New York: Simon and Schuster, 2003. ISBN: 0-684-86348-0, p. 29.

[180]Albert Einstein. *Bite-Size Einstein—Quotations on Just About Everything from the Greatest Mind of the Twentieth Century*. Ed. by Jerry Mayer and John P. Holmes. New York: Thomas Dunne, 1996, p. 61.

"2 Hot Growth Stocks to Buy in the Coming Market Crash"

"2 Reasons Not to Sell in May and Go Away" and

"10 S&P 500 Stocks to Consider... At Much Lower Prices."

There are plenty of fortune-tellers in the industry who claim: "These investments will outperform the S&P 500 over the next decade." Many of these types of headlines come from organizations who, for a fee, will send you monthly, weekly, or even daily newsletters telling you how to manage your (presumably complex) portfolio. Just like the ever-changing advice from nutritionalism, we are barraged with a river of information reportedly claiming to tell us what the "financially-healthy" investment options and strategies are. As the poet Ian S. Thomas said:

> *"And every day, the world will drag you by the hand, yelling, 'This is important! And this is important! And this is important! You need to worry about this! And this! And this!' And each day, it's up to you to yank your hand back, put it on your heart and say, 'No. This is what's important.'"*[181]

To continue the analogy with nutrition, can we, like Michael Pollan, sort through the noise and find just a few principles which, according to the interfaith hermeneutic of evolutionary wisdom, are in some sense "objectively true" guidelines for investing? It's important to note that ancient advice on this topic is sparse, mostly because it is only in the past couple of centuries that investing has become an everyday activity for the working middle-class—the ancient texts are not set up to neatly answer our modern questions. But there does seem to be a few principles which appear to persist over time and are rooted in ancient, time-tested advice. These principles are simplicity, diversity, and consistency.

---

[181] Arianna Huffington. "Commencement Address: Vassar College." In: *Representative American Speeches 2014–2015.* Vol. 87. 6. Amenia, NY: Grey House Publishing, 2015, p. 26; A. Stephen Van Kuiken. *Whom do you serve?* Community Congregational United Church of Christ. 9 Aug. 2020, Pullman, WA. Sermon. URL: www.pullmanucc.org/2020/08/10/whom-do-you-serve/ (visited on 02/13/2021).

Simplicity

The first principle which cuts through the noise is *simplicity*. We here speak of the "true simplicity of a rightly- and nobly-ordered mind and character, not that other simplicity which is only a euphemism for folly,"[182] as Plato said. It is "the relentless pursuit of unrealistic performance, practiced through costly short-term strategies, [which] distracts [us] from one of the most important secrets of investment success: simplicity."[183] Testing the idea of simplicity against the interfaith hermeneutic of evolutionary wisdom shows that this is a concept which has persisted since ancient times and has been championed by some of the greatest minds in investing. Confucius captured this when he said: "Fortitude, resolution, simplicity, and caution in speech are near to the perfect virtue."[184] Lǎozǐ also said: "Look to the simple and treasure the straightforward; Diminish the self and control desire."[185]   Later, Qohelet said: "See, this alone I found, that God made human beings straightforward, but they have devised many schemes."[186] The esteemed investor, John C. Bogle, has written extensively, extolling the virtues of simplicity as *the* most important investment principle:

> *We live in a world where a seemingly infinite amount of information is available to just about everyone. Financial facts, figures, and theories, once available only to investment professionals, are now at the fingertips of individual investors. No longer must the investor depend on the services of an investment professional. Buy and sell to your heart's content over the World Wide Web. The information age has truly transformed the world of investing. Today, investors are bombarded on all sides by investment information—whether they want it or not. Complex quantitative analysis, real-time stock*

---

[182]Plato, Republic 400e.

[183]John C. Bogle. *Common Sense on Mutual Funds.* Hoboken, NJ: John Wiley & Sons, 2010. ISBN: 978-0-470-13813-7, p. 41.

[184]Analects of Confucius 13:27; Kǒng Fūzǐ, *The Analects of Confucius: Chinese–English Bilingual Edition*, op. cit., p. 159.

[185]Tao Te Ching 19.

[186]Ecclesiastes 7:29.

quotes and the like are available at any local library, if not through a personal computer. Investors now ask their mutual fund managers about their 'alpha'; they want to know a fund's 'Sharpe ratio'; they read articles about 'complexity theory' and 'behavioral finance.'

Yet this barrage of information has not necessarily translated into better returns. Instead, we focus on the quantity of data. We want more sophisticated and complex information. Presumably it will enhance our returns. Our world may or may not be any more complex than it has ever been, but we have certainly made the investment process more complicated. In today's environment of a mind-numbing information flow that is at once electrifying and terrifying, where is the intelligent investor to turn?

Turn to simplicity. The great paradox of this remarkable age is that the more complex the world around us becomes, the more simplicity we must seek in order to realize our financial goals. Never underrate either the majesty of simplicity or its proven effectiveness as a long-term strategy for productive investing. Simplicity, indeed, is the master key to financial success. The old Shaker hymn got it just right:

'Tis the gift to be simple;
'Tis the gift to be free;
'Tis the gift to come down
Where we ought to be.[187]

Simplicity has at least three main benefits when applied to investing. First, it has a direct benefit of weeding out financial products which are downright harmful to investors. Many financial products are designed to be overly complex, not because they are better, but because their complexity hides the fact that they are not designed primarily to serve the consumer. Choosing investments which conform to the principle of simplicity automatically weeds out many non-optimal or worse, predatory, financial products. J. L. Collins explains:

---

[187]John C. Bogle, *Common Sense on Mutual Funds*, op. cit., pp. 109–110.

> *"Since the days of Babylon, people have been coming up*
> *with investments, mostly to sell to other people. There*
> *is a strong financial incentive to make these investments*
> *complex and mysterious. But the simple truth is this:*
> *the more complex an investment is, the less likely it is*
> *to be profitable."*[188]

Secondly, if one has a goal to build wealth, a simple investing strategy can actually improve the probability of success for at least two important reasons. First, it is well-known that investors who continually "tinker" with their portfolio tend to underperform the market *on average*. This is mostly a result of our psychological wiring—we tend to buy investments which seem to be performing well and sell those which are doing poorly. The result is the exact opposite of "buy low, sell high." This is not just the case for individual investors. Mutual funds which are actively managed by professional fund managers also underperform the market more often than not. Vanguard, in a study that looked at the performance of 1,540 actively-managed equity funds over 15 years found that "82% failed to outperform the unmanaged index. But 100% of them charged their clients high fees to try."[189] A simple portfolio has less opportunity for tinkering, and less temptation to do so.

The other reason simplicity improves the probability of financial success is that no investment is guaranteed to improve one's financial situation. However, some actions, such as decreasing expenses or increasing one's income, are *mathematically* guaranteed to increase one's wealth. If one has a complex investing strategy (for example, if one's portfolio is so complex it requires paying a professional financial adviser to manage), much time and money can be lost pursuing things that are not guaranteed to improve one's financial status. When the principle of simplicity is employed, it frees time and resources which can then be spent on things which are guaranteed to improve the results, thus improving the probability of success. Or, as John Bogle says: "As they complicate the process, they increase the likelihood of stumbling down an ill-lit

---

[188] J. L. Collins and Peter (Mr. Money Mustache) Adeney, *The Simple Path to Wealth: Your Road Map to Financial Independence and a Rich, Free Life*, op. cit., p. 85.
[189] Ibid., p. 75.

path to disappointment."[190]

Finally, simplicity in investing allows one to focus on more important things in life. The popular yogi, Sadhguru, says: "Wealth is just one of the tools towards human wellbeing, not the whole of it."[191] Lǎozǐ asks rhetorically: "Self or wealth: Which is more precious?"[192] Likewise, Jesus asked: "Is not life more than food, and the body more than clothing?"[193] Thus, tending to a complex investment strategy can suck valuable time away from more meaningful activities. Both the Jewish Proverbs, and the ancient Egyptian wisdom literature, from which some are likely derived, warn: "Do not wear yourself out to get rich; be wise enough to desist."[194] As Henry David Thoreau said: "Our life is frittered away by detail. [...] Simplify, simplify."[195]

In summary, we find that simplicity, rooted in ancient wisdom, has been tested repeatedly over time, and could be *the most* powerful tool for improving the probability of financial success, decreasing stress, and sifting through the never-ending noise.

Diversity

The concept of diversifying investments is so ubiquitous that hardly anything needs to be said about it. The idea of diversification is at least as old as the Old Testament: "Invest in seven ventures, yes, in eight; you do not know what disaster may come upon the land" (Ecclesiastes 11:2). The *Talmud* also encourages diversification: "One should always divide his wealth into three parts: [investing] a third in land, a third in merchandise, and [keeping] a third ready

---

[190]John C. Bogle, *Common Sense on Mutual Funds*, op. cit., p. 41.

[191]Jaggi ("Sadhguru") Vasudev. *Money Matters.* 2014. URL: www . isha . sadhguru . org / us / en / wisdom / article / money - matters (visited on 05/03/2021).

[192]Tao Te Ching 44.

[193]Matthew 6:25.

[194]Proverbs 23:4; Instructions of Amenemope 7 (William K. Simpson. *The Literature of Ancient Egypt: An Anthology of Stories, Instructions, Stelae, Autobiographies, and Poetry.* Ed. by William K. Simpson. Trans. by Rober K. Ritner et al. 3rd ed. New Haven & London: Yale University Press, 2003. ISBN: 0-300-09920-7, p. 230).

[195]Henry David Thoreau. *Walden and Other Writings.* Ed. by Joseph Wood Krutch. New York: Random House, 2004 [1854], p. 182.

to hand."[196] Later, the English proverb, "Don't put all your eggs in one basket," became a familiar mantra. The primary purpose of diversification is to reduce risk. As Shakespeare said:

> My ventures are not in one bottom trusted,
> Nor to one place; nor is my whole estate
> Upon the fortune of this present year:
> Therefore, my merchandise makes me not sad.[197]

Some investments, such as broad-based index funds, satisfy both simplicity and diversity with a single investment strategy and are deeply aligned with these ancient, time-tested principles.

Consistency

The next principle for investing success is *consistency*, or more specifically, *consistency over time*. The idea here is to avoid get-rich-quick schemes, and it applies to both wealth-building and wealth-preservation stages of life. Picking one consistent investment strategy and sticking with it over the long run helps avoid the temptation to "time the market," a temptation which proves financially fatal for the average person because of our psychology. But perhaps even more important is that consistency over time develops the discipline and character that will not squander the wealth. It is well known that lottery winners are statistically more likely to file bankruptcy than the average American.[198] Why? Very likely because they were thrust into an arena for which they had not trained. As Proverbs states: "Wealth hastily gotten will dwindle, but those who gather little by little will increase it."[199] Proverbs 28:20 adds: "The faithful will abound with blessings, but one who is in a hurry to be rich will not go unpunished." And "One who augments wealth by exorbitant interest gathers it for another who is kind to the poor."[200]

---

[196]Tractate Baba Mezi'a 42.

[197]Shakespeare, *Merchant of Venice*, 40.

[198]Ashley Stahl. *You Turn: Get Unstuck, Discover Your Direction, and Design Your Dream Career*. Dallas, TX: BenBella Books, 2021. ISBN: 978-1950665693, p. 69.

[199]Proverbs 13:11.

[200]Proverbs 28:10.

The I-Ching teaches much the same message: "Whatever endures can be created only gradually by long-continued work and careful reflection."[201] And "a tree on a mountain develops slowly according to the law of its being and consequently stands firmly rooted."[202] The familiar Æsop's fable of the hare and the tortoise also comes to mind: "Slow but sure is the quickest way in the long run."[203] Lăozĭ taught a similar message saying, "to hold a steadfast course is to have will."[204]

The time-tested principle is to thus build wealth slowly and consistently over time. This message, of course, is highly countercultural. It is not a quick method; it is difficult and takes time. As the author of Hebrews writes: "Discipline always seems painful rather than pleasant at the time, but later it yields the peaceful fruit of righteousness to those who have been trained by it."[205] Or as Steve Maraboli once tweeted: "Get-rich-quick schemes are for the lazy and unambitious. Respect your dreams enough to pay the full price for them."[206]

Socially Responsible Investing

One might have expected an essay on investing from a Progressive Christian perspective to have focused primarily on choosing socially-responsible investments. To be sure, the idea of socially-responsible investing tests well against the criteria of the interfaith hermeneutic of evolutionary wisdom. The Bible is full of invectives against those who build their wealth through dishonest or immoral means. For example, in Deuteronomy 23:18, money obtained through immoral means such as prostitution cannot be brought into the house of the Lord, used for payment for any vow,

---

[201] I Ching 32; Richard Wilhelm, C. G. Jung, and Hellmut Wilhelm. *The I Ching or Book of Changes*. Trans. by Cary F. Baynes. Norwalk, CT: Easton Press, 2008, p. 127.

[202] I Ching 53; (ibid., p. 204).

[203] Æsop, Fables 2. The Hare and the Tortoise (Æsop and Munro Leaf, *Æsop's Fables—A New Version*, op. cit., pp. 4–5).

[204] Tao Te Ching 33 (Lăozĭ and James Trapp, *Tao Te Ching*, op. cit., p. 41).

[205] Hebrews 12:11.

[206] Steve Maraboli. *"Get rich quick. . . "* Twitter Post [9:11 AM — Aug 16, 2015]. 2015. URL: www . twitter . com / SteveMaraboli / status / 632947703073370112 (visited on 05/14/2021).

as this money is "an abomination to the Lord your God." Proverbs says that, "Oppressing the poor in order to enrich oneself, and giving to the rich, will lead only to loss,"[207] and "Better is a little with righteousness than large income with injustice."[208] The Psalmist also suggested that: "It is well with those who deal generously and lend, who conduct their affairs with justice."[209] And the Apostle Paul said: "Take no part in the unfruitful works of darkness, but instead expose them."[210]

The concept of socially-responsible investing is also clearly in line with the teachings of other faith traditions. It conforms to the concept of "do no harm" or "right livelihood" in Buddhism;[211] Islamic investing principles are primarily focused on choosing *halal*, or "permissible" investments, since many industries do not conform to the values of Islam and are hence *harem* ("forbidden").[212] Even the Law Code of Hammurabi had steep penalties for profiting through dishonest means.[213]

The concept of socially-responsible investing belongs with the other guidelines outlined in this essay. However, a caution label must be attached. This topic has become a major buzzword, with the acronym SRI, in the financial industry in recent decades, and there has been an explosion of investment products targeted at investors who wish to invest in socially-responsible companies. Today, these investment products are heavily marketed, and as with all financial products, especially those which are marketed, a healthy dose of skepticism, thorough research, and wisdom is in order. Not only that, but there are questions about how much impact these investments make. Unless one is directly providing capital, for example, by investing in startups, IPOs, or as an angel

---

[207] Proverbs 22:16.

[208] Proverbs 16:8.

[209] Psalm 112:5.

[210] Ephesians 5:11.

[211] Dhammapada 19:270 (Acharya Buddharakkhita, *The Dhammapada—The Buddha's Path of Wisdom*, op. cit., p. 86); Huston Smith, *The World's Religions*, op. cit., p. 108.

[212] Mohd Ma'Sum Billah. *Modern Islamic Investment Management*. Cham, Switzerland: Springer, 2019. ISBN: 978-3-030-17627-3, p. 56.

[213] Hammurabi's Code 265 (Robert Francis Harper. *The Code of Hammurabi, King of Babylon: About 2250 BC*. Chicago, IL: University of Chicago Press, 1904, p. 91).

investor to socially-responsible companies, the investment may not have much of an impact. Divesting from irresponsible companies and purchasing shares of responsible ones seldom limits access to capital for those companies. Furthermore, many companies claim to be socially responsible, but aren't. There is also a lot of subjectivity surrounding the definition of "socially-responsible" investments, and Progressive Christians must carefully evaluate these products for themselves. As the Buddha said: "A wise man is he who investigates both right and wrong."[214]

But the idea remains an important field of exploration for Progressive Christians who, out of necessity or desire, chose to invest their money. The opportunities to craft a socially-responsible portfolio that targets certain values of interest are practically endless. One can create a portfolio which invests in companies who have philanthropic emphasis, advertise sustainable and green manufacturing, living wages for all workers, or avoid certain industries deemed harmful in society.

Summary

This essay brought our faith tradition into conversation with the financial principle of investing. We first began by examining biblicism, a type of biblical interpretation which often claims to have access to "objective truth." It is argued that even if the biblicist's beliefs about the sacred text are true, such as divine inspiration, inerrancy, and infallibility, these claims simply do not matter in practice due to the phenomenon of pervasive interpretive pluralism. We thus find that while biblicism advertises a narrow menu of interpretation coinciding with objective truth, it instead serves a large buffet of opinions—each dish seasoned with a large helping of pride and arrogance.

Finding biblicism's claims unsubstantiated and unsuitable for understanding how faith can inform investing, we turned to the ancient tradition of multiple creative interpretations. Rather than denying interpretive pluralism (but doing it anyway), this tradition invites everyone to participate at an ancient potluck and delight

---

[214]Dhammapada 19:256.

in diversity as the sacred text is rotated, sliced and carved from every angle, marinated in a variety of presuppositions, and served for our consideration and discussion. But still, for the modern individual seeking "objective" truth, this tradition may also present difficulties, since it lacks a single sustainable hermeneutic—though granted, that is not advertised and is certainly not the point of this tradition.

In an effort to provide a foothold for the modern progressive pilgrim, the interfaith hermeneutic of evolutionary wisdom is proposed. This method notes that even in science, where objective truth is expected, theories tend to be demonstrated by empirical tests rather than proved from *a priori* axioms, resulting in the coveted epistemological certainty. Many theories are proposed in science only to be tested and undergo a cleansing evolutionary process, where the "fittest" theories survive and improve. With this in mind, we examine our sacred text and find a similar phenomenon. Some principles taught in the faith seem to persist across both time, culture, and religion and are independently verified in other faiths. The interfaith hermeneutic of evolutionary wisdom thus attempts to uncover these principles and touts them as "objectively true"—though in the context of a few disclaimers and footnotes. It is thus suggested that this method approaches the goal to which biblicism aspires.

Finally, we looked to our tradition for principles which promote success with investing and find that underneath all the noise and practically infinite amount of information proceeding from the financial industry today, there seem to be just a few underlying principles which have stood the test of time: simplicity, diversity, and consistency. These principles, it is argued, are "objectively true" guidelines for investing which, if practiced, increase the probability of financial success and allow one to focus attention on more important aspects of life. Socially-responsible investing is also explained as being in-line with the interfaith hermeneutic of evolutionary wisdom. Because this is currently an extremely hot topic in the financial industry, it seems the dust has yet to settle to clearly see what investing options allow socially responsible investing without sacrificing the first three guidelines. Accordingly, *all* financial products should be carefully evaluated using wisdom before purchased.

Chapter 4

Minimalism—The New Face of Contentment

*"Poverty consists, not in the decrease of one's posses-
sions, but in the increase of one's greed."*[1] —Plato

"LESS is now" is the title of a new documentary from the
Minimalists.[2] The film's title was inspired by the popular maxim "Less is more," popularized by architect
Ludwig Mies van der Rohe (1886–1969), who used the phrase to
describe his design aesthetic of extreme simplicity. The Minimalists
have reworked this phrase to create a sense of urgency for today's
consumer culture: now is the time for less. In this essay, we bring
faith and personal finance in conversation with each other. Contentment, as a spiritual virtue, is one of the most widely-attested
principles found across religions. However, the message of contentment goes against the grain of our materialistic society. As Progressive Christians, it is our sacred task to update our tradition for
present times. I suggest that the modern minimalism movement is

---

[1] Plato, Laws 736e (Plato. *The Laws of Plato.* Trans. by Thomas L. Pangle.
Chicago, IL: University of Chicago Press, 1988, p. 123 as quoted in Huston
Smith, *The World's Religions*, op. cit., p. 16).

[2] Joshua Fields Millburn, Ryan Nicodemus, and Matt D'Avella. *The Minimalists: Less Is Now [Movie].* Netflix, 2021.

well-suited to be "the new face of contentment." Practicing contentment through minimalism can have enormous benefits in the arena of personal finance. While some may default to compartmentalizing faith and personal finance, this essay presents a positive example of their unification and the profound benefits that can be realized when faith is brought into true dialogue with our personal finances.

A Persistent Ancient Virtue

Recall from Chapter 3 that the interfaith hermeneutic of evolutionary wisdom looks for wisdom in our sacred texts which seem to transcend time, geographical, cultural, and religious boundaries. Of all the general principles, virtues and vices that can be derived with this method, probably none are more well-attested by a great "cloud of witnesses"[3] than *contentment* and material simplicity. Viki Robin gives a succinct summary:

> *"In ancient times, both Socrates and Plato praised the "golden mean." Both the Old Testament ("Give me neither poverty nor wealth, but only enough") and the teachings of Jesus ("Ye cannot serve both God and money") extol the value of material simplicity in enriching the life of the spirit. In American history, well-known individuals (Benjamin Franklin, Henry David Thoreau, Ralph Waldo Emerson, Robert Frost) as well as groups (Amish, Quakers, Hutterites, Mennonites) have carried forward the virtue of thrift—both out of respect for the earth and out of a thirst for a touch of heaven."*[4]

Indeed, the Bible is replete with references to the virtues of contentment. For example, the Apostle Paul said: "There is great gain in godliness combined with contentment"[5] and claimed to "have

---

[3]Hebrews 12:1.

[4]Vicki Robin, Joe Dominguez, and Monique Tilford, *Your Money or Your Life: 9 Steps to Transforming Your Relationship With Money and Achieving Financial Independence*, op. cit., pp. 164–165.

[5]1 Timothy 6:6.

learned to be content with whatever [he had]."[6] The author of
Hebrews also said, "Keep your lives free from the love of money,
and be content with what you have."[7]

Attitudes which are antithetical to contentment are consistently
condemned. Desire, according to the author of James, is the root
of much conflict: "You want something and do not have it; so you
commit murder. And you covet something and cannot obtain it;
so you engage in disputes and conflicts."[8] And in Proverbs, "The
greedy person stirs up strife, but whoever trusts in the Lord will be
enriched."[9] Similarly, Qohelet said, "Better is the sight of the eyes
than the wandering of desire."[10] Jesus was certainly not apathetic
towards greed and discontentment: "Take care! Be on your guard
against all kinds of greed; for one's life does not consist of the
abundance of possessions."[11] And, "All the days of the poor are
hard, but a cheerful heart has a continual feast."[12] In other words,
our satisfaction in life is often more a state of mind than anything
else.

The biblical authors tell us that material wealth is not ultimately satisfying,[13] so we should be content with what we have
and enjoy it, "for this is our lot" in life.[14] Therefore, we should not
worry about the material things of life and focus on more important
spiritual aspects.[15] Spiritual virtues trump material possessions every time.[16] But pure asceticism is not necessarily recommended,
and a teaching similar to the "middle way" in Buddhism is found
in Proverbs: "Give me neither poverty nor riches."[17]

Turning next to Taoism, we find that the old teacher, Lǎozǐ,
praises contentment and the virtue of recognizing what is "enough."
The Tao Te Ching says: "No disaster is worse than not recognizing

---

[6] Philippians 4:11.
[7] Hebrews 13:5.
[8] James 4:2.
[9] Proverbs 28:25.
[10] Ecclesiastes 6:9.
[11] Luke 12:15.
[12] Proverbs 15:15.
[13] Ecclesiastes 5:10.
[14] Ecclesiastes 5:18.
[15] Matthew 6:25.
[16] Psalm 37:16; Proverbs 28:6.
[17] Proverbs 30:8–9.

sufficiency. No crime is greater than acquisitiveness. Thus, recognizing the sufficiency of sufficiency is eternally sufficient."[18] "Coveting precious objects destroys your morals. The wise man is concerned only with having a full belly, not with vain aspirations."[19] "Covetousness brings ruin. Recognizing sufficiency and knowing when to stop avoids these consequences and ensure longevity."[20] "If a vessel you are carrying is already full, it is best not to add anything more."[21] Finally, "To recognize sufficiency is to be rich."[22] Likewise, Buddhism teaches much the same message: "Contentment [is] the greatest wealth."[23]

Buddhism, of course, is deeply interested in contentment. In fact, the whole idea of the Buddha's spiritual path is based on the idea of squelching the flame of desire,[24] which is the cause of suffering: "Beset by craving, people run about like an entrapped hare. Held fast by mental fetters, they come to suffering again and again for a long time. [...] Therefore one who yearns to be passion-free should destroy his own craving."[25] Just like Jesus' teachings about not worrying about material things, the Buddha says: "The fool worries, thinking, 'I have sons, I have wealth.' Indeed, when he himself is not his own, whence are sons, whence is wealth?"[26] Thus, we should focus on renouncing things of "lesser happiness" so we "may realize a greater happiness."[27] "Blessed is contentment with just what one has."[28] Confucius also taught contentment when he said, "A scholar whose heart is set on the truth, but who is still ashamed of poor clothes and bad food, is not worth discussing truth with."[29]

In addition to Plato, we find in ancient Greece that several

[18]Tao Te Ching 46 (Lǎozǐ and James Trapp, *Tao Te Ching*, op. cit., p. 56).

[19]Tao Te Ching 12 (ibid., p. 18).

[20]Tao Te Ching 44 (ibid., p. 54).

[21]Tao Te Ching 9 (ibid., p. 15).

[22]Tao Te Ching 33 (ibid., p. 41).

[23]Dhammapada 15:204 (Acharya Buddharakkhita, *The Dhammapada—The Buddha's Path of Wisdom*, op. cit., p. 71).

[24]Dhammapada 24:359 (ibid., p. 77).

[25]Dhammapada 24:342–343 (ibid., p. 104).

[26]Dhammapada 5:62 (ibid., p. 36).

[27]Dhammapada 21:290 (ibid., p. 91).

[28]Dhammapada 23:331 (ibid., p. 101).

[29]Analects of Confucius 4:9; Kǒng Fūzǐ, *The Analects of Confucius: Chinese–English Bilingual Edition*, op. cit., p. 33.

of Æsop's fables teach the virtue of contentment. "You don't do yourself or anybody else any good when you are dissatisfied with your lot. You might just as well make the best of it."[30] "Many of us who work hard to be somewhere else, don't find that we like it any better when we get there."[31] And, "Don't try to grab everything. You may lose what you have."[32]

Surprisingly, the ancient Egyptian *Pyramid Texts,* which are not exactly known for their philosophical insight, are quite poetic regarding contentment:

> *"Contentment be what is gotten for you,*
> *contentment be what you see, contentment be what you*
> *hear,*
> *contentment be before you, contentment be behind you,*
> *contentment be your lot."*[33]

Even older than the *Pyramid Texts* are the *Instructions of Šuruppak,* a piece of Sumerian/Akkadian wisdom literature, which dates to the early third millennium BCE, making it among the oldest surviving literature. Šuruppak says: "Nothing at all is to be valued, but life should be sweet. You should not serve things; things should serve you."[34] As proof this concept has persisted over time, compare this saying with Dave Ramsey's statement: "I want you to have some nice stuff; I just don't want your nice stuff to have you,"[35] or with Brad Pitt's line in *Fight Club*: "The things

---

[30] Æsop, Fables 29. The Peacock's Complaint (Æsop and Munro Leaf, *Æsop's Fables—A New Version*, op. cit., pp. 42–43).

[31] Æsop, Fables 38. The Mouse & the Weasel (ibid., p. 53).

[32] Æsop, Fables 80. The Man & His Goose (ibid., p. 108).

[33] Pyramid Texts 32 (James Peter Allen and Peter Der Manuelian. *The Ancient Egyptian Pyramid Texts.* Ed. by Peter Der Manuelian et al. Trans. by James P. Allen. Vol. 23. Writings from the Ancient World. Atlanta, GA: Society of Biblical Literature, 2005. ISBN: 978-1-58983-182-7, p. 21).

[34] Instructions of Shuruppak 242–244 (Jeremy A. Black. *The Literature of Ancient Sumer.* Trans. by Jeremy Black et al. New York: Oxford University Press, 2004. ISBN: 0-19-926311-6, p. 290); Stuart Weeks. *Ecclesiastes and Skepticism.* New York: T & T Clark International, 2012. ISBN: 978-0-567-25288-3, p. 164.

[35] Dave Ramsey, *The Legacy Journey: A Radical View of Biblical Wealth and Generosity*, op. cit., p. 60.

you own end up owning you."[36]

We have thus come full circle. Contentment as a guiding principle for our relationship with material things is found in ancient literature over 4,600 years old, in the 21st century as taught by Dave Ramsey, the Minimalists, and others, and everything between. According to the interfaith hermeneutic of evolutionary wisdom, the spiritual discipline of contentment has an enormous body of evidence showing it has been empirically tested and verified by countless individuals and cultures over vast periods of time.

Why is contentment such a powerful spiritual principle? Unfortunately, the interfaith hermeneutic of evolutionary wisdom is not really set up to answer the *why* question, at least in the initial surface-level application. It is better prepared to answer *what* questions. But then again, neither is science. It seems that every mystery in science is answered by yet *more* mysteries.[37] As Janna Levin says: "Each answer I learn releases a rainfall of new questions."[38] Thus, it is advertised by this method that *contentment* is a spiritual principle carrying with it at least similar levels of objectivity and certainty we find in science, and we will do well to pay attention to it and practice it. Although we may theorize about why certain spiritual principles are superior ways of life, we may never really know. Perhaps this is what faith is—remaining faithful to the spiritual path even if (or especially *when*) we lack clarity, certainty and understanding.

---

[36]David Fincher and Chuck Palahniuk. *Fight Club [Movie]*. 20th Century Fox, 1999.

[37]For example, the nature of matter at the quantum level is *far more* mysterious than anyone could have imagined. Sure, we have explained many previously unexplained phenomena with advances in science. But there is no getting around the fact that the explanations are unimaginably complex and raise yet *more* questions. *Why* did the proverbial apple fall on Newton's head? We have found that it is because matter causes a deformation in the space-time continuum. Who would have thought?! This is a far more mysterious "explanation" than anything imagined by Aristotle's gravitational theory, for example. Thus, while science seems to answer the *why* questions, it is in practice answering with simply *more* questions.

[38]Janna Levin. *How the Universe Got Its Spots*. New York: Random House, 2002. ISBN: 1-4000-3272-5, p. 94.

Updating Our Tradition

Although it's clear that contentment is an important principle, taught and practiced over vast time periods, it is highly counter-cultural. Materialism runs rampant in society today, and teaching and practicing contentment and material simplicity is likely to spark criticism, if not fall on deaf ears. Take for example the lyrics from Ariana Grande's "7 rings" (2019), which has become one of the best-selling songs in digital history:

"Whoever said money can't solve your problems
Must not have had enough money to solve 'em
They say, 'Which one?' I say, 'Nah, I want all of 'em'
Happiness is the same price as red bottoms

I want it, I got it, I want it, I got it
I want it, I got it, I want it, I got it
You like my hair? Gee, thanks, just bought it
I see it, I like it, I want it, I got it."

Given the Bible's ever-diminishing status of authority in society, citing it as we did in the previous section is likely to have minimal impact, especially in the younger generation, where religiosity is declining at unprecedented rates. Even worse is citing obscure ancient literature such as the *Instructions of Šhuruppak*. While some may find this interesting, others will likely yawn and ask, "So what?" as they log into their Amazon account to purchase more items they "need" to keep up with the latest trends.

As discussed in the previous chapter, it is our sacred responsibility to update our tradition. This is a major part of what it means to be "progressive." The Jewish religion survived *because it adapted*. The ancient rabbis sought an adaptive faith to maintain relevance as a supreme goal of their work, a model for development of the faith we should take seriously. There is no doubt that "our culture is riddled with jealousy and envy and greed, all of which are by-products of our competitive, consumer driven culture."[39] Thus,

---

[39] Joshua Fields Millburn and Ryan Nicodemus. *Minimalism: Essential Essays*. 1st ed. Mins Publishing, 2011. ISBN: 978-1-9365394-5-1, p. 29.

contentment is in dire need of a facelift. I propose that the modern secular minimalism movement is well-suited to be appropriated by Progressive Christianity as "the new face of contentment." As the Orlando Sentinel said: "The Minimalists made minimalism cool."[40]

Minimalism

Although contentment and simple living has an extremely long history, it has resurged in the past few years through a secular movement called *minimalism*. Some may think of minimalism as a concerted effort to rid oneself of all material possessions and become an ascetic. The example of Colin Wright, who only "owns 51 things and travels all over the world"[41] comes to mind. But minimalism comes in many forms and is just a tool to "simplify our lives so that we could focus on what's important."[42] As the Minimalists say: "There are no rules in minimalism. Rather, minimalism is simply about stripping away the unnecessary things in your life so you can focus on what's important."[43]

Usually, we find that what's actually important to us aren't material possessions at all. For example, one's health, relationships, mission, and passion all overshadow our personal property in importance.[44] Minimalism is not about "reducing the number of possessions that you have [as] a goal unto itself."[45] It is the "the intentional *promotion* of the things we most value and the removal of anything that distracts us from it."[46] The Japanese minimalist Fumio Sasaki describes it as a "prologue for crafting your own

---

[40] *Organize Your Mindset.* 2017. URL: www . orlandosentinel . com / features / os - osig - organize - your - mindset - 20170613 - story . html (visited on 05/21/2021).

[41] Joshua Fields Millburn and Ryan Nicodemus, *Minimalism: Essential Essays*, op. cit., p. 12.

[42] Ibid., p. 23.

[43] Ibid., p. 12.

[44] Ibid., p. 12.

[45] Fumio Sasaki. *Goodbye, Things: On Minimalist Living.* Trans. by Eriko Sugita. New York: W.W. Norton & Company, 2017. ISBN: 978-0393609035, p. 45.

[46] Joshua Becker. *Simplify: 7 Guiding Principles to Help Anyone Declutter Their Home & Life [eBook].* Joshua Becker, 2014, Principle #2.

unique story,"[47] because once we pare down our possessions, we are afforded "more free time and more freedom and a less stressful life,"[48] allowing us to focus on the more important aspects of life.

According to The Minimalists, the average American household has around 300,000 items.[49] These items require time and energy to maintain and financial resources to store. Many people rent storage units just to hold the extra stuff that doesn't fit in the house. Think about all the life energy (time, money, and effort) we often spend acquiring, maintaining, and storing these 300,000 items. As Vicki Robin would analyze it: do we receive fulfillment, satisfaction, and value from these items in proportion to life energy spent? For some possessions, the answer may be a resounding "yes." But others which do not fare so well when held to the light of that question actually *detract* from our happiness, and over time begin to enslave us. Minimalism is a "tool to help you achieve freedom. Freedom from fear, freedom from worry, freedom from [being] overwhelmed, freedom from guilt, freedom from depression, freedom from enslavement. Freedom."[50] It "offers a compelling alternative to the default choice of [...] filling the closets with stuff, and then spending the next 40 years paying it all off."[51]

More philosophically, minimalism is in alignment with our entire life story since "everyone started out as a minimalist"[52] at birth and everyone will likewise leave this life as a minimalist. Or as Qohelet says, "All go to one place; all are from the dust, and all turn to dust again."[53]

Getting started with minimalism is both simple and difficult. It is simple to reduce one's material possessions, but often difficult to let go. It is simple to preach the message of contentment to

---

[47] Fumio Sasaki, *Goodbye, Things: On Minimalist Living*, op. cit., p. 45.

[48] Joshua Fields Millburn and Ryan Nicodemus, *Minimalism: Essential Essays*, op. cit., p. 18.

[49] Dave Ramsey. *Why You Don't Need All Of Your Stuff! | The Minimalists.* YouTube Video. 2021. URL: https://www.youtube.com/watch?v=9IYP5xUoSBE (visited on 05/16/2021).

[50] Joshua Fields Millburn and Ryan Nicodemus, *Minimalism: Essential Essays*, op. cit., p. 11.

[51] J. L. Fisker, *Early Retirement Extreme: A Philosophical and Practical Guide to Financial Independence*, op. cit., back cover.

[52] Fumio Sasaki, *Goodbye, Things: On Minimalist Living*, op. cit., p. 33.

[53] Ecclesiastes 3:20.

those we clearly see need it, but it is difficult to gain traction with a highly counter-cultural message in an ever-materialistic society. The Minimalists agree with the proposal of "Start With the Heart" in Chapter 1:

> "So, how do you become a minimalist, even though your friends or family might not be ready to take the plunge? The answer is easier than you might think: start with yourself. You must first set the example for the people around you."[54]

Although acting out contentment through minimalism can be difficult at first, the modern minimalist movement offers many tools for practice, stories for inspiration, and community for encouragement. As Progressive Christians, I thus suggest that it is a well-suited movement for us to engage with as we explore contentment for ourselves.

The Financial Results of Minimalism

We previously saw that the application of mindfulness to finances may result in dramatic increases in wealth.[55] Minimalism may have similar effects. For example, Marissa Zen reports that minimalism allowed her and her family to save 50 to 70% of their income every year, pay off $250,000 worth of debt, pay for their wedding and honeymoon with cash, move to Europe, buy a home, and furnish it with no debt.[56] Avery Heilbron, another minimalist, claims to have been able to save 80% of his income every month with minimalism.[57] One of the key ways minimalism helps save money is that it cultivates a spirit of contentment which reduces the number of purchases.

---

[54] Joshua Fields Millburn and Ryan Nicodemus, *Minimalism: Essential Essays*, op. cit., p. 74.

[55] See the section "FIRE and Mindfulness" in Chapter 2 on page 25.

[56] Marissa Zen. *10 Extreme Minimalist Budget Tips (Save 70% of Income) | Spend Less | Financial Minimalist Family*. YouTube Video. 2021. URL: www.youtube.com/watch?v=f2u0Tn8esVs (visited on 06/12/2021).

[57] Avery Heilbron. *How I Save 80% Of My Income | Financial Independence | Minimalism*. YouTube Video. 2021. URL: www.youtube.com/watch?v=f2u0Tn8esVs (visited on 06/12/2021).

I love music and books. For several years, I was spending hundreds of dollars a month amassing a collection of books and music CDs. The knock at the door by the Amazon delivery person was a familiar and welcome sound. Once I started practicing minimalism, those purchases practically stopped completely. I went through the difficult process of ridding myself of hundreds of books and CDs. There was a sort of grieving process, followed by a sense of relief. Now, the only books I own are those that fit into the four R's categories: Reread, recommend, reference, and rare.[58] Now the library is my friend. I end up selling most books I purchase after I read them, and only a few pass the test to take place in my permanent library. All the money saved from practicing minimalism goes straight into investments, which, if compounded at 10% interest[59] over 30 years turns into nearly $500,000. While getting rid of the majority of my book and CD collection was emotionally difficult, will I regret not having hundreds of books and CDs which I rarely read or listen to on a regular basis? Probably not.

Additionally, reducing the number of items owned means there is less maintenance and storage costs. As another personal example, before my wife and I started applying mindfulness to our finances and practicing minimalism, we owned an expensive SUV. This was my dream vehicle: shiny black exterior, equally shiny black leather interior. But because it was a nice vehicle and we had spent a lot of money on it, I spent nearly every weekend maintaining and cleaning it, and I always purchased the highest quality parts for it. The end result was that maintenance costs averaged $200 per month. The vehicle also drained our finances due to expensive insurance, money lost due to depreciation, and high fuel consumption. Selling this vehicle was one of the first major steps in our journey. But it was a difficult decision, because I had invested so much time and money into this car. What finally convinced me was when I calculated the financial impact. Selling this vehicle and sharing one car between my wife and me for the next 10 years and investing the savings resulted in nearly $1,000,000 at retirement.

---

[58]Viktoria. *How to Balance Minimalism and a Love Affair with Books.* 2018. URL: www.thelifestyle-files.com/tips-to-balance-minimalism-and-books/ (visited on 06/12/2021).

[59]See Appendix A "Stock Market Growth Calculations" on page 147 for an explanation of long-term stock market returns.

After we sold the vehicle, contrary to the advertisements, our quality of life did not decrease at all. In fact, it increased. Although we were now driving a rusty old beater instead of a fancy SUV, there was suddenly a sense of freedom. Freedom from being worried about maintaining a nice car. Freedom to make progress on our financial goals. Freedom to spend the weekends *not* maintaining the vehicle. Reflecting back, I realize now that I didn't own this SUV; it owned me. Learning to be content with less not only simplified life, but dramatically improved our finances.

When this saved car money eventually turns into $1,000,000, what can we do with it? How can we bless other people with it? How many lives can we save through philanthropic efforts using these resources that would have otherwise been wasted on a possession that was more of a curse than a blessing? These are the types of questions that are sparked when embarking on the Legacy Journey. And such questions wouldn't even be remotely on our minds if it weren't for practicing contentment through minimalism.

Conclusion

In summary, contentment is one of the oldest spiritual principles which pervades religious traditions from the distant past to the present day. In today's materialistic stuff-addicted culture, its message is desperately needed. This essay suggests that the contemporary minimalism movement is well-suited to be appropriated by Progressive Christianity as the new face of contentment. But following the suggested starting place from Chapter 1, we should start with ourselves. What items do we own which get in the way of more important aspects of life? How might our time, energy, and financial resources be better used to change our family, our community, and the world if we didn't spend as much on the acquisition, maintenance, and storage of things which may not always be worthy of our precious God-given life energy? These are questions to first ask ourselves, experiment with changes, and then preach our experience to the culture through our actions and speech. Let us embrace the unification of faith, personal finance, and social justice despite any tensions that may arise!

Chapter 5

Wealth as a Spiritual Amplifier

"Nearly all men can stand adversity, but if you want to test a man's character, give him power."[1] —Abraham Lincoln

THIS journey has so far shown that practices such as mindfulness,[2] simplicity,[3] diversification,[4] consistency,[5] and contentment or minimalism[6] can improve the probability of increasing and preserving one's wealth over time. But this is no prosperity gospel—far from it. If we intend to take this spiritual path seriously, an increase in wealth for any reason is no trivial matter. Where the prosperity gospel is primarily about following God in order that our wealth will increase for our personal enjoyment, the path we are exploring here instead has a more solemn

---

[1]Though not found in the *Collected Works* of Lincoln, this saying is popularly attributed to Lincoln (Clarence Thomas et al. *Lincoln and Liberty: Wisdom for the Ages.* Lexington, KY: University Press of Kentucky, 2014).

[2]See the section "FIRE and Mindfulness" in Chapter 2 on page 25.

[3]See the section "Simplicity" in Chapter 3 on page 86.

[4]See the section "Diversity" in Chapter 3 on 89.

[5]See the section "Consistency" in Chapter 3 on page 90.

[6]See the section "The Financial Results of Minimalism" in Chapter 4 on page 104.

and sacred tone—one that, as we have already seen, sparks pressing questions about the moral status of wealth

Is wealth inherently good?

Is it inherently evil?

How much is morally acceptable to enjoy?

Should all excess be given away?

We found that the Judeo-Christian tradition, rather than providing a single sustainable answer to such questions, not only invites us to participate in a diverse discussion, but actually *canonizes* a plurality of opinions. This signals to us that embedded deep in the fabric of our tradition is a sacred calling to engage with these topics, and avoid compartmentalizing them. We should hold the tension caused by our faith as a sacred and beautiful aspect of our tradition because these tensions encourage true spiritual growth if they are engaged rather than evaded.

But suppose we develop a thoughtful theology of wealth which fully explains our experience of the world. Content with the belief that we've "figured it out," we continue on our way doing much the same as we always have—good or bad—with little additional thought. Perhaps persisting in a stagnant belief,[7] our wealth continues to increase nonetheless. There is a profound danger in this, in not continuing to grow and adapt with changing financial circumstances. But this peril may actually be spiritually healthy if treated with a proper spirit. As with a free-soloing rock climber, the spiritual dangers of wealth can increase focus and attention, providing motivation to hone and sculpt our spirits as we engage more thoroughly with the essence of our faith. On the other hand, an increase in wealth may be detrimental to both our inward and outward journeys, negatively affecting our every relationship in life. The danger is thinking that the frontier of belief—which includes asking questions such as "what is the moral status of wealth?"—is

---

[7]If our views remain largely unchanged over time, this suggests we may not be seeking genuine dialogue with others nor inviting new and rich experiences in life which can shape our worldview. See the section "Engage Rather than Evade" in Chapter 1 on page 14.

the only area that needs to be explored. Instead, our beliefs about wealth likely matter less than our personal spiritual trajectories.

This essay argues that wealth amplifies the effects of our spiritual characteristics—good and bad. As one's wealth increases, the need for spiritual growth, self-examination, and engagement with our tradition increases proportionally. Although we find this fact recorded in our sacred text in the form of strong warnings about the perilous nature of wealth, this essay also attempts to paint a positive vision for the relationship between wealth and spirituality, and suggests that the dangers of wealth can provide momentum to one's spiritual journey, but *only if* we treat wealth with an attitude that embraces the weight of responsibility rather than entitlement or greed.

How Wealth Amplifies Character...

In Ourselves...

Henry Ford once said in an interview with Bruce Barton: "Money doesn't change men, it merely unmasks them. If a man is naturally selfish or arrogant or greedy, the money brings that out, that's all."[8] Many others have also claimed as much, saying: "Money only magnifies who you already are."[9] It is easy to see, by way of

---

[8]Bruce Barton. "It Would Be Fun To Start Over Again—Interview with Henry Ford." In: *The American Magazine* 91 (1921), p. 124; Mark S. Waldman. *The Way of Real Wealth: Creating a Future that is Emotionally Satisfying, Spiritually Fulfilling, Financially Secure.* New York: Harpercollins, 1993. ISBN: 978-0-0625-5283-9, p. 163; Mark S. Waldman. *A Spiritual Guide to Money: How to Use Money for Personal Growth & Genuine Spiritual Experience.* Mark S. Waldman (Xlibris), 2001. ISBN: 0-7388-2821-1, p. 148.

[9]Dave Ramsey, *The Legacy Journey: A Radical View of Biblical Wealth and Generosity*, op. cit., p. 116; Tony Robbins and Peter Mallouk. *Unshakeable: Your Financial Freedom Playbook.* New York: Simon and Schuster, 2017. ISBN: 978-1-5011-6458-3, p. 168; Deion Sanders and Jim Nelson Black. *Power, Money & Sex: How Success Almost Ruined My Life.* Nashville, TN: Word Publishing, 1999. ISBN: 0-8499-1499-X, p. 145; Laura Leigh Clarke. *Wire Yourself for Wealth—Discover Your Personal Money Profile to Effortlessly Attract More Cash.* Carlsbad, CA: Hay House, 2012. ISBN: 978-1-84850-698-5, p. 18; Jeffrey A. Johnson and Tim White. *Get Ready! Get Real! Get Financial Freedom—A Simple Blueprint for Building and Sustaining Financial Freedom.* Atlanta, GA: Opes Publishing, 2020. ISBN: 978-1-7343118-0-8, p.

an analogy, that there is some truth to this claim.

A toddler who rides a tricycle is unlikely to be able to inflict much harm on herself or other's property. Worst case, a bump and a scratch is the result—hardly a story worth sharing at the church potluck. As the child grows, she switches to a bicycle. Riding full speed, she slams into a parked car. The result may be thousands of dollars of damage to the car, coupled with a few broken bones—though hardly an unusual experience. This may catch more people's attention than the toddler incident. As the child grows into a teenager operating a motor vehicle, she drives down a busy highway, carrying the responsibility of ferrying her friends who are passengers. The potential for damage to property is higher, and several lives are at stake—a major mishap would surely reverberate throughout the community, but it still wouldn't make the national, much less international news. Later, she attends flight school and becomes a commercial pilot, routinely transporting hundreds of individuals at a time. A commercial plane crash would be disastrous, not only to the passengers, but potentially to hundreds if not thousands on the ground. There is no doubt that this would catch the attention of international headlines.

There is also a positive side to these scenarios. While the toddler has little potential to do good, save for prompting a smile from onlookers, the child on a bike can use it to ride to visit a neighbor friend who is struggling with depression. The teenager driving a car can deliver meals to those in need. And the pilot can transport life-saving medical supplies across the world and carry passengers who are traveling to reunite with friends and family.

What is the difference between the child on a bike, the teenager in a car, or the adult piloting a plane? In essence, these are all the same type of activity: transportation. The difference lies in the

26; Lisa Crayton. *I Want to Talk With my Teen About Money Management.* Cincinnati, OH: The Standard Publishing, 2006. ISBN: 978-0-7847-1897-0, p. 20; Lee Jenkins. *Taking Care of Business: Establishing a Financial Legacy for Your Family.* Chicago, IL: Moody Publishers, 2001. ISBN: 0-8024-4016-9, p. 56; John Gray. *How to Get What You Want and Want What You Have: A Practical and Spiritual Guide to Personal Success.* New York: HarperOne, 2009. ISBN: 978-0-0619-8443-3; J. D. Hatfield. *A Call to Action—Preaching Through the Book of James.* J. D. Hatfield, 2015. ISBN: 978-1-312-82154-5, p. 217; Larry Winters. *Live the Dream—No More Excuses.* New York: Center Street, 2012. ISBN: 978-1-4555-1362-8, p. 147.

tool that is used. The larger and more powerful the tool, the more potential for good and bad. It's not that a larger tool has better or worse moral status, it's that it amplifies the character of the user.

Likewise, wealth has a tendency to amplify one's spiritual attributes. For example, a landlord who lacks a spirit of mercy may inflict some emotional harm in the world if he owns one or two units. But imagine that same landlord owning a thousand-unit property. How many tenants would be stressed by his lack of mercy? Similarly, someone who is unbelievably generous, but who has little to give, may not make much of a financial impact except by inspiring others—like the poor widow who gave all she had, only two small copper coins (Luke 21:1–4). But using a larger tool, more wealth, the same generous person can change a community, a nation, perhaps even the world.

However, a problem with this argument is that it is almost never accurate to categorize people as solely "unmerciful," wholly "generous," or completely "greedy." Most people are a mixture of good and bad spiritual traits. Take for example, Jeff Bezos, currently one of the richest people on earth with a net worth just shy of $200 billion. While at lower levels of wealth in the past, Bezos' financial decisions were not of much interest. But now the entire world can now see his character in excruciating detail under the microscope of his massive wealth. Recently, Bezos purchased a half-a-billion-dollar superyacht. This yacht is so big that it needs its own support yacht and submarine. Let me say that again—a yacht that is so large, it needs its own support yacht and submarine... a picture completely unimaginable for most people. Materialism in most individuals can never reach levels of this proportion. Around the same time as purchasing his superyacht, Bezos also gave to charity the single largest contribution of the year, a donation of $10 billion.

The point of this essay is not to criticize nor praise Bezos—though perhaps one or both are in order. In the spirit of starting with the heart, that is, starting with *our* heart, the point is simply to illustrate how wealth magnifies both the good and bad aspects of our character.

And In Our Relationships

Wealth not only magnifies *our* virtues and vices, it can have similar effects on those around us. If we start with loving, healthy relationships, then, as wealth builds over time, it can be a blessing.[10] But the opposite is true, too. If our marriage is struggling,[11] or relationships with our children are strained, or if our family and friends harbor envy, a sense of entitlement, or occasionally ask us to fund their unhealthy behavior, the problems only become worse with increased wealth.[12] That is, "your success may reveal the true characters of your friends and family members."[13]

The Inadequacy of Belief Alone

Wealth poses a danger, not just to those of us who are tempted by its power but even to those who remain unchanged in character. To be sure, our good characteristics will be amplified, but so will our bad characteristics. Philosophical questions, such as the moral status of wealth, lay an important foundation for us to begin this journey. As John Shelby Spong says: "What the mind cannot accept, the heart can finally never adore."[14] But mere belief in an idea, a belief which may change over time, is wholly insufficient to overcome the dangers posed by wealth.

It is unfortunate that a dominant form of Christianity has made "believing" the central issue of Christian identity. Marcus Borg claims that this way of viewing the Christian religion is a product of post-Enlightenment modernism.[15] Borg goes on to say:

> *"That Christian faith is about belief is a rather odd notion, when you think about it. It suggests that what*

---

[10]Dave Ramsey, *The Legacy Journey: A Radical View of Biblical Wealth and Generosity*, op. cit., p. 120.

[11]Ibid., p. 121.

[12]Ibid., pp. 131–132.

[13]Ibid., p. 131.

[14]John Shelby Spong. *Rescuing the Bible from Fundamentalism: A Bishop Rethinks the Meaning of Scripture.* HarperSanFransisco, 1991. ISBN: 0-06-067518-8, p. 24.

[15]Marcus J. Borg. *The Heart of Christianity: Rediscovering a Life of Faith.* New York: HarperOne, 2003. ISBN: 978-0-06-073068-0, p. 12.

*God really cares about is the beliefs in our heads—as if
"believing the right things" is what God is most looking
for, as if having "correct beliefs" is what will save us.
And if you have "incorrect beliefs," you may be in trouble. It's remarkable to think that God cares so much
about "beliefs."*

*Moreover, when you think about it, faith as belief is rel-
atively impotent, relatively powerless. You can believe
all the right things and still be in bondage. You can
believe all the right things and still be miserable. You
can believe all the right things and still be relatively unchanged. Believing a set of claims to be true has very
little transforming power."*[16]

As Rachel Held Evans says: "Christianity isn't meant to simply
be believed; it's meant to be lived, shared, eaten, spoken, and
enacted."[17] This is the "heart of Christianity"[18] which is being
resurrected in the Progressive Christian movement. "It is a way
of being Christian in which beliefs are secondary, not primary.[19] It
recognizes that the "task of religion is not to turn us into proper
believers; it is to deepen the personal within us, to embrace the
power of life, to expand our consciousness, in order that we might
see things that eyes do not normally see."[20] It "is a 'way' to be
followed more than it is about a set of beliefs to be believed."[21]
Richard Rohr calls us to action when he says: "We must move
from a belief-based religion to a practice-based religion, or little
will change."[22] Instead of focusing on belief, "the way of Jesus

---

[16]Ibid., pp. 30–31.

[17]Rachel Held Evans, *Searching for Sunday: Loving, Leaving, and Finding
the Church*, op. cit., p. xvi.

[18]Marcus J. Borg, *The Heart of Christianity: Rediscovering a Life of Faith*,
op. cit.

[19]Idem, *Jesus: Uncovering the Life, Teachings, and Relevance of a Religious
Revolutionary*, op. cit., p. 308.

[20]John Shelby Spong. *Eternal Life: A New Vision—Beyond Religion, Beyond Theism, Beyond Heaven and Hell*. New York: HarperOne, 2009. ISBN:
978-0-06-077842-2, p. 185.

[21]Marcus J. Borg, *Jesus: Uncovering the Life, Teachings, and Relevance of
a Religious Revolutionary*, op. cit., p. 308.

[22]Richard Rohr. *The Naked Now: Learning to See as the Mystics See.*

is the way of death and resurrection—the path of transition and transformation from an old way of being to a new way of being."[23]

But this does not mean that "beliefs [are] irrelevant; they do matter. But they are not the object of faith."[24] While we need some element of belief which may put in words some elements of our worldview, this matters far less than our inward transformation, as evidenced by outward results through the practice of our tradition. Huston Smith claims that "ideas are important in life, but of themselves, they seldom provide starting points. They grow out of facts and experiences, and torn from this soil, lose their life, like uprooted trees."[25]

Thus, to think that Christianity is about "getting our intellectual beliefs, our theology right,"[26] is to entirely miss the point. When the topic at hand, wealth, has the power to both give life and destroy it, we dare not stop at merely developing an "intellectually-correct theology"[27] of wealth.

A Call for Spiritual Growth

So far we have argued that if we are on a path of increasing wealth, for whatever reason, our spiritual characteristics will be amplified. Although the magnitude of our generosity may increase, so might our greed. Although we may be able to perform more effective acts of compassion with increased wealth, any actions done with an attitude of indifference, which at lower levels of wealth may go unnoticed, may be plainly evident and harmful to those around us.

While amplification of our virtues is acceptable and welcomed, the danger is amplification of our vices. Thus, as wealth increases, we must dig deeper into our spiritual tradition and be continually

---

Chestnut Ridge, NY: Crossroad Publishing, 2009. ISBN: 978-0-8245-2543-9, p. 108.

[23] Marcus J. Borg. *Reading the Bible Again for the First Time: Taking the Bible Seriously but not Literally.* HarperSanFrancisco, 2001, p. 85.

[24] Idem, *Jesus: Uncovering the Life, Teachings, and Relevance of a Religious Revolutionary,* op. cit., p. 308.

[25] Huston Smith, *The World's Religions*, op. cit., p. 331.

[26] Marcus J. Borg. *Convictions: How I Learned What Matters Most.* New York: HarperCollins, 2014. ISBN: 978-0-06-226998-0, p. 49.

[27] Ibid., p. 49.

transformed by it. This is the call for spiritual growth: every dollar saved must correlate with an equal measure of spiritual growth.

A Vision of Wealth for Spiritual Momentum

If wealth is a spiritual amplifier which magnifies both our virtues and our vices, can we use that to our advantage? Can we use wealth as a spiritual tool to provide momentum to our inward and outward journeys? I suggest that yes, wealth can be used in this manner, but only if we are dedicated to this spiritual path.

James spoke of the word of God as being a mirror which reveals ourselves: "For if any are hearers of the word and not doers, they are like those who look at themselves in a mirror; for they look at themselves and, on going away, immediately forget what they were like."[28] Similarly, the apostle Paul said that "through the law comes the knowledge of sin."[29] That is, the law of God is also like a mirror which reveals our sin. He continues:

> *"Well then, am I suggesting that the law of God is sinful? Of course not! In fact, it was the law that showed me my sin. I would never have known that coveting is wrong if the law had not said, 'You must not covet.' But sin used this command to arouse all kinds of covetous desires within me! If there were no law, sin would not have that power. At one time I lived without understanding the law. But when I learned the command not to covet, for instance, the power of sin came to life, and I died. So I discovered that the law's commands, which were supposed to bring life, brought spiritual death instead. Sin took advantage of those commands and deceived me; it used the commands to kill me. But still, the law itself is holy, and its commands are holy and right and good. But how can that be? Did the law, which is good, cause my death? Of course not! Sin*

---

[28] James 1:23–24.
[29] Romans 3:20.

*used what was good to bring about my condemnation
to death. So we can see how terrible sin really is. It
uses God's good commands for its own evil purposes."*
(Romans 7:7–13)

It seems that wealth operates much in the same way: wealth
reveals and reflects our character. If we are mindful of this fact, I
believe wealth can be used, much like the law, to guide our spiritual
journey. As Dr. Mark S. Waldman says, we can use wealth as a
"source of self-awareness."[30] Wealth, then, if used in this fashion,
may actually have a positive moral status since "anything that
reveals our inner working is far more precious than gold."[31] But
this is only possible if we actively tilt the effects of wealth in our
lives in this direction—otherwise, it will indiscriminately magnify
our character and the nature of our relationships.

Doing by Not-Doing

Our methods of building wealth certainly matter if we wish to use
wealth as a spiritual tool to illuminate our journey. If we try to
pursue wealth through dishonest means, this works against our
spiritual journey, and we would have to try even harder to counter
the effects of that in our life. If we attempt to build wealth through
get-rich-quick schemes, this only promotes attitudes of greed and
impatience which require additional effort to squash. As Brian
Zahnd says: "When we live against the grain of love, we suffer
the shards of self-inflicting suffering."[32] If wealth is to be used
as a positive spiritual tool, our means of building wealth must
not require us to swim upstream on our journey towards spiritual
oneness with the Divine. Instead, our means of building wealth
should carry us along that path effortlessly.

We can take inspiration from Taoism here. Lǎozǐ claimed that
"the wise man acts through Not-doing."[33] This idea of Not-doing,

---

[30] Mark S. Waldman, *A Spiritual Guide to Money: How to Use Money for
Personal Growth & Genuine Spiritual Experience*, op. cit., p. 149.

[31] Ibid., p. 148.

[32] Brian Zahnd. *Sinners in the Hands of a Loving God: The Scandalous
Truth of the Very Good News.* Colorado Springs, CO: WaterBrook, 2017.
ISBN: 978-1-60142-951-3, p. 18.

[33] Tao Te Ching 2; Lǎozǐ and James Trapp, *Tao Te Ching*, op. cit., p. 9.

called *wúwéi,* is "effortless action,"[34] or action which flows with
the natural order of things. In the Tao Te Ching, Lǎozǐ repeatedly
emphasizes the power of *wúwéi* saying, "in doing by Not-doing,
there is nothing that cannot be controlled."[35]

We can apply this idea of *wúwéi* to our wealth-building activities and pursuit of spiritual growth by choosing means of building wealth which naturally propel us towards a higher spiritual
consciousness. For example, it is better to build wealth by the
application of minimalism than by working harder to increase our
income so we can end up with "a garage full of nouns."[36] Since minimalism helps grow a spirit of contentment within us, it naturally
fosters one of the character traits needed to handle wealth well.
It is also better to build wealth by practicing the art of simplicity than through complex investment strategies because simplicity
frees us to focus on further spiritual development. And it is better to build wealth slowly and consistently over time rather than
through get-rich-quick schemes because consistency develops long-
term habits of self-control and discipline that have application to
nearly every other aspect of life. Thus, if we choose our methods of
wealth-building carefully, we can simultaneously build wealth *and*
cultivate the spiritual growth needed to avoid the dangers of amplification. Sūnzǐ would agree that this is a superior way to fight
the spiritual battles posed by wealth:

> *"To fight and conquer in all your battles is not supreme
> excellence; supreme excellence consists in breaking the
> enemy's resistance without fighting."*[37]

In the wildly successful business classic, *The Four Disciplines
of Execution,* the authors describe a powerful method for executing
plans and achieving goals. One of the disciplines they suggest is
to act on leading measures, not lagging measures.[38] For example,

---

[34]Edward Slingerland. *Effortless Action: Wu-wei as Conceptual Metaphor
and Spiritual Ideal in Early China.* New York: Oxford University Press, 2003.

[35]Tao Te Ching 3; Lǎozǐ and James Trapp, *Tao Te Ching,* op. cit., p. 10.

[36]Rob Bell. *Love Wins.* New York: HarperOne, 2011. ISBN: 978-0-06-
204965-0, p. 44.

[37]The Art of War 3:2; Sūnzǐ, *Sun Tzu's The Art of War: Bilingual Edition
Complete Chinese and English Text,* op. cit., p. 10.

[38]Chris McChesney, Sean Covey, and Jim Huling. *The Four Disciplines*

if one wishes to lose weight, focus on diet and exercise—weight loss is a metric which follows, or lags, the leading actions. Put your focus on the actions which *predict* the result, not the result itself. Lǎozǐ said much the same thing when he said: "[the wise man] acts but does not rely on the result."[39] In the same way, if we are to follow this path of ever-increasing spiritual growth, which may directly or indirectly influence our levels of wealth, I suggest that we focus primarily on the spiritual elements which drive those results, not the wealth itself. Perhaps this is what Jesus meant when he said: "Strive first for the kingdom of God and his righteousness, and all these things will be given to you as well."[40] Focus on applying mindfulness to every aspect of life, including finances. Although increased wealth may or may not be a result, don't worry too much about the financial results. Focus on increasing contentment through minimalism. Again, a surplus of wealth may result, but that is secondary, only a lagging measure of the discipline. Hold any riches with an open hand, not with a clenched fist and attitude of pride. As the psalmist said: "If riches increase, do not set your heart on them,"[41] and Marcus Aurelius echoes: "Receive [wealth or prosperity] without arrogance; and be ready to let it go."[42]

Thus, we find the ancient principles of mindfulness, simplicity, consistency, and contentment not only improve the probability of financial success, but also provide the spiritual growth necessary to maximize the effect of our virtues and avoid the negative effects of wealth's amplification of our vices.

However, we must attach a warning to this vision of wealth as a spiritual tool. While Lǎozǐ preached the spiritual discipline of *wúwéi,* he also warned that "the benefits of Not-doing are things achieved by very few."[43] And although Jesus taught a path to-

---

of Execution: Achieving Your Wildly Important Goals. New York: Simon & Schuster, 2012. ISBN: 978-1-4516-2705-3, p. 44.

[39] Tao Te Ching 2; Lǎozǐ and James Trapp, *Tao Te Ching,* op. cit., p. 9.

[40] Matthew 6:33.

[41] Psalm 62:10.

[42] Marcus Aurelius, Meditations 8:33; Marcus Aurelius and George Long. *The Meditations of Marcus Aurelius.* Trans. by George Long. New York: F. M. Lupton Publishing Company, 1887, p. 130.

[43] Tao Te Ching 43; Lǎozǐ and James Trapp, *Tao Te Ching,* op. cit., p. 53.

wards the kingdom of God, he also said: "The gate is narrow and the road is hard that leads to life, and there are few who find it."[44] As we have already seen, wealth's amplification of human character is potentially disastrous, even literally fatal, as history illustrates: "Marriages and families are destroyed by it, nations go to war over it, people are exploited so the powerful can hoard it."[45] Confucius warns: "What truly is within will be manifested without. Therefore, the superior man must be watchful over himself when he is alone."[46] Some may find the responsibility associated with wealth to be too overwhelming to be worth the risk and thus proceed along a different path—an absolutely admirable one, also full of spiritual richness.

For those of us who have been thrust into this arena, where we must deal with questions which do not naturally arise when wealth is absent, it is our sacred calling to struggle with these questions, to live the questions.[47] If wealth magnifies and reflects my character, will I like what I see? Can I use the momentum of the oncoming train of wealth to carry me towards a higher spiritual consciousness? Does that train only drive towards destruction? These are questions we must wrestle with while allowing our tradition to spiritually transform us into a new creation.[48] The sense of responsibility and desire to struggle through the confusion, while working towards knowing God, is what makes a mere pursuit of "God, gold and glory"[49] completely antithetical to the path proposed here.

---

[44]Matthew 7:14.

[45]Peter Enns, *How the Bible Actually Works: In which I Explain How an Ancient, Ambiguous, and Diverse Book Leads us to Wisdom Rather Than Answers—And Why That's Great News*, op. cit., p. 32.

[46]The Great Learning 1:5; Kŏng Fūzĭ, *The Sacred Books of China: The Texts of Confucianism*, op. cit., p. 413.

[47]David M. Felten and Jeff Procter-Murphy. *Living the Questions: The Wisdom of Progressive Christianity*. New York: HarperOne, 2012. ISBN: 978-0-06-210936-1.

[48]2 Corinthians 5:17.

[49]Luis N. Rivera and Luis Rivera Pagán. *A Violent Evangelism: The Political and Religious Conquest of the Americas*. Louisville, KY: Westminster John Knox Press, 1992. ISBN: 0-664-25367-9, p. 261.

Chapter 6

Cultivating the Kingdom of God on Earth in Our Afterlife

"If I worship You for fear of Hell, burn me in Hell. And if I worship You in hope of Paradise, exclude me from Paradise. But if I worship You for Your Own sake, grudge me not Your everlasting Beauty."[1] —Rabia, Sufi Poetess, 8th century

HEAVEN and Hell, and other visions of the afterlife have perpetually captured the human imagination, offering uplifting hope and profound dread. One thinks of pearly gates and never-ending fires, of judgment and justice, and one's eternal fate being dependent on actions or beliefs in a finite life. What happens when our beliefs about the afterlife are brought into conversation with personal finance and our work for social justice? To find out, this essay examines how the biblical authors thought about the afterlife. We find that the authors keep ideas about the

---

[1] Gunnar Norlén. *Islam and its World.* Vol. 3. Usa River, Tanzania: Research Institute of Makumira University College, 2001. ISBN: 9789987657025, p. 252.

afterlife in the *periphery* of their spiritual vision. Instead of focusing on details about the afterlife, they tend to emphasize bringing the kingdom of God *on earth*. If we follow their example, we should also attempt to bring the kingdom of God on earth now... and in our afterlife, whatever that might be. While the details of how to accomplish this goal may differ between individuals, progress towards this goal is not helped when we keep faith, personal finance, and social justice from dialogue with each other.

There is no Afterlife in the Hebrew Bible

The human eye presents a clear image of things it focuses on. Items centered in the optical path are sharp and detailed. But the eye has notoriously poor peripheral vision and has difficulty distinguishing detail, color, and shape for objects outside a narrow band around the point of fixation. Ideas about the afterlife in the Old Testament are decidedly in the peripheral vision of the biblical authors. There are hardly any passages in the Old Testament which bring into focus a clear notion of what happens after death.

We will first examine the Old Testament. While "the Jewish scriptures contain a variety of views about what happens to a person at death,"[2] the idea of Sheol is the most common.

Sheol is almost always described incidentally, as a synonym for death and the grave.[3] Such incidental phrases include "going down to Sheol,"[4] "bring down my gray hairs in sorrow to Sheol,"[5] and "they go down alive into Sheol."[6] And God's anger is described as burning "to the depths of Sheol."[7] Virtually *all* uses of the term Sheol are vague and peripheral.[8] Based on how Sheol is used,

---

[2]Bart D. Ehrman. *Heaven and Hell: A History of the Afterlife*. New York: Simon & Schuster, 2020. ISBN: 978-1-5011-3673-3, p. 83.

[3]Ibid., p. 85.

[4]Genesis 37:35.

[5]Genesis 42:38; Genesis 44:29; Genesis 44:31.

[6]Numbers 16:30; Numbers 16:33.

[7]Deuteronomy 32:22.

[8]2 Samuel 22:6; 1 Kings 2:6; 1 Kings 2:9; Job 7:9; Job 11:8; Job 14:13; Job 17:13; Job 17:16; Job 21:13; Job 24:19; Job 26:6; Psalm 6:5; Psalm 9:17; Psalm 16:10; Psalm 18:5; Psalm 30:3; Psalm 31:17; Psalm 49:14; Psalm 49:15; Psalm 55:15; Psalm 86:13; Psalm 88:3; Psalm 89:48; Psalm 116:3; Psalm 139:8;

we find that it is the resting place for *both* the righteous and the wicked, but it is clearly not a place of reward for the righteous and is to be avoided as long as possible.[9] In fact, it seems that Sheol is more akin to annihilation. God does not remember those who descend into Sheol, since God is the god of the living.[10] Likewise, those who die do not praise God anymore: "For in death there is no remembrance of you; in Sheol who can give you praise?" (Psalm 6:5); and "Sheol cannot thank you, death cannot praise you; those who go down to the Pit cannot hope for your faithfulness" (Isaiah 38:18). The author of Ecclesiastes provides a good summary of these ancient views about what happens after death: "The living know that they will die, but the dead know nothing; they have no more reward, and even the memory of them is lost."[11] Thus: "Whatever your hand finds to do, do with your might; for there is no work or thought or knowledge or wisdom in Sheol, to which you are going."[12]

Earlier in his career, John Shelby Spong set out to write a "definitive book"[13] about the afterlife. But after several years of research, he abandoned the project. He describes his frustration with the lack of clarity in the Old Testament data:

> *"I first searched out the concept of life after death as it appeared in the Hebrew scriptures. I was amazed to find how scanty that material was. My Jewish ancestors in faith were so concerned about this life that they had little time to invest much of their energy in the fantasy land of life after death. One finds early in Hebrew history a sense of a place called Sheol, which simply meant the*

Psalm 141:7; Proverbs 1:2; Proverbs 5:5; Proverbs 7:27; Proverbs 9:18; Proverbs 15:11; Proverbs 15:24; Proverbs 23:14; Proverbs 27:20; Proverbs 30:16; Isaiah 5:14; Isaiah 7:11; Isaiah 14:9; Isaiah 14:11; Isaiah 14:15; Isaiah 28:15; Isaiah 28:18; Isaiah 38:10; Isaiah 38:18; Isaiah 57:9; Ezekiel 31:15; Ezekiel 31:16; Ezekiel 31:17; Ezekiel 32:21; Ezekiel 32:27; Hosea 13:14; Amos 9:2; Jonah 2:2; Habakkuk 2:5.

[9] Bart D. Ehrman, *Heaven and Hell: A History of the Afterlife*, op. cit., p. 86.

[10] Psalm 88:11.

[11] Ecclesiastes 9:5.

[12] Ecclesiastes 9:10.

[13] John Shelby Spong, *Eternal Life: A New Vision—Beyond Religion, Beyond Theism, Beyond Heaven and Hell*, op. cit., p. 8.

> *abode of all the dead. It was generally located, in the
> minds of the people, somewhere beneath the earth. This
> Sheol, however, was never a motivating realm or an
> anticipated destiny.*"[14]

Outside of the strange story in 1 Samuel 28 where Saul communicates with the spirit of Samuel, who was recently deceased, through the "witch of Endor,"[15] there is hardly any indication of an afterlife in the Old Testament—at least not a conscious one. But as we have already discussed, views change over time. And "after the period of the classical prophets, Jewish thinkers came to imagine that in fact there would be life for the individual who had died."[16] This was the idea of bodily resurrection for judgment. Although scholars aren't sure how or why this doctrine of bodily resurrection came about,[17] it is clear that it is intimately linked with a desire to see justice done to the wicked, who seem to have "gotten away with it."[18] Thus, we begin to see in the later Jewish scriptures, a rise of apocalyptic thinking where the dead are raised to have their sins accounted for on Judgment Day. This view is described in the Book of Daniel, often considered the first real apocalypse: "Many of those who sleep in the dust of the earth shall awake, some to everlasting life, and some to shame and everlasting contempt. Those who are wise shall shine like the brightness of the sky, and those who lead many to righteousness, like the stars forever and ever" (Daniel 12:2–3).

It wasn't until the apocrypha and the time of Jesus that Jewish thoughts shifted towards a more familiar vision of the afterlife, mostly driven by the concept of divine justice.[19] But even in the New Testament, it "doesn't seem to be that important to the bib-

---

[14] Ibid., pp. 8–9.

[15] Ibid., p. 9.

[16] Bart D. Ehrman, *Heaven and Hell: A History of the Afterlife*, op. cit., p. 103.

[17] Ibid., p. 104.

[18] Ibid., p. 106.

[19] Martha Himmelfarb. "Afterlife and Resurrection." In: *The Jewish Annotated New Testament.* Ed. by Amy-Jill Levine and Marc Zvi Brettler. 2nd ed. New York: Oxford University Press, 2017, p. 692; John Shelby Spong, *Eternal Life: A New Vision—Beyond Religion, Beyond Theism, Beyond Heaven and Hell*, op. cit., p. 9.

lical writers to get really clear on what happens when you die."[20]

The Afterlife in the New Testament

The world of the New Testament appears vastly different than the Old Testament. While there are only a few references to demons in the Old Testament,[21] it seems that every time Jesus and his followers turn a corner, they run into a demon-possessed person. In fact, there are nearly ten times more references to demons in the New Testament,[22] even though the New Testament accounts for only 25% of the Bible. Not only is the spiritual world vastly different in the New Testament, but this comes with no clear explanation—it is just *assumed* by the biblical authors that demons exist and can possess people.

In the same way, we find a sudden difference in eschatological views. While the Old Testament has only a few minor references to the possibility of a resurrection of the dead, we find that this seems to have been a hot topic in the time of Jesus. Two major groups of religious leaders at the time differed about the afterlife. The Sadducees held to the traditional concept of Sheol, whereas the Pharisees generally ascribed to some sort of resurrection and judgment.[23] Although some of Jesus' harshest words were directed at the hypocrisy of the Pharisees,[24] it seems that he agreed with them on the belief about the resurrection of the dead. In one

---

[20]Peter Enns and Jared Byas. "Episode 121: Pete and Jared—Pete and Jared Talk About the Afterlife." In: *The Bible for Normal People [Podcast]*. 2021. URL: www.peteenns.com/episode-121-the-afterlife/ (visited on 06/09/2021).

[21]Leviticus 17:7; Deuteronomy 32:17; 2 Chronicles 11:15; Psalm 106:37; Isaiah 13:21; Isaiah 34:14.

[22]Matthew 4:24; Matthew 7:22; Matthew 8:16; Matthew 8:28; Matthew 8:31; Matthew 8:33; Matthew 9:32–34; Matthew 10:8; Matthew 10:8; Matthew 11:18; Matthew 12:22; Matthew 12:22–28; Matthew 15:22; Matthew 17:14–18; Mark 1:32; Mark 1:39; Mark 3:15; Mark 3:22; Mark 5:1–18; Mark 6:13; Mark 7:26; Mark 7:29–30; Mark 9:38; Mark 16:9; Mark 16:17; Luke 4:33–35; Luke 4:41; Luke 7:33; Luke 8:2; Luke 8:26–38; Luke 9:1; Luke 9:37–42; Luke 9:49; Luke 10:17; Luke 11:14; Luke 11:18–20; Luke 13:32; John 7:20; John 8:48–52; John 10:20–21; 1 Corinthians 10:20–21; Galatians 2:18; 1 Timothy 4:1; James 2:19; Revelation 9:20; Revelation 16:14; Revelation 18:2.

[23]Acts 23:8.

[24]Matthew 23:1–29.

instance, the Sadducees ask Jesus a question about marriage at the resurrection, a question which seems to have been designed to force anyone who believes in the resurrection to admit that the belief is ridiculous.[25] Jesus, however, supports the idea of resurrection, not by citing one of the passages which seem clearest on the topic, such as in Daniel[26] or Isaiah,[27] but by creatively reinterpreting an obscure phrase in Exodus,[28] a passage we previously looked at regarding the tradition of creative biblical interpretation within the Bible itself.[29]

However, the resurrection of the dead at the end of time was not the focus of Jesus' teachings. In the judgment of virtually all scholars, the kingdom of God was the central point of his teachings.[30] To speak of this kingdom, Jesus uses parables, metaphors, analogies, and symbolism. But these modes of communication are inherently subject to various interpretations, and "ambiguity attends some of the crucial sayings,"[31] as Marcus Borg says. To make matters more confusing, the Gospel of Matthew changes every instance of the phrase "the kingdom of God" to "the kingdom of Heaven," which to modern readers may unfortunately evoke all the imagery of Heaven, the location of the afterlife for the faithful or, as the evangelicals have claimed, for those who intellectually assent to certain "correct" beliefs. Despite its centrality, "a century of scholarly activity has produced no consensus regarding [interpretation of the phrase "the kingdom of God"], suggesting some fundamental difficulties."[32] To add to the complexity, it is not clear from Jesus' teachings whether the kingdom of God was to come in a future event on earth or whether it was already a present mystical reality.[33] According to Jesus' use of the phrase, the kingdom of God

---

[25] Matthew 22:23–33; Mark 12:18–27; Luke 20:27–40.

[26] Daniel 12:2–3.

[27] Isaiah 26:19.

[28] Exodus 3:6.

[29] See the section "Inner-biblical Interpretation" in Chapter 3 on page 68.

[30] Marcus J. Borg, *Conflict, Holiness, and Politics in the Teachings of Jesus*, op. cit., p. 256.

[31] Ibid., p. 256.

[32] Ibid., p. 256.

[33] Ibid., p. 256.

has already come,[34] is coming soon,[35] has already come, and will come in the future.[36] The kingdom of God has drawn near,[37] and it is among you.[38]

In contrast to the kingdom of God, Jesus also mentions in some instances the fate of those who are not able to gain entrance to God's kingdom on earth. But there is no consistent treatment of the subject throughout the New Testament. Instead, "the fiery punishment that marks the traditional understanding of hell is mostly the gift of Matthew, with some heavy assistance from the book of Revelation."[39] It is not a point that seems really important to Jesus on which to impart clarity. There are at least three terms, Hell, Hades, and Gehenna[40] used in the New Testament to describe the fate of those who don't make it into the kingdom of God. Unfortunately, many English translations simply use the term Hell, which hides the fact that many of these references use the term "Gehenna," which referred to a literal valley outside Jerusalem. It was thought to be the place where the kings of Judah sacrificed their children by fire, and therefore it was considered cursed. It is not clear whether Jesus used the term to refer to the physical location of the valley (i.e., God would set up his kingdom and Gehenna would be the place of the damned), or whether it was just a symbol or figure of speech that evoked the wrath of God, or both. Whatever the historical Jesus' views on the afterlife were, he clearly believed in a day of reckoning which was coming very soon and involved a resurrection, judgment, and establishment of God's kingdom.[41]

In addition to the teachings and sayings of Jesus, the majority of the New Testament was written by Paul, a self-proclaimed Phar-

---

[34]Matthew 12:28; Luke 11:20.

[35]Mark 9:1; Luke 9:27.

[36]Luke 13:28–29.

[37]Mark 1:15; Luke 10:9; Luke 10:11.

[38]Luke 17:21.

[39]John Shelby Spong, *Eternal Life: A New Vision—Beyond Religion, Beyond Theism, Beyond Heaven and Hell*, op. cit., pp. 9.

[40]Matthew 5:22; Matthew 5:29; Matthew 5:30; Matthew 10:28;Matthew 18:9; Matthew 23:15; Matthew 23:33; Mark 9:45; Mark 9:45; Mark 9:47; Luke 12:5; James 3:6.

[41]Mark 9:1; Bart D. Ehrman, *Heaven and Hell: A History of the Afterlife*, op. cit., p. 167.

isee,[42] and his belief in the resurrection of the dead seems to have played an enormous role in shaping his theology. So the logic goes: if the dead are to be raised at the end times before God sets up his kingdom on earth, and having now seen that Jesus was raised from the dead, the end must indeed be near. Much of Paul's writings seem to be wrestling with the theological implications of this idea, but they don't give us a very clear picture of the afterlife.

Having a clear view of the afterlife also didn't seem an important factor in the early church. In fact, the Thessalonian church didn't know what happened after death and asked Paul about it.[43] Dale B. Martin, professor of Religious Studies at Yale University, remarks:

> "Now isn't that curious that Paul has to fill in this big gap in their knowledge. The very thing that most of us modern people think you become a Christian for— which is immortal life or the immortality of the soul, or life after death—the Thessalonians didn't know anything about. [...] They were upset because people in their community had died and they didn't know what was going to happen to them."[44]

First Things First

While the dominant form of Christianity that has evolved over the past 2,000 years sometimes makes the claim that "scripture makes clear that the one central business of this life is to prepare for the next,"[45] even a cursory examination of the sacred text shows this claim fails tremendously to match the actual data of the Bible. The Old Testament, which makes up 75% of the entire Bible, does not make any teachings about an afterlife even remotely central. That leaves the remaining 25% of the Bible which makes no efforts to promote a systematic and clear discussion about the afterlife,

---

[42] Acts 23:6.

[43] 1 Thessalonians 4:13–18.

[44] Dale B. Martin. *Introduction to the New Testament History and Literature*. 2009. URL: https://oyc.yale.edu/religious-studies/rlst-152/lecture-14 (visited on 06/06/2021).

[45] Randy Alcorn, *Money, Possessions, and Eternity*, op. cit., p. 109.

as we think of it today. Instead, we find views about the afterlife inextricably intertwined with ancient Jewish apocalyptic thinking that developed during the Second Temple period.[46]

To unpack the views of the afterlife in the New Testament would take us far from our present purposes and would in fact indulge in the opposite of what this essay intends to promote: ideas about the afterlife tend to distract us from more important pursuits. So long as we believe that justice will be done in the afterlife, social justice on earth will not be our passion.[47] Although eschatology plays a much more central role in the New Testament than the Old Testament, it's clear that what happens after death is *still* in the periphery. If the earliest Christians converted to this new religious movement, it doesn't seem to be out of fear of Hell or greed for Heaven—something else drew them to the Jesus movement. And that's the point: if we were to truly adopt a "biblical" view of the afterlife, we should live as if it were only a peripheral notion, and focus on other more central issues such as cultivating the kingdom of God on earth.

The point is not to dismantle or promote any particular notion about the afterlife. We find in the scriptures and tradition a variety of views. It seems that the Christian tradition is wide enough to include many different perspectives about the afterlife. If you don't believe there is any consciousness after death, that's fine; many of the Old Testament authors apparently believed the same thing. Do you believe that we are ushered into Paradise after death? Apparently, some of the gospel writers also believe this.[48] We thus find that a variety of views are acceptable, even canonized, but the tradition doesn't really answer our question: what *actually* happens after death? It seems the best response is to hold our views loosely, as the author of Ecclesiastes models and says, "Who knows?"

> *"All go to one place; all are from the dust, and all turn to dust again. Who knows whether the human spirit goes upward and the spirit of animals goes downward*

---

[46]Martha Himmelfarb, "Afterlife and Resurrection," op. cit., p. 692.

[47]John Shelby Spong, *Eternal Life: A New Vision—Beyond Religion, Beyond Theism, Beyond Heaven and Hell*, op. cit., p. 133.

[48]Luke 23:43.

> *to the earth? So I saw that there is nothing better than*
> *that all should enjoy their work, for that is their lot;*
> *who can bring them to see what will be after them?"*
> (Ecclesiastes 3:20–22)

Finding that we are apparently tasked with living a meaningful life without certainty about what happens next, we must ask, as Francis Schaeffer did, "How then should we live?"[49] Perhaps we should first live according to the things we *know*. For example, we know that we have this life here and now. Even the most extreme forms of skepticism can admit this, as René Descartes argued.[50] We also know that we are part of an ever-unfolding story, a grand process of causality. Just as the present begets the future, our lives and actions also beget a new chapter in this evolving story. Just as our lives and environment have been shaped by that which precedes us, so too our legacy. Maybe our sacred responsibility is to cultivate the kingdom of God *on earth* now... and in our afterlife.

Cultivating the Kingdom of God on Earth in our Afterlife

Progressive Christian, Mike McHargue, after deconstructing the fundamentalist version of Christianity he was raised with, rebuilt his faith on a series of axioms, or statements which can be assumed as true without requiring any argumentation. For him,

> *"The Afterlife is <u>at least</u> the persistence of our physical*
> *matter in the ongoing life-cycle on Earth, the memes we*
> *pass on to others, and our unique neurological signature*
> *in the brains of those who knew us. <u>Even if</u> this is all*
> *the afterlife is, the consequences of <u>our</u> actions persist*

---

[49]Francis Schaeffer. *How Should We Then Live? The Rise and Decline of Western Thought and Culture*. Wheaton, IL: Crossway, 2005. ISBN: 978-1-58134-536-0.

[50]René Descartes, *Discourse on Method and Meditations on First Philosophy*, op. cit.; John Shelby Spong, *Eternal Life: A New Vision—Beyond Religion, Beyond Theism, Beyond Heaven and Hell*, op. cit., p. 20.

> *beyond our death, and our ethical considerations must*
> *include a timeline beyond our death.* "[51]

As followers of Jesus, one of our primary aims is to cultivate the kingdom of God on earth, as Jesus so consistently discussed. This means working towards peace and justice for all people. Imagining the kingdom of God, and what it would be like, and working towards *that* is a sacred duty of the Christian faith. Regardless of what happens to us after *we* die, as Mike McHargue says, the consequences of our actions persist beyond our death. There are two aspects of this charge:

1. cultivate the kingdom of God on earth *now*, and

2. consider how our actions ripple through time to the next generation.

In practice, there may be little difference between these, since our actions in the present influence the future. Someday, our time will come, and we will no longer be able to actively cultivate God's kingdom *on earth* ourselves; that will be left to the next generation. Cultivating healthy relationships in our present will undoubtedly have an impact in the future after we are gone. Saving someone's life by providing needed food, clothing, or shelter in the present may allow them to carry on a spirit of generosity after we die. And involving our kids with philanthropic efforts can instill in them an importance of continuing that work when it is up to them. Thus, our actions *now* can theoretically continue cultivating the kingdom of God even after our life on earth is over.

However, some special considerations are in order for ensuring that our legacy continues to bear fruit. This is the task of estate planning. The problem is that once we die, our estate is left to others to handle, and what if they don't use it to further the kingdom of God but instead use it for their own selfish pleasure? Qohelet bemoans this fact, saying:

> *"I hated all my toil in which I had toiled under the sun,*
> *seeing that I must leave it to those who come after me—*
> *and who knows whether they will be wise or foolish? Yet*

---

[51]Mike McHargue, *Finding God in the Waves: How I Lost My Faith and Found It Again Through Science*, op. cit., pp. 253–254.

*they will be master of all for which I toiled and used my
wisdom under the sun. This also is vanity. So I turned
and gave my heart up to despair concerning all the toil
of my labors under the sun, because sometimes one who
has toiled with wisdom and knowledge and skill must
leave all to be enjoyed by another who did not toil for
it. This also is vanity and a great evil."* (Ecclesiastes
2:18–21)

In fact, several major studies have shown that, worldwide,
about 70% of estates are involuntarily lost after their transition
into the hands of heirs.[52] The problem of inter-generational failure
to retain or grow assets is so common that many cultures have
traditional phrases that refer to that phenomenon. The cause of
this is suggested by a Williams Group study of 3,250 families who
transitioned their wealth.[53] The study found that there was "no
relationship between post-transition failure and tax laws, culture,
economic cycles, wars, or any other economic factors."[54] Instead,
the primary reasons had to do with the fact that, while people
do spend time planning for the transition of their assets, much
less time is spent planning the transition of the *family.*[55] Based
on their research, the authors of this study describe ten questions
which predict with 95% confidence[56] whether an estate transition
will be successful or not:[57]

1. Our family has a mission statement that spells out the overall
   purpose of our wealth.

---

[52] Roy Orville Williams and Vic Preisser. *Philanthropy, Heirs & Values:
How Successful Families Are Using Philanthropy To Prepare Their Heirs for
Post-transition Responsibilities.* Robert D. Reed Publishers, 2005. ISBN: 1-
931741-51-4, p. 19.

[53] Ibid., p. 20.

[54] Ibid., p. 20.

[55] Ibid., p. 20.

[56] Ibid., p. 24.

[57] Roy Orville Williams and Vic Preisser. *Preparing Heirs: Five Steps to a
Successful Transition of Family Wealth and Values.* Robert D. Reed Publish-
ers, 2003. ISBN: 1-931741-31-X, p. 57; (idem, *Philanthropy, Heirs & Values:
How Successful Families Are Using Philanthropy To Prepare Their Heirs for
Post-transition Responsibilities,* op. cit., p. 26).

2. The entire family participates in most important decisions, such as defining a mission for our wealth.

3. All family heirs have the option of participating in the management of the family's assets.

4. Heirs understand their future roles, have "bought into" those roles, and look forward to performing those roles.

5. Heirs have actually reviewed the family's estate plans and documents.

6. Our current wills, trusts, and other documents make most asset distributions based upon heir readiness, not heir age.

7. Our family mission includes creating incentives and opportunities for our heirs.

8. Our younger children are encouraged to participate in our family's philanthropic grant-making decisions.

9. Our family considers family unity to be just as important as family financial strength.

10. We communicate well throughout our family and regularly meet as a family to discuss issues and changes.

Families who answered "Yes" to 7 or more of these questions before the transition were most likely to be a post-transition success story.[58] Thus, ensuring a successful transition of wealth, one that encourages and furthers the kingdom of God in our afterlife, requires far more than simply having a will. It requires cultivating trust, sincerity, and competence with others.[59] It means developing a unifying philanthropic mission,[60] involving family members and other vested parties prior to the transition,[61] and facilitating meaningful communication.[62]

---

[58] Ibid., p. 24.

[59] Ibid., p. 39.

[60] Ibid., p. 6.

[61] Ibid., p. 35.

[62] Ibid., p. 133.

In the end, the goal is to cultivate the kingdom of God in our present and in such a way that increases the probability of our mission being carried forward in the future after we are no longer able. It involves doing philanthropic and social justice work *now* as well as preparing the next generation to carry that mission forward. It involves not only financial and estate planning, but intentional efforts in creating a unifying mission among our current relationships and with those who will continue to carry to the torch. Perhaps Qohelet is right: "The people of long ago are not remembered, nor will there be any remembrance of people yet to come by those who come after them."[63] Yet the conclusion of Ecclesiastes is to continue being faithful anyway.[64]

Conclusion

For those of us who believe in an afterlife, we should not let those beliefs become the focus of our life. If we take the biblical authors as our models, these beliefs may give us hope, but they should be in the periphery. Confucius himself "dismissed speculation about life after death on the grounds that it was hard enough to deal with the current reality, never mind the reality of another world!"[65]

And for those of us who think there is nothing to be experienced in the afterlife and say, like the ancients did: "We must all die; we are like water spilled on the ground, which cannot be gathered up"[66]—the "ancient expression of the law of entropy: once dispersed, life can never be retrieved."[67]—hedonism is probably not the most meaningful life to be pursued. Qohelet claims to have tried that and found it unsatisfactory. Instead, it's likely that the most satisfying life is one that appreciates the simple pleasures of

---

[63] Ecclesiastes 1:11.

[64] Peter Enns. *Ecclesiastes*. Ed. by J. Gordon McConville and Craig Bartholomew. The Two Horizons Old Testament Commentary. Grand Rapids, MI: Wm. B. Eerdmans Publishing, 2011. ISBN: 978-0-8028-6649-3, p. 219.

[65] Martin Palmer. *The Elements of Taoism*. Barnes & Noble Books, 1999. ISBN: 978-0-7607-1078-3, p. 70.

[66] 2 Samuel 14:14.

[67] Bart D. Ehrman, *Heaven and Hell: A History of the Afterlife*, op. cit., p. 81.

life: eating, drinking, and taking pleasure in our toil,[68] while continuing our search for meaning through true communion with the sacred[69] and through cultivating the kingdom of God on earth, now... and in our afterlife. And it is difficult to make this happen without seeking a unification of our faith, personal finance, and work in social justice.

---

[68] Ecclesiastes 3:13.

[69] A. Stephen Van Kuiken. *Desiring True Communion*. 6 June 2021, Pullman, WA. Sermon. URL: `https://pullmanucc.org/2021/06/07/desiring-true-communion/` (visited on 06/11/2021).

Chapter 7

A Vision of Unity and Emergence

"From chaos to cosmos, this cause-and-effect relationship crosses more than thirty-eight powers of ten in size and forty-two powers of ten in time. [...] We feel it when we look up. We feel it when we look down. We feel it when we look within."[1] *—Neil deGrasse Tyson*

YEARS ago I made a list of things I wanted to purchase. I had just started working full-time as an engineer, making a decent salary. After 5 years of being a poor college student, I wanted to start saving money and spending it on a bunch of *things* that I wanted—and a few necessities. The list included a new laptop, various accessories for my SUV, including a high-brightness light bar, equipment for a home music studio, and new smart phones for my wife and me. The list totaled over $32,000. There were two problems with this. First, I hadn't practiced saving money, so progress on purchasing these items was slow. To buy all the items on the list would require over a year of working full time. A year of my life energy would be spent on these *things*.

---

[1]Neil deGrasse Tyson and Donald Goldsmith. *Origins: Fourteen Billion Years of Cosmic Evolution.* New York: W. W. Norton & Company, 2004. ISBN: 0-393-05992-8, p. 143.

The second issue is that it was entirely focused on myself. There was no thought put towards generosity or saving money to help others. I eventually changed course by practicing mindfulness in finance through the teachings of the FIRE community and Dave Ramsey. I was shocked to find that my desire for those things vanished rapidly. Not only was making my personal finances self-focused cementing an enslavement to a lifetime of fruitless labor, but it was also unsatisfying.

In this essay, we turn up the intensity on our *outward* focus. I argue that the trajectory of the human story, and the story of the entire universe in fact, is one of *emergence*. For 13.8 billion years, the universe has evolved, with individual elements combining to produce new things which have behaviors unlike its constituents. For this to happen, individual elements must cooperate with each other. And this is what humans have been struggling to do for a long time. In order for a new human oneness to emerge, we must be less focused on ourselves, and have more concern for others. I believe that compartmentalizing personal finance, faith, and social justice only hinders this vision. Aligning our sights with the trajectory of the universe is more likely to help such a vision succeed. And, I suspect, focusing on a concern for others is also more satisfying.

The Continual Birth of Emergence

Our story begins with the creation event approximately 13.8 billion years ago. Some call this epic story "cosmic evolution."[2] Others call it "Darwinian cosmology."[3] It is a story which "resonates with a myth that is deeper than the sin/redemption story, and which our culture shares with all others: the myth of order out of chaos."[4]

---

[2] Eric J. Chaisson. "Using Complexity Science to Search for Unity in the Natural Sciences." In: *Complexity and the Arrow of Time*. Ed. by Charles H. Lineweaver, Paul C. W. Davies, and Michael Ruse. New York: Cambridge University Press, 2013. Chap. 4. ISBN: 978-1-107-02725-1, p. 4.

[3] Stanley N. Salthe. *Development and Evolution: Complexity and Change in Biology*. Cambridge, MA: MIT Press, 1993. ISBN: 0-262-19335-3, p. 248.

[4] Brian Goodwin. *How the Leopard Changed its Spots: The Evolution of Complexity*. London: Weidenfeld & Nicolson, 1994. ISBN: 0-297-81499-0, p. 181.

Most models of the Big Bang singularity describe it as an infinitely dense, yet homogeneous, point of pure energy where the four fundamental forces were unified into one. And then...an explosion...or, more properly, an expansion. We don't know the details because there is no way to directly observe the event—only its aftermath. Yet this modern creation story tells us that soon after the initial expansion, the four fundamental forces separated. After about 379,000 years, electrons and nuclei combined into giant clouds of atoms—predominantly hydrogen, with lesser amounts of helium and lithium.[5] Later, gravitational instability made matter clump together, causing stars and planets to form.[6] While the Big Bang gave rise to only three elements, the periodic table today boasts of almost 100 naturally-occurring chemical elements[7] because of nuclear fusion taking place in the stars which then explode as supernovae and distribute those elements throughout the universe.

Somehow, from the dust of the Earth, the breath of life was given to inanimate matter, giving birth to single-celled life. Later, cells combined to create more complex multicellular organisms which evolved into yet more complex organisms. The social organisms then formed societies, and in the case of humans, tribes and cultures. In summary, "the Big Bang happened, gravitational instability made matter clump together, stars started to shine, planets formed, life began, humans showed up, societies formed," and as Seth Lloyd says, "all hell broke loose."[8]

Despite the apparent randomness of this tale, there are some underlying unifiers that give us a sense of a consistent, albeit mean-

[5]Robert M. Hazen. "The Emergence of Chemical Complexity: An Introduction." In: *Chemical Evolution Across Space & Time: From the Big Bang to Prebiotic Chemistry*. Ed. by Lori Zaikowski and Jon M. Friedrich. Vol. 981. ACS Symposium Series. Proceedings of the American Chemical Society Symposium Spring 2007 ACS National Meeting, Chicago, IL. American Chemical Society Publications, 2008. Chap. 1. ISBN: 978-0-8412-7431-0, p. 3.

[6]Seth Lloyd. "On the Spontaneous Generation of Complexity in the Universe." In: *Complexity and the Arrow of Time*. Ed. by Charles H. Lineweaver, Paul C. W. Davies, and Michael Ruse. New York: Cambridge University Press, 2013. Chap. 5. ISBN: 978-1-107-02725-1, p. 80.

[7]Robert M. Hazen, "The Emergence of Chemical Complexity: An Introduction," op. cit., p. 3.

[8]Seth Lloyd, "On the Spontaneous Generation of Complexity in the Universe," op. cit., p. 80.

dering, trajectory. For example, "evolution is one of those unifiers, incorporating physical, biological, and cultural changes within a broad and inclusive cosmic-evolutionary scenario."[9] This common thread, in fact, "runs through all science disciplines."[10] Another unifier is complexity, "delineating the growth of structure, function, and diversity within and among galaxies, stars, planets, life, and society throughout natural history."[11] Combined, evolution and complexity produce the phenomenon of new behavior generated from the combination of constituent elements. This phenomenon is called *emergence,* and it has become a new focus in biology and cosmology in the past couple decades.[12]

Neil deGrasse Tyson notes that "throughout the cosmos, matter has consistently organized itself into structure. From its nearly perfectly-smooth distribution soon after the Big Bang, matter has clumped itself together on all size scales."[13] Emergence began in the early universe when particles collected together to form atoms which exhibited completely new behavioral characteristics. These atoms became arranged in various ways to produce more complex materials—molecules which act in very different ways than their underlying atomic elements. Molecules are combined together to produce single-celled organisms which, again, exhibit remarkably more complex behavior that does not even remotely resemble that of the constituent molecules. Similarly, a collection of cells in a multi-celled organism produced yet more complex behavior unlike that of the underlying individual cells. Finally, when multiple multi-celled organisms of a similar kind are organized together,

[9] Eric J. Chaisson, "Using Complexity Science to Search for Unity in the Natural Sciences," op. cit., p. 4.

[10] Lori Zaikowski, Richard T. Wilkens, and Kurt Fischer. "Science and the Concept of Evolution: From the Big Bang to the Origin and Evolution of Life." In: *Chemical Evolution Across Space & Time: From the Big Bang to Prebiotic Chemistry.* Ed. by Lori Zaikowski and Jon M. Friedrich. Vol. 981. ACS Symposium Series. Proceedings of the American Chemical Society Symposium Spring 2007 ACS National Meeting, Chicago, IL. American Chemical Society Publications, 2008. Chap. 18. ISBN: 978-0-8412-7431-0, p. 326.

[11] Eric J. Chaisson, "Using Complexity Science to Search for Unity in the Natural Sciences," op. cit., p. 4.

[12] Brian Goodwin, *How the Leopard Changed its Spots: The Evolution of Complexity*, op. cit., p. 181.

[13] Neil deGrasse Tyson and Donald Goldsmith, *Origins: Fourteen Billion Years of Cosmic Evolution*, op. cit., p. 122.

even higher-order phenomena occurs.[14] For example, in some parts of southeast Asia, thousands of male fireflies gather in trees at night and flash on and off in unison.[15] Likewise, as Brian Goodwin explains:

> *"Ants and other social insects such as termites and bees present us with a paradox that is good for proverbs. The activity patterns of individuals often appear to be very disorganized, and by any of the normal criteria they cannot be described as intelligent. No-one has succeeded in teaching individual ants anything; for instance, they are simply incapable of learning to discriminate one direction from another in finding a food source, always making a random choice at a Y-junction, even if the food is always in the same place. However, put a bunch of ants together, and what marvels of collective activity result! Individual neurons are not very intelligent either, but a lot of them hooked up together can result in remarkably interesting and quite unexpected behavior. This is the very essence of emergent behavior."*[16]

Emergent behavior is also found in birds which flock together. When a simple set of rules are followed by the individuals, the overall phenomenon is the entire flock swooping and soaring as if controlled by one central mind, yet it remarkably does not involve any central coordination. The story continues with what is commonly suggested to be "the most complex structure in the universe"[17]— the human brain. Humans, on their own, are able to create and invent things. But when brought together under the umbrella of a

---

[14]John Tyler Bonner. *The Evolution of Complexity by Means of Natural Selection.* Princeton, NJ: Princeton University Press, 1988. ISBN: 0-691-08493-9, p. 189.

[15]Steven H. Strogatz. *Nonlinear Dynamics and Chaos: With Applications to Physics, Biology, Chemistry, and Engineering.* Boulder, CO: Westview Press, 1994. ISBN: 0-7382-0453-6, p. 103.

[16]Brian Goodwin, *How the Leopard Changed its Spots: The Evolution of Complexity,* op. cit., p. 65.

[17]Simon Conway Morris. "Life: The Final Frontier for Complexity?" In: *Complexity and the Arrow of Time.* Ed. by Charles H. Lineweaver, Paul C. W. Davies, and Michael Ruse. New York: Cambridge University Press, 2013. Chap. 7. ISBN: 978-1-107-02725-1, p. 140.

unified goal, more complex entities with emergent behavior, such as businesses, are formed. From these entities are birthed a multitude of inventions, such as modern commercial airplanes, of unimaginable complexity and which no individual human could design and build on his own from raw materials in a single lifetime.

Robert M. Hazen, one of the world's topmost influential Earth scientists, summarizes this story: "The history of the universe has been one inexorable, inevitable, chemical complexification—a sequence of emergent evolutionary episodes from nucleosynthesis, to planet formation, to life." [18]

The Trajectory of Our Story

If the entire story of the universe were to take place in one twenty-four-hour period, humans would arrive at 23:59:59. That is, we *just* got here. Something new and unusual is emerging, and I believe it has been the raging talk of our religious traditions. What is this new thing? If we learn anything from the common threads of this story it's that new and beautiful complexity is being birthed from individual elements cooperating together. This, then, is the trajectory of our story: the death of individualism and the emergence of a new collective oneness. Our faith traditions speak of a unified humanity and of the essential behaviors needed to achieve this vision.

It is what Jesus prayed for: "that they may all be one. As you, Father, are in me and I am in you, may they also be in us." [19] Paul spoke of this in his famous passage about the body of Christ:

> "For just as the body is one and has many members, and all the members of the body, though many, are one body, so it is with Christ. For in the one Spirit we were all baptized into one body—Jews or Greeks, slaves or free— and we were all made to drink of one Spirit. Indeed, the body does not consist of one member but of many. If the foot would say, 'Because I am not a hand, I do

---

[18] Robert M. Hazen, "The Emergence of Chemical Complexity: An Introduction," op. cit., p. 3.
[19] John 17:21.

not belong to the body,' that would not make it any less a part of the body. And if the ear would say, 'Because I am not an eye, I do not belong to the body,' that would not make it any less a part of the body. If the whole body were an eye, where would the hearing be? If the whole body were hearing, where would the sense of smell be? But as it is, God arranged the members in the body, each one of them, as he chose. If all were a single member, where would the body be? As it is, there are many members, yet one body. The eye cannot say to the hand, 'I have no need of you,' nor again the head to the feet, 'I have no need of you.' On the contrary, the members of the body that seem to be weaker are indispensable, and those members of the body that we think less honorable we clothe with greater honor, and our less respectable members are treated with greater respect; whereas our more respectable members do not need this. But God has so arranged the body, giving the greater honor to the inferior member, that there may be no dissension within the body, but the members may have the same care for one another. If one member suffers, all suffer together with it; if one member is honored, all rejoice together with it. Now you are the body of Christ and individually members of it." (1 Corinthians 12:12–27)

The psalmist also spoke of a blessed unity, saying: "How very good and pleasant it is when kindred live together in unity!"[20] Confucius called it the "Great Unity"—a Chinese utopian vision of the world in which everyone and everything is at peace. Similarly, the unity of humanity is one of the central teachings of the Bahá'í Faith. And of course, the central tenet of Hinduism is that all existence is pervaded by a Oneness.

The Lifeblood of Unity

If the new thing that is being birthed on the world's stage is a unified humanity, then what is the lifeblood which courses through its

---

[20] Psalm 133:1.

veins? What lubricates its operations? And what nutrients flow between individual members of the body of Christ to produce a healthy and flourishing whole? When people bump against each other in life, or work together to accomplish a singular vision, is it not the fruit of the Spirit which provide the nutrients for humanity's emergent behavior? Love, joy, peace, patience, kindness, gentleness, and self-control?[21] I believe that our religious traditions have been trying to articulate this vision all along.

The Bible, Dhammapada, Koran, and Chinese classics are all replete with references to these virtues and call for their cultivation in our lives. As people moved from hunter-gatherer societies to living in great metropolises, understanding not only how to tolerate one another, but how to live in unity and harmony became a major focus which we find recorded in our sacred texts. Paul tells us to "Above all, clothe yourselves with love, which binds everything together in perfect harmony."[22]

A Vision of Unity

What if we aligned our personal finances with the trajectory of our story? What would this look like? What if the aim of our financial journey was to nurture the new Oneness being birthed on the world's stage and not just satisfy our fleshly desires? Would not generosity be a primary goal? Social justice? A reduction of the ego and an increased concern for others? A unification of personal finance, social justice, and our faith has the potential to shake the very foundations of developed societies. It calls into question the underlying assumptions of the so-called "American dream." It suggests that a vicious pursuit of accumulation for our own purposes is actually swimming against the tides of emergence—against the trajectory of our story. It is in stark contrast to individual and corporate greed. Success in this vision is not defined by the magnitude of one's net worth at death, nor is it defined by the dollar amount of items purchased during one's life. While our society tends to define one's success based on one's ability to *spend* money, this vision

---

[21]Galatians 5:22–23.
[22]Colossians 3:14.

suggests that "success" is not even the opposite of spending. It is something different altogether and is better defined in relation to how well we align our whole lives with the lifeblood of emergence—that is, how aligned we are with the collective Oneness.

Are we digging deep into our tradition to cultivate the nutrients of this Oneness, such as the fruits of the Spirit: love, joy, peace, patience, kindness, generosity, faithfulness, gentleness, and self-control?[23] Do we have the courage to dissolve compartmental barriers and let our faith overflow into our finances? Are we mindful of our status in the existing socioeconomic systems—of our privileges or disadvantages—lest we harbor the debilitating attitudes of pride or victimhood? Do we further our concerns for others, especially the poor and disadvantaged, using our time and finances? What does "alignment with the collective Oneness" *actually* look like in our daily lives?

These are not easy questions, and they demonstrate that this vision of unity is more of a goal to be struggled towards rather than a logical conclusion to be believed. This vision does not offer an easy, step-by-step path to alignment. Instead, it is contextual and depends on our individual background, current situations, beliefs, relationships, socioeconomic status, spiritual maturity, etc. It's likely that everyone's path towards aligning our finances with this vision of unity will look different, maybe even antithetical to others' journeys at times. That's why this vision is less of a "how-to" and more of a "what if?" As Joel Primack and Nancy Abrams said: "Big changes are happening on our planet, and shepherding ourselves through them successfully is gong to require tremendous creativity."[24]

But this vision of unity will be difficult to achieve if we compartmentalize our faith, personal finances, and social justice. Is generosity not just an individual act of wealth redistribution? Aren't concerns about social justice deeply embedded in the Christian faith? Do we limit the effectiveness of our part in the whole when we are blind to the social systems that have played a major role in

---

[23] Galatians 5:22–23.
[24] Joel R. Primack and Nancy Ellen Abrams. *The View From the Center of the Universe: Discovering Our Extraordinary Place in the Cosmos.* New York: Penguin, 2006. ISBN: 1-59448-914-9, p. 11.

dictating our personal financial successes or failures?

Unity does not necessarily mean homogeneity. I don't think this vision requires us all to act the same, believe the same, or even have the same levels of wealth. As Paul described, different body parts have different critical functions. Perhaps some people are called to challenge the systems of the world and enact social justice that way. Maybe others are meant to gain as much as possible from the system and redistribute it themselves through acts of generosity.

What if our whole being, including our faith, finances, and concerns about social justice, was aligned with a trajectory of emergence where all of humanity is unified and further, one with the rest of creation and with God? What if our personal finances existed, as Immanuel Kant wrote, not only "by means of the other parts, but [...] for the sake of the others and the whole?"[25] Let's participate together in this emerging phenomenon where the common good is "the new frontier,"[26] as Walter Brueggemann says, and ask, "What if?"

---

[25]Immanuel Kant. *Critique of Judgment.* Trans. by J. H. Bernard. Mineola, NY: Dover, 2012. ISBN: 978-0-486-12220-5, p. 164; cited in Stuart A. Kauffman. "Evolution Beyond Newton, Darwin, and Entailing Law: The Origin of Complexity in the Evolving Biosphere." In: *Complexity and the Arrow of Time.* Ed. by Charles H. Lineweaver, Paul C. W. Davies, and Michael Ruse. New York: Cambridge University Press, 2013. Chap. 8. ISBN: 978-1-107-02725-1, p. 168.

[26]Walter Brueggemann, Peter Block, and John McKnight, *An Other Kingdom: Departing the Consumer Culture*, op. cit., p. 45.

Appendix A

Stock Market Growth Calculations

Long-Term Growth Rate (20 years)

Per Dave Ramsey, the average growth rate of the stock market, as measured by the S&P 500, is about 12%.[1] Note that this is the simple average of the percent return during each year from 1926 to 2010.[2] However, a more useful measure of growth rate is the compound annual growth rate (CAGR), which is what we use in a compound interest rate calculator. Given the initial value (IV) at t_0 and final value (FV) at t_n, the CAGR can be calculated with (A.1). Assuming dividends are reinvested, $1 invested Jan. 1, 1926

---

[1]Dave Ramsey, *Dave Ramsey's Complete Guide to Money*, op. cit., pp. 211–212; idem, *The Legacy Journey: A Radical View of Biblical Wealth and Generosity*, op. cit., pp 215–216.

[2]We know the 12% figure is a simple average because in a blog post explaining the 12%, Ramsey quotes an average return of 12.25% from 1923 to 2016 by citing the Moneychimp calculator (Dave Ramsey. *Return on Investment: the 12% Reality*. 2021. URL: www.ramseysolutions.com/retirement/the-12-reality (visited on 06/12/2021); Moneychimp. *CAGR of the Stock Market: Annualized Returns of the S&P 500*. 2018. URL: www.moneychimp.com/features/market_cagr.htm (visited on 06/12/2021)). This 12.25% number is contrasted by the CAGR of 10.34% in the same calculator for the same time period.

S&P 500 - Growth of $1

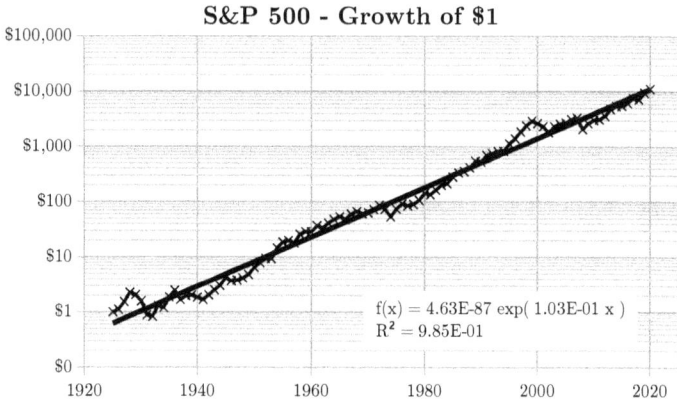

Figure A.1: Growth of $1 invested in S&P 500 from 1926 to 2017. The compound annual growth rate (CAGR) is 10.3% (Moneychimp. *CAGR of the Stock Market: Annualized Returns of the S&P 500.* 2018. URL: www.moneychimp.com/features/market_cagr.htm (visited on 06/12/2021)).

to Jan. 1, 2021 grew to $11,185.62.[3] This translates to a 10.31% CAGR as shown in (A.2).

$$\text{CAGR} = \left(\frac{\text{FV}}{\text{IV}}\right)^{\frac{1}{t_n - t_0}} - 1 \qquad (A.1)$$

$$\text{CAGR} = \left(\frac{\$11,185.62}{\$1}\right)^{\frac{1}{2021 - 1926}} - 1 = 10.31\% \qquad (A.2)$$

However, this method calculates a CAGR based on only two data points and is thus sensitive to those initial and final values. Another method which uses all the data points in between is a least squares curve fit of the data with the compound interest formula. Figure A.1 shows the growth of $1 invested from 1926 to 2017. The curve fit shows a 10.3% CAGR.

---

[3] Ibid.

It is easy to pick and choose dates that change the CAGR slightly, so this analysis assumes a *long-term* CAGR of **10%** for any investment that is in the stock market for 20 years or more. Since the simple average annual growth rate is usually 1–2% larger than the CAGR,[4] calculations using the 10% figure are in-line with Dave Ramsey's 12%.

Shorter-Term Growth (10 years)

As the investment time increases, the range of historical annualized returns shrinks.[5] For example, 1 year holding periods had annualized returns from -44.4% to $+57.5\%$ while 75 year holding periods had annualized returns between $+9.4\%$ to $+11.7\%$.[6] Thus, for very long-terms (> 20 years), the estimate of 10% CAGR is realistic based on the history. However, the variation in return from one decade to the next is substantial[7] with historical results ranging from -2% to $+19\%$.[8] If one plans for a 10% CAGR over the next 10 years, there is significant risk of undershooting a target by not contributing enough to account for the possibility of lower return.

Bogle Sources of Return Model for Stocks

This section uses the Bogle Sources of Return Model for Stocks (BSRM/S) as a basis for developing "reasonable expectations for future equity market returns."[9] From the outset, it should be made clear that this is *not a forecast* of future returns, only a method for setting *expectations* on an investment using a simple common

---

[4] Ibid.

[5] R. P. DeGennaro. *How the Stock Market Works Course Guidebook*. The Great Courses, 2014, p. 27.

[6] Ibid., p. 26.

[7] John C. Bogle. *Bogle on Mutual Funds: New Perspectives for the Intelligent Investor*. John Wiley & Sons, 2015, p. 9.

[8] R. P. DeGennaro, *How the Stock Market Works Course Guidebook*, op. cit., p. 26.

[9] John C. Bogle and M. W. Nolan. "Occam's Razor Redux: Establishing Reasonable Expectations for Financial Market Returns." In: *Journal of Portfolio Management* 42.1 (2015).

sense analysis. According to Bogle, there are only three elements which contribute to returns of common stocks:[10]

1. Dividends

2. Earnings growth

3. Speculative return (change in price to earnings (P/E) ratio)

In the long run, it is dividend yields and earnings growth that are the driver of stock returns.[11] For example, the average dividend yield of the S&P 500 from 1871 to 2017 is 4.38%[12] while long-term earnings growth has averaged 6%[13] resulting in a 10.38% annualized return. Compared to the average return of 10.79% over the same period,[14] we see that the long term return on stocks is "substantially about the economics of business, not the emotions of speculators."[15]

Speculative returns, on the other hand, have no such long-term trend. Bogle shows a plot of cumulative investment return and cumulative speculative return from 1871–2015 in Fig. A.2. Investment returns (dividends and earnings growth) clearly comprise the bulk of returns. The speculative return (changes in price to dividend ratio) has no cumulative impact over long periods of time, suggesting a strong pattern of reversion to the mean.[16]

However, changes in the price to earnings ratio can have huge impact on stock returns over shorter periods of time (e.g., a

---

[10]John C. Bogle, *Bogle on Mutual Funds: New Perspectives for the Intelligent Investor*, op. cit., p. 9.

[11]idem, *John Bogle on Investing: The First 50 Years*, op. cit., p. 159; E. Tyson. *Investing in Your 20s and 30s For Dummies*. Wiley, 2017. ISBN: 9781119431428, p. 95.

[12]multpl. *S&P 500 Dividend Yield by Year*. 2018. URL: http://www.multpl.com/s-p-500-dividend-yield/table (visited on 09/22/2018).

[13]John C. Bogle, *John Bogle on Investing: The First 50 Years*, op. cit., p. 159.

[14]Moneychimp, *CAGR of the Stock Market: Annualized Returns of the S&P 500*, op. cit.

[15]John C. Bogle and M. W. Nolan, "Occam's Razor Redux: Establishing Reasonable Expectations for Financial Market Returns," op. cit., p. 121.

[16]Ibid., p. 121.

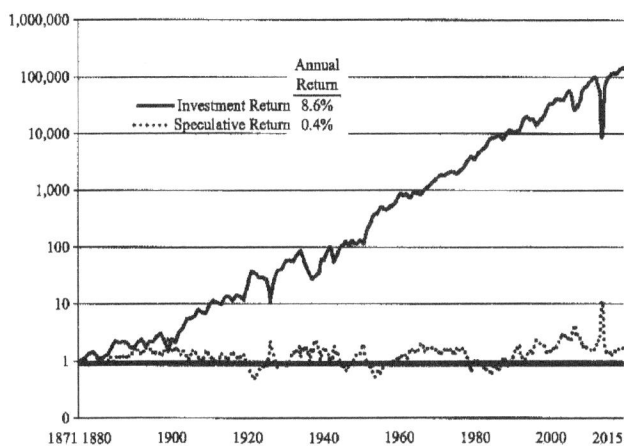

Figure A.2: Cumulative Investment Return and Cumulative Speculative Return, 1871–2015 (John C. Bogle and M. W. Nolan. "Occam's Razor Redux: Establishing Reasonable Expectations for Financial Market Returns." In: *Journal of Portfolio Management* 42.1 (2015), p. 120).

decade)[17], and it is important to set future expectations in accordance with the historical pattern of reversion to the mean. To account for the speculative return, the BSRM/S makes one simple assumption: *the speculative return (P/E ratio) will revert to its mean within about a decade.* This will add to or subtract from the expected return from dividends and earnings growth. This is summarized by Bogle in the formula of (A.3),

$$R_t = D_0 + G_t + \Delta P/E_t \qquad (A.3)$$

where R_t is the return over some period of time t (ten years), D_0 is the dividend yield at the beginning of the period t, G_t is the annual expected growth in nominal earnings per share during period t, and $\Delta P/E_t$ is the expected annualized rate of change in the price/earnings multiple over period t.[18]

This model not only makes intuitive sense but apparently has an impressive history of forecasting the actual returns as shown in Fig. A.3.

Calculation of Expected Returns

Long-term earnings growth has averaged 6%[19] and current dividend yields are 2%. So we expect investment returns to be 8% over the next decade. However, the current P/E ratio is 25, but the average P/E ratio from the last 50 years is 19.[20] If we expect the current P/E ratio of 25 to drop back to 19 over the next decade, we should expect a change in valuation as shown in (A.4).

$$\Delta P/E_t = \frac{(19 - 25)}{19} = -32\% \qquad (A.4)$$

Thus, while we expect our investment to grow by 8% per year over the next decade, we also expect the price of our investment to drop by about 3% per year giving a total return of about 5%.

---

[17] John C. Bogle, *Bogle on Mutual Funds: New Perspectives for the Intelligent Investor*, op. cit., p. 11.

[18] John C. Bogle and M. W. Nolan, "Occam's Razor Redux: Establishing Reasonable Expectations for Financial Market Returns," op. cit., p. 120.

[19] John C. Bogle, *John Bogle on Investing: The First 50 Years*, op. cit., p. 159.

[20] Calculated from data in: multpl, *S&P 500 Dividend Yield by Year*, op. cit.

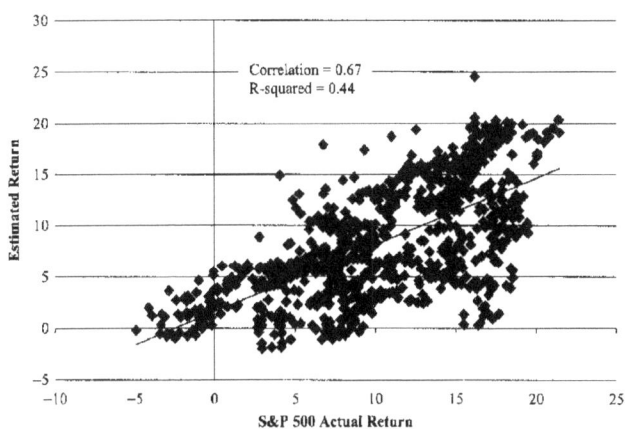

Figure A.3: Actual Equity Returns vs. Predicted Returns Moving 10-Year Periods, 1915–2014 (John C. Bogle and M. W. Nolan. "Occam's Razor Redux: Establishing Reasonable Expectations for Financial Market Returns." In: *Journal of Portfolio Management* 42.1 (2015), p. 123).

Thus, we can reasonably expect a **5%** growth rate of investments over the next decade.[21]

---

[21] Note that Bogle thinks the earnings growth rate will only be 5% and thus expects a 4% return on common stock over the next decade. He makes it clear, however, that low expectations for return is *not* a reason to not invest, but a reason to increase contributions to meet goals (John C. Bogle and M. W. Nolan, "Occam's Razor Redux: Establishing Reasonable Expectations for Financial Market Returns," op. cit., p. 130).

Appendix B

Future Value of Annuity with Increasing Contributions

This appendix calculates the future value of an annuity when the contributions increase by some percentage every period. The problem is setup by considering each contribution as growing according to the usual compound growth. However, contributions can increase each year and will grow for a different amount of time.[1] Assuming an initial contribution, C_0, increases by r_c each year, the initial value of each deposit, C_n, is given in (B.1) when the year of the deposit is $t \in [1, t_n]$.

$$C_n = C_0 r_c^{t-1} \qquad \text{(B.1)}$$

Each deposit then compounds from the date of the deposit to the time t_n. If a year is divided into n periods (e.g., $n = 12$ gives 1

---

[1]Example: a contribution of $3,000 at the beginning of a 10 year period has 120 months to compound. If contribution amounts increase by 4% each year, then a contribution of $3,120 at the beginning of the second year has 108 months to compound.

month periods), then the length of time (in months) each deposit is allowed to grow, t_{n_i}, is given in (B.2), knowing the month $n_i \in [0, n-1]$ and year t when the contribution was deposited.

$$t_{n_i} = nt_n - n_i - n(t-1) \tag{B.2}$$

The final value of each contribution, FV_{C_0}, is found by compounding the initial value of the deposit, C_n, at the yearly interest rate of the investment, r_i, for the time each contribution is allowed to compound, t_{n_i}, as shown in (B.3).

$$\mathrm{FV}_{C_0} = C_n \left(r_i^{1/n} \right)^{t_{n_i}} \tag{B.3}$$

If the account begins with an initial value (IV), we can calculate the final value of the whole account, FV, by simply summing the final values of all the contributions as shown in (B.4), which is reduced to a closed form in (B.6).

$$\mathrm{FV} = \mathrm{IV} r_i^{t_n} + \sum_{t=0}^{t=t_n} \sum_{n_i=0}^{n-1} C_n \left(r_i^{1/n} \right)^{t_{n_i}} \tag{B.4}$$

$$= \mathrm{IV} r_i^{t_n} + \sum_{t=0}^{t=t_n} \sum_{n_i=0}^{n-1} \left(C_0 r_c^{t-1} \right) \left(r_i^{1/n} \right)^{nt_n - n_i - n(t-1)} \tag{B.5}$$

$$= \mathrm{IV} r_i^{t_n} + \frac{C_0 r_i^{\frac{1}{n}} [1 - r_i] \left[r_c^{t_n} - r_i^{t_n} \right]}{\left(r_i^{\frac{1}{n}} - 1 \right) (r_i - r_c)} \tag{B.6}$$

The reduction in (B.6) is valid when $r_i \neq 1$ and $r_i \neq r_c$. In some cases, we may require the initial contribution amount, C_0, which produces a particular final value. Solving (B.6) for C_0 gives (B.7).

$$C_0 = \frac{\left(1 - r_i^{-\frac{1}{n}} \right) (r_i - r_c) \left(\mathrm{FV} - \mathrm{IV} r_i^{t_n} \right)}{[1 - r_i] \left[r_c^{t_n} - r_i^{t_n} \right]} \tag{B.7}$$

Furthermore, if we require the initial value (IV) that will create a particular final value, we can use the form in (B.8).

$$IV = r_i^{-t_n} \left(FV - \frac{C_0 r_i^{\frac{1}{n}} \left[1 - r_i\right] \left[r_c^{t_n} - r_i^{t_n}\right]}{\left(r_i^{\frac{1}{n}} - 1\right)(r_i - r_c)} \right) \qquad (B.8)$$

BIBLIOGRAPHY

Adams, James Luther. *The Essential James Luther Adams: Selected Essays and Addresses.* Ed. by George Kimmich Beach.
Boston, MA: Skinner House Books, 1998. ISBN: 978-1558963528.

Æsop and Munro Leaf. *Æsop's Fables—A New Version.* Trans. by
John Warrington. Norwalk, CT: Easton Press, 1979.

Alcorn, Randy. *Money, Possessions, and Eternity.* Carol Stream,
IL: Tyndale House Publishers, Inc., 2011. ISBN: 978-0-8423-
5360-1.

Allen, James Peter and Peter Der Manuelian. *The Ancient Egyptian Pyramid Texts.* Ed. by Peter Der Manuelian et al. Trans.
by James P. Allen. Vol. 23. Writings from the Ancient World.
Atlanta, GA: Society of Biblical Literature, 2005. ISBN: 978-1-
58983-182-7.

Allison, Dale C. *The Sermon on the Mount: Inspiring the Moral
Imagination.* New York: Crossroad Publishing Company, 1999.

Andrews, Edward D. et al. *Biblical Criticism: Beyond the Basics.*
Cambridge, Ohio: Christian Publishing House, 2017. ISBN: 978-
1-945757-71-6.

Arthur, Chris. "Financial Literacy Education for Citizens: What
Kind of Responsibility, Equality and Engagement?" In: *Citizenship, Social and Economics Education* 11.3 (2012), pp. 163–
176.

Aurelius, Marcus and George Long. *The Meditations of Marcus Aurelius.* Trans. by George Long. New York: F. M. Lupton Publishing Company, 1887.

Bannerman, James. *Inspiration: The Infallible Truth and Divine Authority of the Holy Scriptures*. Edinburgh: T. and T. Clark, 1865.

Barton, Bruce. "It Would Be Fun To Start Over Again—Interview with Henry Ford." In: *The American Magazine* 91 (1921).

Basinger, David. "Biblical Paradox: Does Revelation Challenge Logic?" In: *Journal of the Evangelical Theological Society* 30.2 (1987), pp. 205–213.

Beal, John P., James A. Coriden, and Thomas Joseph Green. *New Commentary on the Code of Canon Law*. Paulist Press, 2000.

Beale, Gregory K. and Donald A. Carson. *Commentary on the New Testament Use of the Old Testament*. Grand Rapids, MI: Baker Books, 2007. ISBN: 978-0-8010-2693-5.

Becker, Joshua. *Simplify: 7 Guiding Principles to Help Anyone Declutter Their Home & Life [eBook]*. Joshua Becker, 2014.

Bell, Rob. *Love Wins*. New York: HarperOne, 2011. ISBN: 978-0-06-204965-0.

— *Velvet Elvis: Repainting the Christian Faith*. Grand Rapids, MI: Zondervan, 2006.

Bennison, J. W. *The Affliction of Affluence: Reconciling Gratitude, Generosity and Greed*. 2012. URL: www.wordsnways.com/the-affliction-of-affluence-reconciling-gratitude-greed-generosity (visited on 02/13/2021).

Berlin, Adele and Marc Zvi Brettler. "Introduction: What is The Jewish Study Bible?" In: *The Jewish Study Bible: Jewish Publication Society Tanakh Translation*. Ed. by Adele Berlin, Marc Zvi Brettler, et al. 2nd ed. Oxford University Press, USA, 2014.

Berlin, Adele, Marc Zvi Brettler, et al. *The Jewish Study Bible: Jewish Publication Society Tanakh Translation*. 2nd ed. Oxford University Press, USA, 2014.

Billah, Mohd Ma'Sum. *Modern Islamic Investment Management*. Cham, Switzerland: Springer, 2019. ISBN: 978-3-030-17627-3.

Black, Jeremy A. *The Literature of Ancient Sumer*. Trans. by Jeremy Black et al. New York: Oxford University Press, 2004. ISBN: 0-19-926311-6.

Boff, Leonardo. *Francis of Assisi: A Model for Human Liberation*. Trans. by John W. Diercksmeier. Maryknoll, NY: Orbis Books, 2006.

Bogle, John C. *Bogle on Mutual Funds: New Perspectives for the Intelligent Investor.* John Wiley & Sons, 2015.

— *Common Sense on Mutual Funds.* Hoboken, NJ: John Wiley & Sons, 2010. ISBN: 978-0-470-13813-7.

— *John Bogle on Investing: The First 50 Years.* Hoboken, NJ: John Wiley & Sons, 2015. ISBN: 978-1-119-08836-3.

Bogle, John C. and M. W. Nolan. "Occam's Razor Redux: Establishing Reasonable Expectations for Financial Market Returns." In: *Journal of Portfolio Management* 42.1 (2015), pp. 119–134.

Bonner, John Tyler. *The Evolution of Complexity by Means of Natural Selection.* Princeton, NJ: Princeton University Press, 1988. ISBN: 0-691-08493-9.

Borg, Marcus J. *Conflict, Holiness, and Politics in the Teachings of Jesus.* London: Continuum International Publishing Group, 1998.

— *Convictions: How I Learned What Matters Most.* New York: HarperCollins, 2014. ISBN: 978-0-06-226998-0.

— *Jesus: Uncovering the Life, Teachings, and Relevance of a Religious Revolutionary.* New York: HarperCollins e-books, 2006.

— *Reading the Bible Again for the First Time: Taking the Bible Seriously but not Literally.* HarperSanFrancisco, 2001.

— *The Heart of Christianity: Rediscovering a Life of Faith.* New York: HarperOne, 2003. ISBN: 978-0-06-073068-0.

Boyd, Gregory A. *Benefit of the Doubt: Breaking the Idol of Certainty.* Grand Rapids, MI: Baker Books, 2013.

Brenoff, Ann. *7 Things You Can Learn From The 'FIRE' Early Retirement Movement.* 2018. URL: https://bit.ly/3ncRv4I (visited on 04/21/2021).

Brettler, Marc Zvi. "Jewish Interpretation in the Premodern Era." In: *The New Oxford Annotated Bible with Apocrypha: New Revised Standard Version.* Ed. by Michael D. Coogan et al. 5th ed. New York: Oxford University Press, 2010.

— "The Hebrew Bible's Interpretation of Itself." In: *The New Oxford Annotated Bible with Apocrypha: New Revised Standard Version.* Ed. by Michael D. Coogan et al. 5th ed. New York: Oxford University Press, 2010.

Broughton, Geoff. "Restorative Justice and Jesus Christ: Why Restorative Justice Requires a Holistic Christology." PhD thesis. Charles Sturt University, 2011.

Brueggemann, Walter. *Journey to the Common Good.* Louisville, KY: Westminster John Knox Press, 2010. ISBN: 978-0-664-23516.

— *Money and Possessions: Interpretation: Resources for the Use of Scripture in the Church.* Louisville, KY: Westminster John Knox Press, 2016. ISBN: 9780664233648.

Brueggemann, Walter, Peter Block, and John McKnight. *An Other Kingdom: Departing the Consumer Culture.* Hoboken, NJ: John Wiley & Sons, 2015. ISBN: 978-1-119-19472-9.

Buddharakkhita, Acharya. *The Dhammapada—The Buddha's Path of Wisdom.* Trans. by Acharya Buddharakkhita. Kandy, Sri Lanka: Buddhist Publication Society, 2003. ISBN: 978-955-24-0131-2.

Burk, Denny et al. *Four Views on Hell.* Ed. by Preston Sprinkle and Stanley N. Gundry. 2nd ed. Grand Rapids, MI: Zondervan Academic, 2016.

Buxbaum, Yitzhak. *The Life and Teachings of Hillel.* Plymouth, UK: Rowman & Littlefield Publishers, 2004.

Byas, Jared. *Love Matters More: How Fighting to Be Right Keeps Us from Loving Like Jesus.* Grand Rapids, MI: Zondervan, 2020.

Callahan, Richard J. "R3AL HOPE: Living with the End in Mind." PhD thesis. George Fox University, 2013.

Calvin, John. *Institutes of the Christian Religion.* Trans. by John Allen. Vol. 1. 1816.

Carson, Donald A. *Exegetical Fallacies.* Grand Rapids, MI: Baker Books, 1996.

Castelein, John et al. *Understanding Four Views on Baptism.* Ed. by John H. Armstrong and Paul E. Engle. Grand Rapids, MI: Zondervan Academic, 2009.

Cautero, Rachel. *Are You in the Top 1%?* 2021. URL: `www . smartasset . com / financial - advisor / are - you - in - the - top-1-percent` (visited on 04/19/2021).

Chaisson, Eric J. "Using Complexity Science to Search for Unity in the Natural Sciences." In: *Complexity and the Arrow of Time.*

Ed. by Charles H. Lineweaver, Paul C. W. Davies, and Michael Ruse. New York: Cambridge University Press, 2013. Chap. 4, pp. 68–79. ISBN: 978-1-107-02725-1.

Clarke, Laura Leigh. *Wire Yourself for Wealth—Discover Your Personal Money Profile to Effortlessly Attract More Cash.* Carlsbad, CA: Hay House, 2012. ISBN: 978-1-84850-698-5.

Clason, George S. *The Richest Man in Babylon.* New American Library, 1988.

Cloninger, C. *More E-Mail from God for Teens.* David C. Cook Publishing Company, 2003.

Collins, J. L. and Peter (Mr. Money Mustache) Adeney. *The Simple Path to Wealth: Your Road Map to Financial Independence and a Rich, Free Life.* Scotts Valley, CA: CreateSpace Independent Publishing Platform, 2016. ISBN: 9781533667922.

Conway, Bobby. *Doubting Toward Faith: The Journey to Confident Christianity.* Harvest House Publishers, 2015.

Cowan, Steven B., Stanley N. Gundry, and William Lane Craig. *Five Views on Apologetics.* Grand Rapids, MI: Zondervan, 2000.

Crayton, Lisa. *I Want to Talk With my Teen About Money Management.* Cincinnati, OH: The Standard Publishing, 2006. ISBN: 978-0-7847-1897-0.

Crossan, John Dominic. *God and Empire: Jesus Against Rome, Then and Now.* New York: HarperCollins e-books, 2007.

Culpepper, Polk. *Churches Teaching the Doctrine of Shame.* 2015. URL: www.progressivechristianity.org/resources/churches-teaching-the-doctrine-of-shame/ (visited on 02/13/2021).

— *Shame Based Prayers: 'You May Be a Child of God, But You Are Still an Unworthy Human Being'.* 2015. URL: https://www.progressivechristianity.org/resources/shamed-based-prayers-you-may-be-a-child-of-god-but-you-are-still-an-unworthy-human-being/ (visited on 02/13/2021).

Darnell, Charles Van Divier. *Who Art Thou, Lord?—The Good News Jesus Preached.* Xlibris, 2013.

Daugherty, Greg. *What 30-Year-Old Retirees Can Teach The Rest Of Us.* 2014. URL: www.forbes.com/sites/nextavenue/2014/03/21/what-30-year-old-retirees-can-teach-the-rest-of-us/?sh=12ac29e437b0 (visited on 04/21/2021).

De Cremer, David and Kees Van den Bos. "Justice and Feelings: Toward A New Era in Justice Research." In: *Social Justice Research* 20.1 (2007), pp. 1–9.

DeGennaro, R. P. *How the Stock Market Works Course Guidebook*. The Great Courses, 2014.

Descartes, René. *Discourse on Method and Meditations on First Philosophy*. Trans. by Donald A. Cress. 4th ed. Indianapolis, IN: Hackett Publishing, 1998.

DiAngelo, Robin. *White Fragility: Why It's So Hard for White People to Talk about Racism*. Boston, MA: Beacon Press, 2018. ISBN: 978-0-8070-4741-5.

Diehl, David W. "Evangelicalism and General Revelation: An Unfinished Agenda." In: *Journal of the Evangelical Theological Society* 30.2 (1987), pp. 441–455.

Dieter, Melvin E. et al. *Five Views on Sanctification*. Ed. by Stanley N. Gundry. Grand Rapids, MI: Zondervan Academic, 1996.

Donahue, John R. "Guidelines for Reading and Interpretation." In: *The New Interpreter's Study Bible: New Revised Standard Version with the Apocrypha*. Ed. by Walter J. Harrelson et al. Nashville, TN: Abingdon Press, 2003, pp. 2261–2267. ISBN: 978-0-687-27832-9.

Done, Dominic. *When Faith Fails: Finding God in the Shadow of Doubt*. Thomas Nelson, 2019.

Earley, D. *The 21 Most Dangerous Questions of the Bible*. Barbour Publishing, Incorporated, 2013.

Ehrman, Bart D. *Heaven and Hell: A History of the Afterlife*. New York: Simon & Schuster, 2020. ISBN: 978-1-5011-3673-3.

— *How Jesus Became God: The Exaltation of a Jewish Preacher from Galilee*. 2014.

— *Jesus: Apocalyptic Prophet of the New Millennium*. New York: Oxford University Press, 1999.

— *Jesus, Interrupted: Revealing the Hidden Contradictions in the Bible (And Why We Don't Know About Them)*. New York: HarperOne, 2009.

— *The New Testament: A Historical Introduction to the Early Christian Writings*. 2nd ed. Oxford: Oxford University Press, 2000.

Einstein, Albert. *Bite-Size Einstein—Quotations on Just About Everything from the Greatest Mind of the Twentieth Century*. Ed. by Jerry Mayer and John P. Holmes. New York: Thomas Dunne, 1996.

Elman, Yaakov. "Classical Rabbinic Interpretation." In: *The Jewish Study Bible: Jewish Publication Society Tanakh Translation*. Ed. by Adele Berlin, Marc Zvi Brettler, et al. 2nd ed. Oxford University Press, USA, 2014, pp. 1859–1878.

Enns, Peter. *Ecclesiastes*. Ed. by J. Gordon McConville and Craig Bartholomew. The Two Horizons Old Testament Commentary. Grand Rapids, MI: Wm. B. Eerdmans Publishing, 2011. ISBN: 978-0-8028-6649-3.

— *How the Bible Actually Works: In which I Explain How an Ancient, Ambiguous, and Diverse Book Leads us to Wisdom Rather Than Answers—And Why That's Great News*. New York: HarperOne, 2019. ISBN: 978-0-06-268674-9.

— *Inspiration and incarnation: Evangelicals and the Problem of the Old Testament*. 2nd ed. Grand Rapids: MI: Baker Academic, 2015. ISBN: 978-0-8010-9748-5.

— *The Bible Tells Me So: Why Defending Scripture Has Made Us Unable to Read It*. New York: HarperOne, 2014.

— *The Sin of Certainty: Why God Desires Our Trust More Than Our 'Correct' Beliefs*. New York: HarperOne, 2016. ISBN: 978-0-06-227208-9.

Enns, Peter. "Episode 54: Ask Pete—Answering Questions from The Bible For Normal People Community." In: *The Bible for Normal People [Podcast]*. 2019. URL: `www.peteenns.com/ask-pete-episode-55/` (visited on 05/02/2021).

Enns, Peter and Jared Byas. "Episode 121: Pete and Jared—Pete and Jared Talk About the Afterlife." In: *The Bible for Normal People [Podcast]*. 2021. URL: `www.peteenns.com/episode-121-the-afterlife/` (visited on 06/09/2021).

Enns, Peter et al. *Five Views on Biblical Inerrancy*. Ed. by James R. A. Merrick, Stephen M. Garrett, and Stanley N. Gundry. Grand Rapids, MI: Zondervan Academic, 2013.

Evans, Rachel Held. *A Year of Biblical Womanhood: How a Liberated Woman Found Herself Sitting on Her Roof, Covering*

Her Head, and Calling Her Husband 'Master'. Nashville, TN: Thomas Nelson, 2012. ISBN: 978-1-59555-367-6.

Evans, Rachel Held. *Evolving in Monkey Town: How a Girl Who Knew All the Answers Learned to Ask the Questions*. Grand Rapids, MI: Zondervan, 2010. ISBN: 978-0-310-29399-6.

— *Inspired: Slaying Giants, Walking on Water, and Loving the Bible Again*. Nashville, TN: Thomas Nelson, 2018. ISBN: 978-0-7180-2231-0.

— *Searching for Sunday: Loving, Leaving, and Finding the Church*. Nashville, TN: Thomas Nelson, 2015. ISBN: 978-0-7180-2212-9.

Farnell, F. David et al. *Vital Issues in the Inerrancy Debate*. Wipf & Stock Publishers, 2016.

Felten, David M. and Jeff Procter-Murphy. *Living the Questions: The Wisdom of Progressive Christianity*. New York: Harper-One, 2012. ISBN: 978-0-06-210936-1.

Fensham, F. Charles. "Widow, Orphan, and the Poor in Ancient Near Eastern Legal and Wisdom Literature." In: *Journal of Near Eastern Studies* 21.2 (1962), pp. 129–139.

Fincher, David and Chuck Palahniuk. *Fight Club [Movie]*. 20th Century Fox, 1999.

Fisher, Margaret W. "The Collected Works of Mahatma Gandhi, Volumes I–XII (1884–1914)." In: *American Political Science Review* 60.1 (1966), pp. 123–124.

Fisker, J. L. *Early Retirement Extreme: A Philosophical and Practical Guide to Financial Independence*. Scotts Valley, CA: CreateSpace Independent Publishing Platform, 2010.

Frame, John M. *The Doctrine of the Word of God*. P&R Publishing, 2010.

Friel, Todd. *Reset for Parents: How to Keep Your Kids from Backsliding*. New Leaf Publishing Group, 2017.

Fūzǐ, Kǒng. *The Analects of Confucius: Chinese–English Bilingual Edition*. Trans. by Pan Fuen et al. 1st ed. Jinan, China: Qi Lu Press, 1993. ISBN: 7-5333-0283-4.

— *The Sacred Books of China: The Texts of Confucianism*. Ed. by Friedrich Max Müller. Trans. by James Legge. Vol. 28. The Sacred Books of the East. Oxford: Clarendon Press, 1885.

Gafney, Wilda C. *Womanist Midrash: A Reintroduction to the Women of the Torah and the Throne.* Louisville, KY: Westminster John Knox Press, 2017.

Galilei, Galileo. "Letter to the Grand Duchess Christina of Tuscany." In: *Published online at Modern History Sourcebook* (1999).

— *The Galileo Affair: A Documentary History.* Vol. 1. Univ of California Press, 1989.

Gannon, Niall J. *Tailored Wealth Management: Exploring the Cause and Effect of Financial Success.* Springer, 2019.

Gard, Daniel L. et al. *Show Them No Mercy: 4 Views on God and Canaanite Genocide.* Ed. by Stanley N. Gundry. Grand Rapids, MI: Zondervan Academic, 2003.

Global Wealth Databook. 2019. URL: `www.credit-suisse.com/media/assets/corporate/docs/about-us/research/publications/global-wealth-databook-2019.pdf` (visited on 04/20/2021).

Goldman, A. *Debt: A Love Story.* 2018. URL: `www.wealthsimple.com/en-us/magazine/couple-debt` (visited on 02/27/2021).

Goodwin, Brian. *How the Leopard Changed its Spots: The Evolution of Complexity.* London: Weidenfeld & Nicolson, 1994. ISBN: 0-297-81499-0.

Gray, John. *How to Get What You Want and Want What You Have: A Practical and Spiritual Guide to Personal Success.* New York: HarperOne, 2009. ISBN: 978-0-0619-8443-3.

Grenz, Stanley J. *Renewing the Center: Evangelical Theology in a Post-theological Era.* Grand Rapids, MI: Baker Academic, 2006. ISBN: 0-8010-2239-8.

Ham, Ken and Britt Beemer. *Already Gone: Why Your Kids Will Quit Church and What You Can Do To Stop It.* New Leaf Publishing Group, 2009.

Harper, Robert Francis. *The Code of Hammurabi, King of Babylon: About 2250 BC.* Chicago, IL: University of Chicago Press, 1904.

Hatfield, J. D. *A Call to Action—Preaching Through the Book of James.* J. D. Hatfield, 2015. ISBN: 978-1-312-82154-5.

Hayek, Friedrich August. *Law, Legislation and Liberty: A New Statement of the Liberal Principles of Justice and Political Economy.* Oxfordshire, UK: Routledge, 2012.

Hazen, Robert M. "The Emergence of Chemical Complexity: An Introduction." In: *Chemical Evolution Across Space & Time: From the Big Bang to Prebiotic Chemistry.* Ed. by Lori Zaikowski and Jon M. Friedrich. Vol. 981. ACS Symposium Series. Proceedings of the American Chemical Society Symposium Spring 2007 ACS National Meeting, Chicago, IL. American Chemical Society Publications, 2008. Chap. 1, pp. 1–15. ISBN: 978-0-8412-7431-0.

Hedstrom, Matthew S. *My Brother's Keeper: George McGovern and Progressive Christianity.* Oxford University Press, 2018.

Heijer, Alexander den. *Nothing You Don't Already Know: Remarkable Reminders About Meaning, Purpose, and Self-realization.* Scotts Valley, CA: CreateSpace Independent Publishing Platform, 2020.

Heilbron, Avery. *How I Save 80% Of My Income | Financial Independence | Minimalism.* YouTube Video. 2021. URL: www.youtube.com/watch?v=f2uOTn8esVs (visited on 06/12/2021).

Henderson, Robert T. *The Church and the Relentless Darkness.* Wipf and Stock Publishers, 2013.

Henry, Carl F. H. "The Priority of divine revelation: a review article." In: *Journal of the Evangelical Theological Society* 27.1 (1984), pp. 77–92.

Henry, Theresa F., Athar Murtuza, Renee E. Weiss, et al. "Accounting as an Instrument of Social Justice." In: *Open Journal of Social Sciences* 3.01 (2015), p. 66.

Herbert, Wray. "Mindfulness and Heuristics." In: *The Wiley Blackwell Handbook of Mindfulness* (2014), pp. 279–289.

Hick, John, Clark H. Pinnock, and Alister E. McGrath. *Four Views on Salvation in a Pluralistic World.* Ed. by Stanley N. Gundry, Dennis L. Okholm, and Timothy R. Phillips. Counterpoints. Grand Rapids, MI: Zondervan, 1996.

Himmelfarb, Martha. "Afterlife and Resurrection." In: *The Jewish Annotated New Testament.* Ed. by Amy-Jill Levine and Marc Zvi Brettler. 2nd ed. New York: Oxford University Press, 2017, pp. 691–695.

Holmes, Stephen R. et al. *Two Views on the Doctrine of the Trinity.* Ed. by Jason S. Sexton and Stanley N. Gundry. Grand Rapids, MI: Zondervan Academic, 2014.

Hopkins, G. M. *"God's Grandeur" and Other Poems*. Dover Publications, 1995.

Horton, Michael et al. *Four Views on Eternal Security*. Ed. by J. Matthew Pinson and Stanley N. Gundry. Grand Rapids, MI: Zondervan Academic, 2011.

Housel, Morgan. *The Psychology of Money: Timeless Lessons on Wealth, Greed, and Happiness*. Hampshire, UK: Harriman House Limited, 2020.

Huffington, Arianna. "Commencement Address: Vassar College." In: *Representative American Speeches 2014–2015*. Vol. 87. 6. Amenia, NY: Grey House Publishing, 2015, pp. 21–26.

Ingrouille, Stuart. *Unbelievable: Christianity as a House of Cards*. Lulu.com, 2013.

Jacobson, Howard. "Biblical Interpretation in Pseudo-Philo's *Liber Antiquitatum Biblicarum*." In: *A Companion to Biblical Interpretation in Early Judaism*. Ed. by Matthias Henze. Grand Rapids, MI: Wm. B. Eerdmans Publishing, 2012.

Jasnow, Richard L. *A Late Period Hieratic Wisdom Text (P. Brooklyn 47.218.135)*. Ed. by Thomas A. Holland and Thomas G. Urban. Vol. 52. Studies in Ancient Oriental Civilization. Oriental Institution of the University of Chicago, 1992. ISBN: 0-918986-85-0.

Jenkins, Lee. *Taking Care of Business: Establishing a Financial Legacy for Your Family*. Chicago, IL: Moody Publishers, 2001. ISBN: 0-8024-4016-9.

Johnson, Jeffrey A. and Tim White. *Get Ready! Get Real! Get Financial Freedom—A Simple Blueprint for Building and Sustaining Financial Freedom*. Atlanta, GA: Opes Publishing, 2020. ISBN: 978-1-7343118-0-8.

Kahan, Alan S. *Mind vs. Money: The War Between Intellectuals and Capitalism*. New Brunswick, New Jersey: Transaction Publishers, 2010. ISBN: 978-1-4128-1063-0.

Kainer, Gordon. *God's Solution to the Doubting Dilemma*. Lulu, 2016.

Kaiser, Walter C. et al. *Four Views on Moving Beyond the Bible to Theology*. Ed. by Stanley N. Gundry and Gary T. Meadors. Counterpoints. Grand Rapids, MI: Zondervan Academic, 2009. ISBN: 978-0-310-27655-5.

Kant, Immanuel and H. J. Paton. *The Moral Law—Kant's Groundwork of the Metaphysic of Morals.* Trans. by H. J. Paton. 3rd ed. London: Hutchinson & Co., 1964 [1797].

Kant, Immanuel. *Critique of Judgment.* Trans. by J. H. Bernard. Mineola, NY: Dover, 2012. ISBN: 978-0-486-12220-5.

Kant, Immanuel. *Critique of Pure Reason.* Trans. by Paul Guyer and Allen W. Wood. 1998.

Kauffman, Stuart A. "Evolution Beyond Newton, Darwin, and Entailing Law: The Origin of Complexity in the Evolving Biosphere." In: *Complexity and the Arrow of Time.* Ed. by Charles H. Lineweaver, Paul C. W. Davies, and Michael Ruse. New York: Cambridge University Press, 2013. Chap. 8, pp. 162–190. ISBN: 978-1-107-02725-1.

Keller, Catherine. *Cloud of the Impossible: Negative Theology and Planetary Entanglement.* New York: Columbia University Press, 2015. ISBN: 978-0-231-17114-4.

Khaled, Fatma. *This is How Much You Need to be Worth to be in the Richest 1% in the US—And Other Countries.* 2021. URL: www . businessinsider . com / net - worth - to - be - in - 1 - percent - top - richest - wealth - 2021 - 2 (visited on 04/19/2021).

Kinder, George. *The Seven Stages of Money Maturity: Understanding the Spirit and Value of Money in Your Life.* New York: Dell Publishing, 2012.

Klein, Linda Kay. *Pure: Inside the Evangelical Movement that Shamed a Generation of Young Women and How I Broke Free.* Simon and Schuster, 2018.

Kline, Morris. *Mathematics for the Nonmathematician.* Courier Corporation, 1967.

Knox, John S. *John Wesley's 52 Standard Sermons: An Annotated Summary.* Eugene, OR: Wipf and Stock Publishers, 2017.

Koetsier, Teun and Luc Bergmans. *Mathematics and the Divine: A Historical Study.* Elsevier, 2004.

Kolb, Robert. "Reality Rests on the Word of the Lord: Martin Luther's Understanding of God's Word." In: *Reformation & Revival* 9.4 (2000), pp. 47–63.

Kuiken, A. Stephen Van. *Bibliolatry.* Community Congregational United Church of Christ. 22 Jan. 2017, Pullman, WA. Sermon.

URL: www.pullmanucc.org/2017/01/26/bibliolatry/ (visited on 05/01/2021).

— *Demonizing the Other*. Community Congregational United Church of Christ. 15 July 2018, Pullman, WA. Sermon. URL: www.pullmanucc.org/2018/07/18/demonizing-the-other/ (visited on 05/22/2021).

— *Desiring True Communion*. 6 June 2021, Pullman, WA. Sermon. URL: https://pullmanucc.org/2021/06/07/desiring-true-communion/ (visited on 06/11/2021).

— *Disagreeing with Jesus*. Community Congregational United Church of Christ. 22 Mar. 2021, Pullman, WA. Sermon. URL: www.pullmanucc.org/2021/03/22/disagreeing-with-jesus/ (visited on 05/06/2021).

— *Everyone Does Better When Everyone Does Better*. 3 September 2017, Pullman, WA. Sermon. URL: https://pullmanucc.org/2017/09/06/everyone-does-better-when-everyone-does-better/ (visited on 01/02/2022).

— *Whom do you serve?* Community Congregational United Church of Christ. 9 Aug. 2020, Pullman, WA. Sermon. URL: www.pullmanucc.org/2020/08/10/whom-do-you-serve/ (visited on 02/13/2021).

Kuyper, Abraham. *The Work of the Holy Spirit*. Cosimo, Inc., 2007.

Lamoureux, Denis O. et al. *Four Views on the Historical Adam*. Grand Rapids, MI: Zondervan Academic, 2013.

Lapin, Rabbi Daniel. *Thou Shall Prosper: Ten Commandments for Making Money*. Hoboken, NJ: John Wiley & Sons, 2002.

Lérins, Vincent of. "A Commonitory." In: *Nicene and post-Nicene fathers—Second Series*. Ed. by Philip Schaff and Henry Wallace. Vol. 11. (originally published circa 434). New York: Cosmo Classics, 2007, pp. 131–159.

Lesko, Frank. *Bootstraps*. 2017. URL: www.progressivechristianity.org/resources/bootstraps/ (visited on 06/12/2021).

— *How Toxic Shame Turns Evangelization Into Abuse*. 2015. URL: www.progressivechristianity.org/resources/how-toxic-shame-turns-evangelization-into-abuse/ (visited on 02/13/2021).

Levin, Janna. *How the Universe Got Its Spots*. New York: Random House, 2002. ISBN: 1-4000-3272-5.

Lewis, Gordon R. "Is Propositional Revelation Essential to Evangelical Spiritual Formation?" In: *Journal of the Evangelical Theological Society* 46.2 (2003), pp. 269–298.

Lewis, Walter H. and Memory P. F. Elvin-Lewis. *Medical Botany: Plants Affecting Human Health*. John Wiley & Sons, 2003.

Lewis-Anthony, Justin. *You Are the Messiah and I Should Know: Why Leadership is a Myth (and Probably a Heresy)*. London: Bloomsbury Publishing, 2013.

Limbaugh, David. *Finding Jesus in the Old Testament*. Simon and Schuster, 2015.

Lloyd, Seth. "On the Spontaneous Generation of Complexity in the Universe." In: *Complexity and the Arrow of Time*. Ed. by Charles H. Lineweaver, Paul C. W. Davies, and Michael Ruse. New York: Cambridge University Press, 2013. Chap. 5, pp. 80–112. ISBN: 978-1-107-02725-1.

Lucey, Thomas A. "A Critically Compassionate Approach to Financial Literacy: A Pursuit of Moral Spirit." In: *Education Sciences* 8.4 (2018), p. 152.

— "The Art of Relating Moral Education to Financial Education: An Equity Imperative." In: *Social Studies Research and Practice* 2.3 (2007), pp. 486–500.

Lusardi, Annamaria. *Americans' Financial Capability*. Tech. rep. National Bureau of Economic Research, 2011.

Lusardi, Annamaria, Pierre-Carl Michaud, and Olivia S. Mitchell. "Optimal Financial Knowledge and Wealth Inequality." In: *Journal of Political Economy* 125.2 (2017), pp. 431–477.

Lǎozǐ and James Trapp. *Tao Te Ching*. Ed. by Sarah Uttridge. Trans. by James Trapp. New York: Chartwell Books, 2015. ISBN: 978-0-7858-3319-2.

Machen, J. Gresham. *Christianity and Liberalism*. J. J. Little & Ives Company, 1923.

Malchow, Bruce V. *Social Justice in the Hebrew Bible: What is New and What is Old*. Collegeville, MN: Liturgical Press, 1996.

Maraboli, Steve. *"Get rich quick..."* Twitter Post [9:11 AM — Aug 16, 2015]. 2015. URL: www.twitter.com/SteveMaraboli/status/632947703073370112 (visited on 05/14/2021).

Martin, Dale B. *New Testament History and Literature*. New Haven: Yale University Press, 2012.

Martin, William J. "Special Revelation as Objective." In: *Revelation and the Bible: Contemporary Evangelical Thought*. Edited by Carl F. H. Henry (1958), pp. 61–72.

Martin, Dale B. *Introduction to the New Testament History and Literature*. 2009. URL: https://oyc.yale.edu/religious-studies/rlst-152/lecture-12 (visited on 05/01/2021).

— *Introduction to the New Testament History and Literature*. 2009. URL: https://oyc.yale.edu/religious-studies/rlst-152/lecture-14 (visited on 06/06/2021).

Mayer, John D. *Why Confucius Had No Time to Judge*. 2009. URL: www.psychologytoday.com/us/blog/the-personality-analyst/200903/why-confucius-had-no-time-judge (visited on 04/18/2021).

McChesney, Chris, Sean Covey, and Jim Huling. *The Four Disciplines of Execution: Achieving Your Wildly Important Goals*. New York: Simon & Schuster, 2012. ISBN: 978-1-4516-2705-3.

McHargue, Mike. *Finding God in the Waves: How I Lost My Faith and Found It Again Through Science*. New York: Convergent Books, 2016. ISBN: 978-1-101-90605-7.

McLaren, Brian D. *A Generous Orthodoxy: Why I am a Missional, Evangelical, Post/Protestant, Liberal/Conservative, Mystical/Poetic, Biblical, Charismatic/Contemplative, Fundamentalist/Calvinist, Anabaptist/Anglican, Methodist, Catholic, Green, Incarnational, Depressed-yet-hopeful, Emergent, Unfinished Christian*. Grand Rapids, MI: Zondervan, 2004. ISBN: 978-0-310-25803-2.

— *A New Kind of Christianity: Ten Questions That are Transforming the Faith*. New York: HarperOne, 2010. ISBN: 978-0-06-185398-2.

Mèngzǐ. *Mencius*. Ed. by Philip J. Ivanhoe. Trans. by Irene Bloom. Translations from the Asian Classics. New York: Columbia University Press, 2009. ISBN: 978-0-231-12204-7.

Merrill, Eugene H., Mark F. Rooker, and Michael A. Grisanti. *The World and the Word: An Introduction to the Old Testament*. B&H Publishing Group, 2011.

Millburn, Joshua Fields and Ryan Nicodemus. *Minimalism: Essential Essays*. 1st ed. Mins Publishing, 2011. ISBN: 978-1-9365394-5-1.

Millburn, Joshua Fields, Ryan Nicodemus, and Matt D'Avella. *The Minimalists: Less Is Now [Movie]*. Netflix, 2021.

Milne, Bruce. *Know the Truth: A Handbook of Christian Belief*. InterVarsity Press, 2009.

Milton, John, E. Fenton, and S. Johnson. *Paradise Lost*. John Bumpus, 1821.

Miranda, José Porfirio. *Marx and the Bible: A Critique of the Philosophy of Oppression*. Eugene, OR: Wipf and Stock Publishers, 2004.

Money. *A Growing Cult of Millennials Is Obsessed With Early Retirement. This 72-Year-Old Is Their Unlikely Inspiration*. 2018. URL: www . money . com / vicki - robin - financial - independence-retire-early/ (visited on 04/21/2021).

Moneychimp. *CAGR of the Stock Market: Annualized Returns of the S&P 500*. 2018. URL: www . moneychimp . com / features / market_cagr.htm (visited on 06/12/2021).

Moor, Leonard de. "The Idea of Revelation in the Early Church." In: *The Evangelical Quarterly* 50.3 (1978), pp. 166–172.

Morris, Henry. *Defending the Faith: Upholding Biblical Christianity and the Genesis Record*. New Leaf Publishing Group, 1999.

Morris, Simon Conway. "Life: The Final Frontier for Complexity?" In: *Complexity and the Arrow of Time*. Ed. by Charles H. Lineweaver, Paul C. W. Davies, and Michael Ruse. New York: Cambridge University Press, 2013. Chap. 7, pp. 135–161. ISBN: 978-1-107-02725-1.

Morrow, J. G. *The Listening Heart: Hearing God in Prayer*. Baker Publishing Group, 2013.

multpl. *S&P 500 Dividend Yield by Year*. 2018. URL: http://www. multpl . com / s - p - 500 - dividend - yield / table (visited on 09/22/2018).

Myers, Ched. *The Biblical Vision of Sabbath Economics*. Tell The Word, 2002.

Najman, Hindy. "Early Nonrabbinic Interpretation." In: *The Jewish Study Bible: Jewish Publication Society Tanakh Translation*.

Ed. by Adele Berlin, Marc Zvi Brettler, et al. 2nd ed. Oxford University Press, USA, 2014, pp. 1841–1850.

Niebuhr, Reinhold. *Moral Man and Immoral Society: A Study in Ethics and Politics*. New York: Continuum, 2005. ISBN: 0-8264-7714-3.

Norlén, Gunnar. *Islam and its World*. Vol. 3. Usa River, Tanzania: Research Institute of Makumira University College, 2001. ISBN: 9789987657025.

Novak, Michael. "Defining Social Justice." In: *First things* (2000), pp. 11–12.

Olson, Roger E. *Reformed and Always Reforming (Acadia Studies in Bible and Theology): The Postconservative Approach to Evangelical Theology*. Grand Rapids, MI: Baker Academic, 2007. ISBN: 978-0-8010-3169-4.

Organize Your Mindset. 2017. URL: www.orlandosentinel.com/features/os-osig-organize-your-mindset-20170613-story.html (visited on 05/21/2021).

Packer, James I. "Contemporary Views of Revelation." In: *Revelation and the Bible: Contemporary Evangelical Thought. Edited by Carl F. H. Henry* (1959), pp. 89–104.

Palmer, Martin. *The Elements of Taoism*. Barnes & Noble Books, 1999. ISBN: 978-0-7607-1078-3.

Parker, Theodore. "The Transient and Permanent in Christianity." In: *Electronic Texts in American Studies* (1908). Ed. by George Willis Cookie.

Patterson, Kerry et al. *Crucial Conversations: Tools for Talking When Stakes are High*. McGraw-Hill Education, 2012.

Perkins, Pheme. "The New Testament Interprets the Jewish Scriptures." In: *The New Oxford Annotated Bible with Apocrypha: New Revised Standard Version*. Ed. by Michael D. Coogan et al. 5th ed. New York: Oxford University Press, 2010.

Perrotta, Cosimo. *Consumption as an Investment: The Fear of Goods from Hesiod to Adam Smith*. Trans. by Joan McMullin. New York: Routledge, 2004. ISBN: 0-415-30619-1.

Phipps, William E. *The Wisdom & Wit of Rabbi Jesus*. Louisville, KY: Westminster John Knox Press, 1993.

Pink, Arthur W. *The Divine Inspiration of the Bible*. Swengel, PA: Bible Truth Depot, 1917.

Pinto, Laura Elizabeth and Hannah Chan. "Social Justice and Financial Literacy." In: *Our Schools, Our Selves* 19.2 (2010), pp. 61–77.

Pinto, Laura Elizabeth and Elizabeth Coulson. "Social Justice and the Gender Politics of Financial Literacy Education." In: *Journal of the Canadian Association for Curriculum Studies* 9.2 (2011), pp. 54–85.

Piper, John. *How Are General and Special Revelation Different?* 2009. URL: www.desiringgod.org/interviews/how-are-general-and-special-revelation-different (visited on 04/17/2020).

Plato. *The Laws of Plato*. Trans. by Thomas L. Pangle. Chicago, IL: University of Chicago Press, 1988.

Pollan, Michael. *Food Rules: An Eater's Manual*. New York: Penguin Group USA, 2009. ISBN: 978-0-14-311638-7.

— *In Defense of Food: An Eater's Manifesto*. New York: Penguin Group USA, 2008. ISBN: 978-1-59420-145-5.

Poucher, David R. "Teaching Personal Finance as a General Education Course in a Liberal Arts Institution." In: *Christian Business Academy Review* 12 (2017).

Powell, Corey. *God in the Equation: How Einstein Transformed Religion*. New York: Simon and Schuster, 2003. ISBN: 0-684-86348-0.

Primack, Joel R. and Nancy Ellen Abrams. *The View From the Center of the Universe: Discovering Our Extraordinary Place in the Cosmos*. New York: Penguin, 2006. ISBN: 1-59448-914-9.

Ramsey, Dave. *Dave Ramsey's Complete Guide to Money*. Brentwood, TN: Ramsey Press, 2011.

— *The Legacy Journey: A Radical View of Biblical Wealth and Generosity*. Brentwood, TN: Ramsey Press, 2014. ISBN: 978-1-937-07771-6.

Ramsey, Dave. *Return on Investment: the 12% Reality*. 2021. URL: www.ramseysolutions.com/retirement/the-12-reality (visited on 06/12/2021).

— *Why You Don't Need All Of Your Stuff! | The Minimalists*. YouTube Video. 2021. URL: https://www.youtube.com/watch?v=9IYP5xUoSBE (visited on 05/16/2021).

Reid, John Kelman Sutherland. *The Authority of Scripture: A Study of the Reformation and Post-Reformation Understanding of the Bible.* Methuen, 1962.

Rieckens, Scott and Peter Adeney. *Playing with FIRE (Financial Independence Retire Early).* Novato, CA: New World Library, 2019.

Rivera, Luis N. and Luis Rivera Pagán. *A Violent Evangelism: The Political and Religious Conquest of the Americas.* Louisville, KY: Westminster John Knox Press, 1992. ISBN: 0-664-25367-9.

Robbins, Tony and Peter Mallouk. *Unshakeable: Your Financial Freedom Playbook.* New York: Simon and Schuster, 2017. ISBN: 978-1-5011-6458-3.

Roberts, E. and J. Eyl. *Christian Tourist Attractions, Mythmaking, and Identity Formation.* Bloomsbury Publishing, 2018.

Robin, Vicki, Joe Dominguez, and Monique Tilford. *Your Money or Your Life: 9 Steps to Transforming Your Relationship With Money and Achieving Financial Independence.* New York: Penguin, 2008.

Robin, Vicki. *Your Money or Your Life: An Interview with Author Vicki Robin [Podcast].* 2017. URL: www.madfientist.com/ vicki-robin-interview/ (visited on 04/20/2021).

Rohr, Richard. *Falling Upward: A Spirituality for the Two Halves of Life.* San Francisco, CA: John Wiley & Sons, 2011. ISBN: 978-0-470-90775-7.

— *The Naked Now: Learning to See as the Mystics See.* Chestnut Ridge, NY: Crossroad Publishing, 2009. ISBN: 978-0-8245-2543-9.

— *Universal Christ: How a Forgotten Reality Can Change Everything We See, Hope For, and Believe.* New York: Convergent Books, 2019.

Rumford, Douglas J. *Questions God Asks, Questions Satan Asks.* Wheaton, Ill. : Tyndale House, 1998.

Salthe, Stanley N. *Development and Evolution: Complexity and Change in Biology.* Cambridge, MA: MIT Press, 1993. ISBN: 0-262-19335-3.

Sandel, Michael J. "Lecture 1: The Moral Side of Murder." In: *Harvard University's Justice [Online Course]* (2005). URL:

www.justiceharvard.org/themoralsideofmurder/ (visited on 04/17/2021).

Sanders, Deion and Jim Nelson Black. *Power, Money & Sex: How Success Almost Ruined My Life*. Nashville, TN: Word Publishing, 1999. ISBN: 0-8499-1499-X.

Sandlin, P. Andrew. "Two Paradigms for Adherents of Sola Scriptura." In: *Reformation & Revival* 9.4 (2000), pp. 36–46.

Sasaki, Fumio. *Goodbye, Things: On Minimalist Living*. Trans. by Eriko Sugita. New York: W.W. Norton & Company, 2017. ISBN: 978-0393609035.

Schaeffer, Francis. *How Should We Then Live? The Rise and Decline of Western Thought and Culture*. Wheaton, IL: Crossway, 2005. ISBN: 978-1-58134-536-0.

Schwab-Pomerantz, Carrie. *Financial Literacy: A Great Equalizer in the Battle Against Social Injustice*. 2020. URL: www.aboutschwab.com/financial-literacy-a-great-equalizer-in-the-battle-against-social-injustice (visited on 03/28/2021).

— *Financial Literacy: A Powerful Tool for Social Justice in 2020 and Beyond*. 2020. URL: www.schwab.com/resource-center/insights/content/financial-literacy-powerful-tool-social-justice-2020-and-beyond (visited on 03/31/2021).

Sheridan, Ruth. "Scripture Fulfillment." In: *The Jewish Annotated New Testament*. Ed. by Amy-Jill Levine and Marc Zvi Brettler. 2nd ed. New York: Oxford University Press, 2011, pp. 727–730. ISBN: 978-0-19-046185-0.

Simpson, William K. *The Literature of Ancient Egypt: An Anthology of Stories, Instructions, Stelae, Autobiographies, and Poetry*. Ed. by William K. Simpson. Trans. by Rober K. Ritner et al. 3rd ed. New Haven & London: Yale University Press, 2003. ISBN: 0-300-09920-7.

Slingerland, Edward. *Effortless Action: Wu-wei as Conceptual Metaphor and Spiritual Ideal in Early China*. New York: Oxford University Press, 2003.

Smith, Christian. *The Bible Made Impossible: Why Biblicism Is Not a Truly Evangelical Reading of Scripture*. Grand Rapids, MI: Brazos Press, 2012.

Smith, Huston. *The World's Religions*. New York: HarperOne, 2009. ISBN: 978-0-06-166018-4.

Sommer, Benjamin D. "Inner-biblical Interpretation." In: *The Jewish Study Bible: Jewish Publication Society Tanakh Translation*. Ed. by Adele Berlin, Marc Zvi Brettler, et al. 2nd ed. Oxford University Press, USA, 2014, pp. 1835–1841.

Spong, John Shelby. *Biblical Literalism: A gentile Heresy: A Journey Into a New Christianity Through the Doorway of Matthew's Gospel*. New York: HarperCollins, 2016.

— *Eternal Life: A New Vision—Beyond Religion, Beyond Theism, Beyond Heaven and Hell*. New York: HarperOne, 2009. ISBN: 978-0-06-077842-2.

— *Liberating the Gospels: Reading the Bible with Jewish Eyes*. HarperSanFrancisco, 1996.

— *Why Christianity Must Change or Die: A Bishop Speaks to Believers in Exile*. HarperSanFrancisco, 1998. ISBN: 0-06-067536-5.

Spong, John Shelby. *Rescuing the Bible from Fundamentalism: A Bishop Rethinks the Meaning of Scripture*. HarperSanFransisco, 1991. ISBN: 0-06-067518-8.

— *The Sins of Scripture: Exposing the Bible's Texts of Hate to Reveal the God of Love*. New York: HarperOne, 2005. ISBN: 978-0-06-077840-8.

Sproul, Robert Charles. *The Consequences of Ideas*. Wheaton, IL: Crossway Books, 2000. ISBN: 978-1-4335-0314-6.

Stahl, Ashley. *You Turn: Get Unstuck, Discover Your Direction, and Design Your Dream Career*. Dallas, TX: BenBella Books, 2021. ISBN: 978-1950665693.

Stark, Thom. *The Human Faces of God: What Scripture Reveals When it Gets God Wrong (and Why Inerrancy Tries to Hide It)*. Eugene, OR: Wipf and Stock Publishers, 2011. ISBN: 978-1-60899-323-9.

Stern, David. "Midrash and Jewish Exegesis." In: *The Jewish Study Bible: Jewish Publication Society Tanakh Translation*. Ed. by Adele Berlin, Marc Zvi Brettler, et al. 2nd ed. Oxford University Press, USA, 2014, pp. 1879–1891.

— "Midrash and Parables." In: *The Jewish Annotated New Testament*. Ed. by Amy-Jill Levine and Marc Zvi Brettler. 2nd ed.

New York: Oxford University Press, 2011, pp. 707–710. ISBN: 978-0-19-046185-0.

Stone, Dan. "Cultivating Financial Mindfulness: A Dual-process Theory." In: *Consumer Knowledge and Financial Decisions.* Springer, 2011, pp. 15–27.

Strogatz, Steven H. *Nonlinear Dynamics and Chaos: With Applications to Physics, Biology, Chemistry, and Engineering.* Boulder, CO: Westview Press, 1994. ISBN: 0-7382-0453-6.

Suchocki, Marjorie. *The Fall to Violence: Original Sin in Relational Theology.* A&C Black, 1994.

Sūnzĭ. *Sun Tzu's The Art of War: Bilingual Edition Complete Chinese and English Text.* Ed. by John Minford. Trans. by Lionel Giles. 1st ed. Tokyo: Tuttle Publishing, 2012. ISBN: 978-0-8048-3944-0.

Taylor, Nick and William Davies. "The Financialization of Anti-capitalism? The Case of the 'Financial Independence Retire Early' Community." In: *Journal of Cultural Economy* (2021), pp. 1–17.

Thomas, Clarence et al. *Lincoln and Liberty: Wisdom for the Ages.* Lexington, KY: University Press of Kentucky, 2014.

Thoreau, Henry David. *Walden and Other Writings.* Ed. by Joseph Wood Krutch. New York: Random House, 2004 [1854].

Tolstoy, Leo. *War and Peace.* Trans. by Ann Dunnigan. New York: Penguin Group (USA), 1968 [1869].

Toon, Peter et al. *Who Runs the Church?: 4 Views on Church Government.* Ed. by Steven B. Cowan and Stanley N. Gundry. Grand Rapids, MI: Zondervan Academic, 2009.

Treadway, Anna J. "The Revolution Begins in the Heart: Exploring the Spiritual Lives of Women Activists for Social Justice." PhD thesis. University of British Columbia, 2005.

Tyson, E. *Investing in Your 20s and 30s For Dummies.* Wiley, 2017. ISBN: 9781119431428.

Tyson, Neil deGrasse and Donald Goldsmith. *Origins: Fourteen Billion Years of Cosmic Evolution.* New York: W. W. Norton & Company, 2004. ISBN: 0-393-05992-8.

Vasudev, Jaggi ("Sadhguru"). *Money Matters.* 2014. URL: www.isha.sadhguru.org/us/en/wisdom/article/money-matters (visited on 05/03/2021).

Viktoria. *How to Balance Minimalism and a Love Affair with Books*. 2018. URL: `www.thelifestyle-files.com/tips-to-balance-minimalism-and-books/` (visited on 06/12/2021).

Voltaire. *The Works of Voltaire: A Contemporary Version*. Vol. 18. St. Hubert Guild, 1901.

Waldman, Mark S. *A Spiritual Guide to Money: How to Use Money for Personal Growth & Genuine Spiritual Experience*. Mark S. Waldman (Xlibris), 2001. ISBN: 0-7388-2821-1.

— *The Way of Real Wealth: Creating a Future that is Emotionally Satisfying, Spiritually Fulfilling, Financially Secure*. New York: Harpercollins, 1993. ISBN: 978-0-0625-5283-9.

Ward, Mark L. *Goodreads Review of Five Views on Apologetics*. 2013. URL: `www.goodreads.com/review/show/639892599?book_show_action=true&from_review_page=1` (visited on 05/01/2021).

Weeks, Stuart. *Ecclesiastes and Skepticism*. New York: T & T Clark International, 2012. ISBN: 978-0-567-25288-3.

Wenham, Gordon John, William A. Heth, and Craig S. Keener. *Remarriage after Divorce in Today's Church*. Ed. by Mark L. Strauss. Grand Rapids, MI: Zondervan Academic, 2009.

Wheeler, Sondra Ely. *Wealth as Peril and Obligation: The New Testament on Possessions*. Grand Rapids, MI: Wm. B. Eerdmans Publishing, 1995.

Wilhelm, Richard, C. G. Jung, and Hellmut Wilhelm. *The I Ching or Book of Changes*. Trans. by Cary F. Baynes. Norwalk, CT: Easton Press, 2008.

Williams, Roy Orville and Vic Preisser. *Philanthropy, Heirs & Values: How Successful Families Are Using Philanthropy To Prepare Their Heirs for Post-transition Responsibilities*. Robert D. Reed Publishers, 2005. ISBN: 1-931741-51-4.

— *Preparing Heirs: Five Steps to a Successful Transition of Family Wealth and Values*. Robert D. Reed Publishers, 2003. ISBN: 1-931741-31-X.

Willis, Lauren E. "Against Financial-literacy Education." In: *Iowa Law Review* 94 (2008), p. 197.

Wills, S. *Meet the Young People Who Are Retiring in Their 30s*. 2018. URL: `www.vice.com/en/article/qvnwvq/financial-independence-retire-early` (visited on 04/21/2021).

Winters, Larry. *Live the Dream—No More Excuses.* New York: Center Street, 2012. ISBN: 978-1-4555-1362-8.

Wong, Kristin. *The Basics of FIRE (Financial Independence and Early Retirement).* 2019. URL: www.twocents.lifehacker.com/the-basics-of-fire-financial-independence-and-early-re-1820129768 (visited on 04/21/2021).

Wright, Nicholas Thomas. "How Can the Bible be Authoritative?" In: *Vox Evangelica* 21.1991 (1991), pp. 7–29.

Wylen, Stephen M. *The Seventy Faces of Torah: The Jewish Way of Reading the Sacred Scriptures.* New York: Paulist Press, 2005.

Zahnd, Brian. *Sinners in the Hands of a Loving God: The Scandalous Truth of the Very Good News.* Colorado Springs, CO: WaterBrook, 2017. ISBN: 978-1-60142-951-3.

Zaikowski, Lori, Richard T. Wilkens, and Kurt Fischer. "Science and the Concept of Evolution: From the Big Bang to the Origin and Evolution of Life." In: *Chemical Evolution Across Space & Time: From the Big Bang to Prebiotic Chemistry.* Ed. by Lori Zaikowski and Jon M. Friedrich. Vol. 981. ACS Symposium Series. Proceedings of the American Chemical Society Symposium Spring 2007 ACS National Meeting, Chicago, IL. American Chemical Society Publications, 2008. Chap. 18, pp. 326–342. ISBN: 978-0-8412-7431-0.

Zen, Marissa. *10 Extreme Minimalist Budget Tips (Save 70% of Income) | Spend Less | Financial Minimalist Family.* YouTube Video. 2021. URL: www.youtube.com/watch?v=f2u0Tn8esVs (visited on 06/12/2021).

INDEX OF ANCIENT SOURCES

---

[2]Robert Francis Harper. *The Code of Hammurabi, King of Babylon: About 2250 BC*. Chicago, IL: University of Chicago Press, 1904.

[3]Jeremy A. Black. *The Literature of Ancient Sumer*. Trans. by Jeremy Black et al. New York: Oxford University Press, 2004. ISBN: 0-19-926311-6.

[4]William K. Simpson. *The Literature of Ancient Egypt: An Anthology of Stories, Instructions, Stelae, Autobiographies, and Poetry*. Ed. by William K. Simpson. Trans. by Rober K. Ritner et al. 3rd ed. New Haven & London: Yale University Press, 2003. ISBN: 0-300-09920-7.

[5] James Peter Allen and Peter Der Manuelian. *The Ancient Egyptian Pyramid Texts*. Ed. by Peter Der Manuelian et al. Trans. by James P. Allen. Vol. 23. Writings from the Ancient World. Atlanta, GA: Society of Biblical Literature, 2005. ISBN: 978-1-58983-182-7.

[6] Richard L. Jasnow. *A Late Period Hieratic Wisdom Text (P. Brooklyn 47.218.135)*. Ed. by Thomas A. Holland and Thomas G. Urban. Vol. 52. Studies in Ancient Oriental Civilization. Oriental Institution of the University of Chicago, 1992. ISBN: 0-918986-85-0.

[7] Acharya Buddharakkhita. *The Dhammapada—The Buddha's Path of Wisdom*. Trans. by Acharya Buddharakkhita. Kandy, Sri Lanka: Buddhist Publication Society, 2003. ISBN: 978-955-24-0131-2.

[8] Richard Wilhelm, C. G. Jung, and Hellmut Wilhelm. *The I Ching or Book of Changes*. Trans. by Cary F. Baynes. Norwalk, CT: Easton Press, 2008.

[9] Sūnzǐ. *Sun Tzu's The Art of War: Bilingual Edition Complete Chinese and English Text*. Ed. by John Minford. Trans. by Lionel Giles. 1st ed. Tokyo: Tuttle Publishing, 2012. ISBN: 978-0-8048-3944-0.

[10] Lǎozǐ and James Trapp. *Tao Te Ching*. Ed. by Sarah Uttridge. Trans. by James Trapp. New York: Chartwell Books, 2015. ISBN: 978-0-7858-3319-2.

[11] Kǒng Fūzǐ. *The Analects of Confucius: Chinese–English Bilingual Edition*. Trans. by Pan Fuen et al. 1st ed. Jinan, China: Qi Lu Press, 1993. ISBN: 7-5333-0283-4.

---

[12] Kǒng Fūzǐ. *The Sacred Books of China: The Texts of Confucianism.* Ed. by Friedrich Max Müller. Trans. by James Legge. Vol. 28. The Sacred Books of the East. Oxford: Clarendon Press, 1885.

[13] Mèngzǐ. *Mencius.* Ed. by Philip J. Ivanhoe. Trans. by Irene Bloom. Translations from the Asian Classics. New York: Columbia University Press, 2009. ISBN: 978-0-231-12204-7.

[14] Æsop and Munro Leaf. *Æsop's Fables—A New Version.* Trans. by John Warrington. Norwalk, CT: Easton Press, 1979.

[15] Plato. *The Laws of Plato.* Trans. by Thomas L. Pangle. Chicago, IL: University of Chicago Press, 1988.

[16] Marcus Aurelius and George Long. *The Meditations of Marcus Aurelius.* Trans. by George Long. New York: F. M. Lupton Publishing Company, 1887.

INDEX OF TOPICS

INDEX OF MODERN AUTHORS

NOTES

US $14.95   Christian Living / General

ISBN 978-1-953516-07-7 (paperback)

5 1 4 9 5

9 781953 516077

www.vorstossen.com